PAINTING
with
ACRYLICS

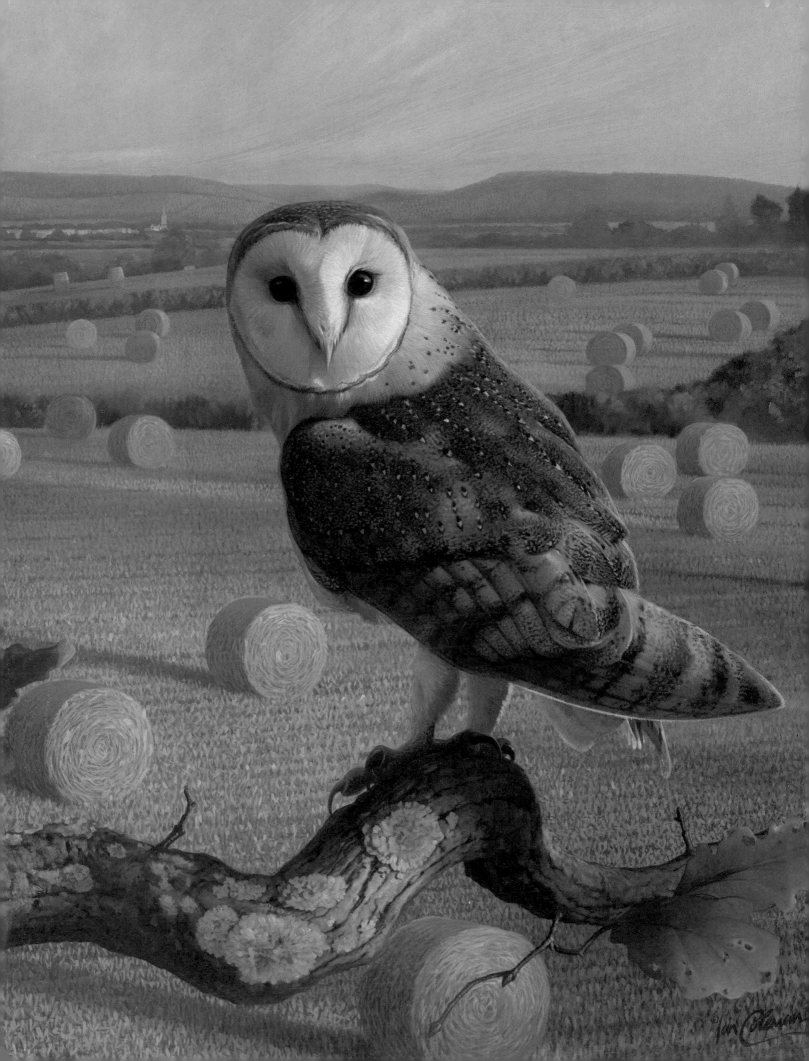

PAINTING
with
ACRYLICS

Ian Coleman

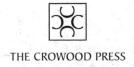

THE CROWOOD PRESS

First published in 2015 by
The Crowood Press Ltd
Ramsbury, Marlborough
Wiltshire SN8 2HR

www.crowood.com

British Library Cataloguing-in-Publication Data
A catalogue record for this book is available from the British Library.

ISBN 978 1 84797 883 7

Frontispiece: Detail of *Barn Owl near Ross-on-Wye*. Acrylic on MDF board by Ian Coleman.
61x64cm (24x18in).
Painted on gesso board using tints, semi-opaque layers and thicker opaque layers. Blue wash
tints in the sky on top of a base cream colour.

Dedication
To Becky and our three sons Huxley, Dexter and Jasper, a constant source of inspiration.

Typeset by Kelly-Anne Levey
Printed and bound in Malaysia by Times Offset (M) Sdn Bhd.

CONTENTS

Introduction 7

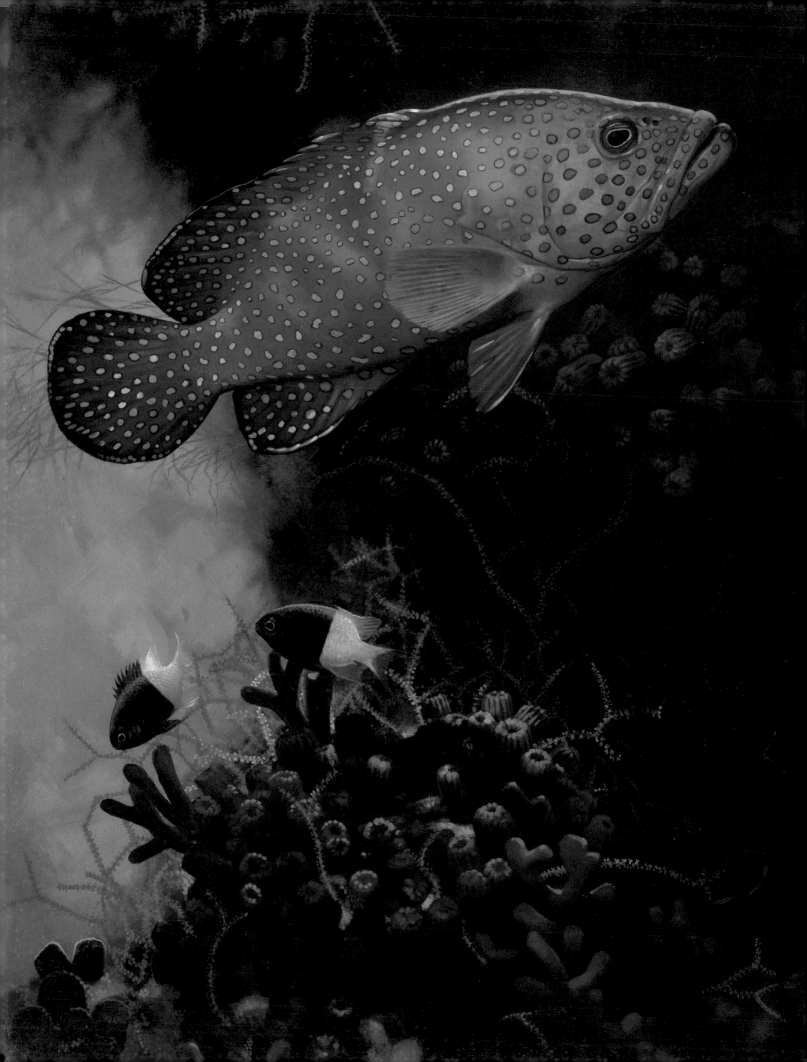

INTRODUCTION

This is a book that takes a technical and detailed approach to learning a wide range of effects within this forgiving medium of acrylic paint.

In this book I aim to show you how to control its fast drying quality to your advantage. It's a tough paint which takes all sorts of handling, especially multiple layers of thick and thin textures and best of all it's very forgiving with mistakes. In a nutshell there are no rules with Acrylics.

Acrylic paintings can take on so many styles with results that look like flowing watercolours, solid gouache colours or luscious oil paintings. The type of painting you would like to create is achievable with this versatile medium. The core techniques in this book illustrate what you can do with a limited set of materials to then go on to include all the wonderful additives, brushes and mediums available today.

This book demonstrates eleven classic paint techniques with each image predominantly rendered in that featured style to encourage you to either copy it directly or use a similar image in the same technique.

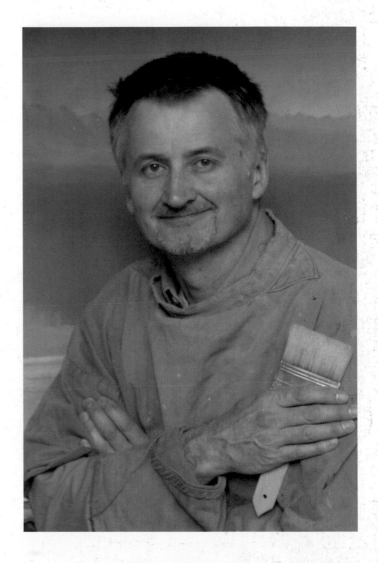

THE AIM OF THE BOOK

I'd like to introduce you to a set of useful brush skills to manipulate acrylic paint to achieve a range of styles and finishes. Each example has been kept to within a single technique as far as possible, using a core range of brushes with a basic range of paint colours, without the huge range of specialised products.

All these techniques could be combined in one work of art and in a style that is so far removed from the craftsmanship approach taken in this book. However, completing a painting solely in one technique can rapidly help you to learn a new skill. The principals of how to handle the paint could be applied to any style of painting no matter how loose, expressive and abstract the image may be.

I hope you enjoy playing with these core techniques and in the process find one or two that fire you off into a new direction of imagination. Acrylics are so versatile there are plenty more styles and techniques to show you but for now, have fun, experiment and get to love this medium.

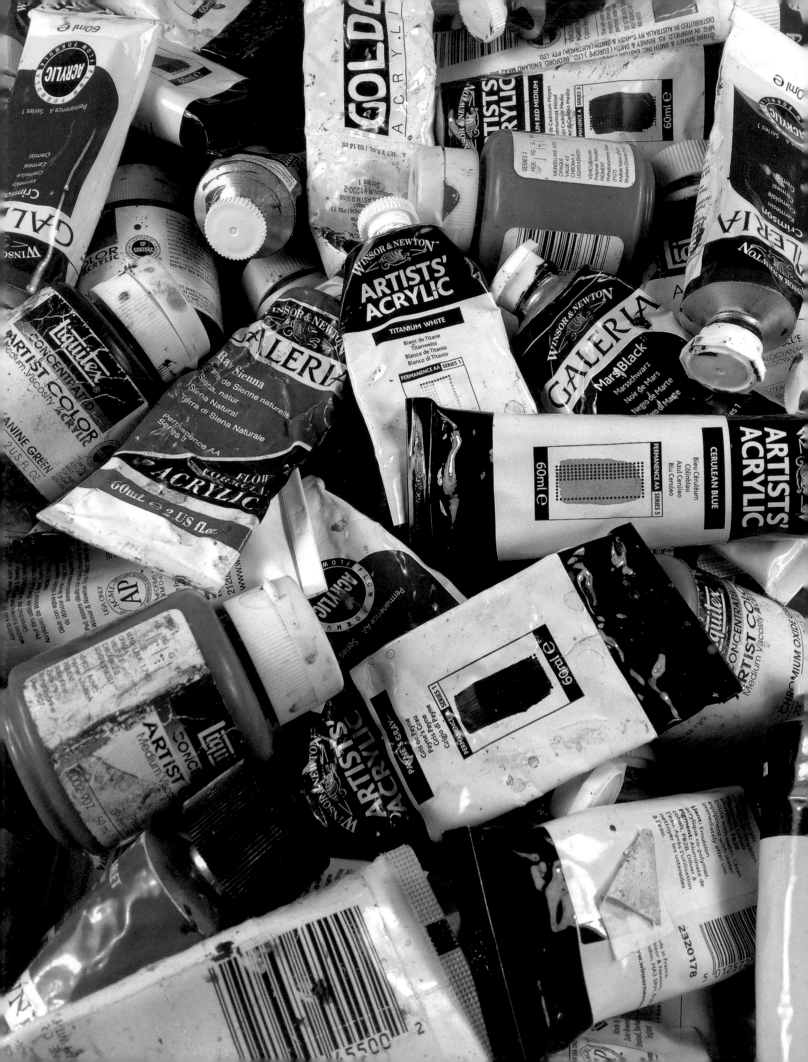

CHAPTER 1

TOOLS AND MATERIALS

BRUSHES

All the images were painted at this book size of 220 × 280mm, with the brushes and paints featured in each chapter. I've selected a relatively small range of brush types to cover many of the popular and classic ways of mark making, to show how they may become your core favourites. However, don't be worried if you can't obtain the same brands or sizes: these are just a guide to the brush type, and ones that are similar will be fine. I use a mix of artist's grade brushes and budget brushes.

Obviously it's true that you get what you pay for, but if an old decorating brush gives the marks required, then that's the best one for the job! So generally my advice is always to get the best brush for the purpose. My studio is full of old and out-of-shape brushes which do make an appearance every now and then, so I never throw them away.

Quality, well made synthetics and Hog brushes hold their shape and last longer. Painting with a cheap detail brush which has a tip that doesn't spring back, or splays at the slightest pres-

sure, is completely frustrating. However, occasionally a budget paint brush does the very job you want, and that's why I've included them here in the book – namely the black-handled Winsor & Newton Azanta range for blocking in, and the Royal & Langnickel Soft Grip Nylon Bright Brushes for detailing. Langnickel Hogs are also good value.

The only down side to acrylic is that it will ruin your clothes unless you remove it immediately; also, to some extent working with acrylics will have you replacing your brushes more frequently than oils or watercolours. But that's the only down side!

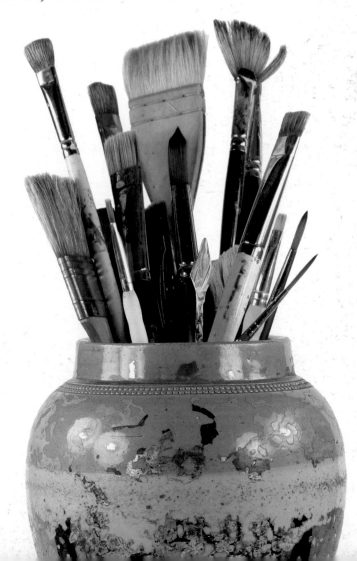

ABOVE: Fig. 1.1 An all-round palette with small and large wells for thick and thin mixes of colour.

RIGHT: Fig. 1.2 All the brushes used in the making of this book.

BRUSH TIPS

- Don't let the paint dry on the brushes.

- Wash your brushes well.

- Use a mixing brush to save the tip of the painting brush.

- To revive a brush, soak before applying a mechanic's hand cleaner.

- Treat your brush gently: for example, load a round brush by rotating it in colour and not dabbing or swishing.

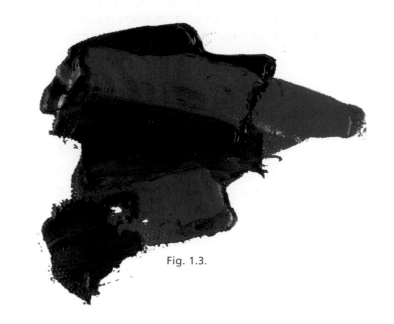

Fig. 1.3.

ACRYLIC PAINTS

Acrylic paint is a water-soluble, fast-drying paint. Once dry it cannot be re-hydrated, and so any number of thick and thin layers can be applied on top. They bond to a huge range of surfaces, which is why they are so popular in the crafts and arts world.

The range of acrylics comes in three distinct viscosities: liquid, soft and heavy-bodied, each being created for a different purpose. This book features the soft-bodied range, which has a medium viscosity enabling it to overlap with both the other ranges. It's a great place to start because you can then see in which direction you would like to go.

Super-budget acrylic paints have an inherent poor quality, and using them could give you a disappointing experience of what these amazing paints can do. I would therefore recommend using the recognized mainstream brands in either student's grades or preferably artist's grades.

I have used the most commonly available for this book so as to keep things straightforward: Winsor and Newton Artists' Acrylics, but Golden and Liquitex brands, amongst others, make an excellent alternative.

Fig. 1.4.

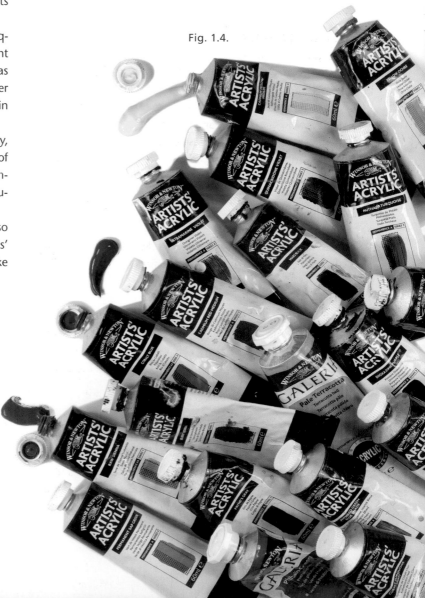

COLOURS

The range of colours selected has been kept to a relative few to suit the examples, and those choices are sometimes arbitrary and approximate. Certain types of painting, like the ones in this book, are not based on critical colour choices. Worrying about the exact colours can get in the way of creativity and work flow, so if a mid brown such as burnt sienna is not handy, use a burnt umber instead, and so on. If it turns out to be not quite right it's easy to tweak.

Our sense of colour can be a very personal choice; thus some artists prefer a palette of muted colours, some like bright, and some just go completely crazy – but this all adds up to creating our own unique style. So although I give a colour its specific name in the step-by-step chapters, for example a 'pthhalo blue-green shade', it can in fact be any blue that's close enough.

PAINT TIPS

- Don't let paint get on your clothes.

- Always put the caps back on the tubes of paints no matter how short a time before the next squirt.

- Soak plastic or ceramic well palettes in hot soapy water before peeling and scrubbing off.

SURFACES AND OTHER ITEMS

Besides the usual items such as pencils, charcoal, tape, jars and so on, the following may be useful with acrylic painting.

ACRYLIC WHITE GESSO

All white gessos are not equal: some are chalky and opaque, and others more gel-like in their viscosity. As it is the base to the painting, an opaque and 'toothy' finish is what is required, so Liquitex, Winsor & Newton and Golden currently make great gesso.

A wide 2in to 4in hog brush or 'varnish' brush makes an excellent gesso brush. Gesso can be sanded to the required texture or smoothed to an impractical glass finish if so desired, with wet and dry paper and a little water.

STRETCHED CANVAS

There is a huge variety of artist's canvas rolls, so stretching your own canvases gives the widest choice of finish.

CANVAS BOARD

Canvas board comes in many finishes, but the best advice is to take a close look and avoid very open weaves as more of the pigment then sits in between the cotton and less on top of it.

MDF, HARDBOARD, PLYBOARD, MARINE PLYBOARD

All these surfaces require a light sanding before application of three or four thin coats of paint for a smoother finish. Lightly sand with fine sandpaper between coats; use two generous coats for a rougher finish. Use a foam roller for a fine pimply or egg-shell finish. Board is best suited for small to medium paintings.

WATERCOLOUR BOARD

Watercolour paper is pre-bonded on to a board in order to resist warping. It is especially good for very watery paintings and linework.

WATERCOLOUR PAPER

Watercolour paper is ideal for bringing granulation effects into washes: choose rough papers and use the paper texture with opaque drybrush techniques.

STAY-WET PALETTE

This sort of palette is a very useful item to have as it keeps paint usable for days. It is especially good when painting delicate and illustrative paintings with small amounts of fluid colour mixes.

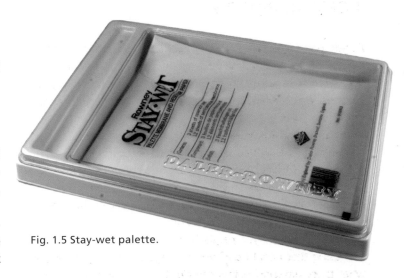

Fig. 1.5 Stay-wet palette.

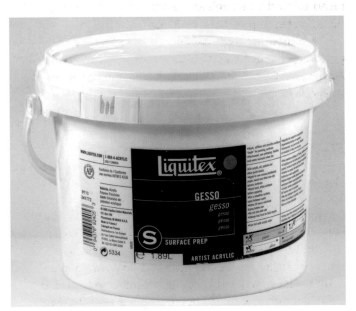

Fig. 1.6.

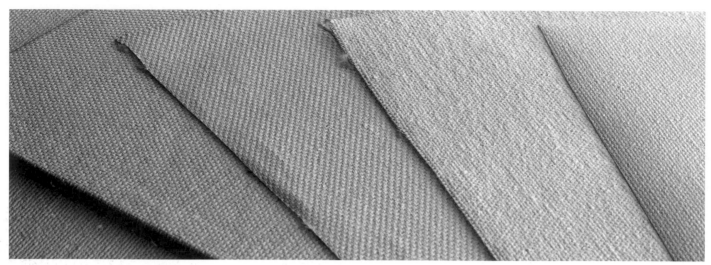

Fig. 1.7 A range of canvas textures.

TEAR-OFF PALETTES, PAINT WELLS, CONTAINERS WITH LIDS, OR A GLASS PALETTE

Tear-off palettes work well with small amounts of paint using small brushes, and charging the brush from the bottom of the paint blob.

Paint wells are best suited for large, liquid applications. Air-tight containers and jars may be used for large paintings with mixed colours which are being painted over many days.

Glass palettes are used for medium to high viscosity thick paints, mixing with brushes or a palette knife. They are easy to clean as the paint comes off in large strips, like plastic.

IMAGETRACE® PAPER, TRACING PAPER

This is a convenient way of transferring drawings in five colour choices. Tracing paper will be needed for photocopying drawings and drawing outlines.

OPACITY

Opacity describes how transparent or opaque the paint is. Depending on the colour, some will appear very transparent when diluted thinly with water, but when applied neat from the tube they appear almost opaque. The most opaque colours appear to have a small amount of white to get that solid look.

They are not as opaque as gouache paints, for example, and therefore often need another coat to achieve that opacity when used as a low to medium viscosity paint.

This range of opacity is because some colours are more naturally opaque or have had an opacity agent added to them. There are opacity ratings on some brands of paint, such as Winsor and Newton's Artists' Acrylics, with 'O' for opaque, 'SO' for semi-opaque, 'ST' for semi-transparent, and 'T' for transparent.

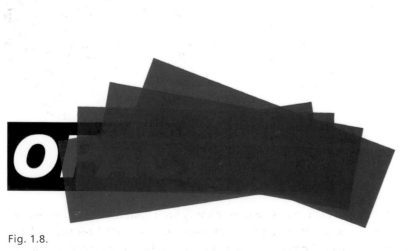

Fig. 1.8.

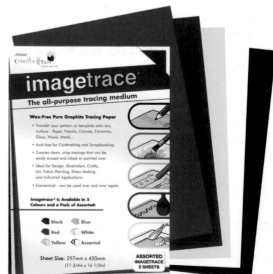

The manufacturer wants to supply the pigment in its strongest form and colour, such as viridian and magenta, but it won't have that vivid 'wow' factor if it's opaque. So the trick is to add a little white into the colour to make it opaque, and then when it's dry, finish it off with a transparent layer to bring back its intensity of colour.

Opaqueness is used to put in that final highlight or reflection with a solid non see-through effect. Or it can be diluted to create fog, mist, dust and so on with a semi-opaque quality. An example of this is in the next chapter, Chapter 2 Shading and Blending, the Stippling Technique, where semi-opaqueness is used to build up an image.

With every successive layer of diluted paint the opacity builds up to a solid colour, and by controlling this property, subtle, smooth and striking effects can be achieved.

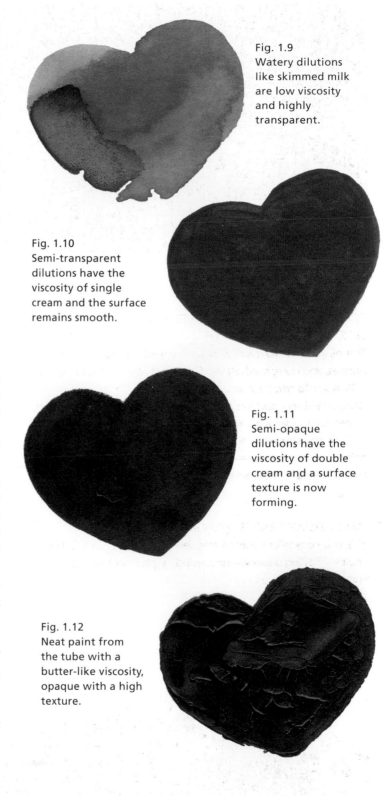

Fig. 1.9
Watery dilutions like skimmed milk are low viscosity and highly transparent.

Fig. 1.10
Semi-transparent dilutions have the viscosity of single cream and the surface remains smooth.

Fig. 1.11
Semi-opaque dilutions have the viscosity of double cream and a surface texture is now forming.

Fig. 1.12
Neat paint from the tube with a butter-like viscosity, opaque with a high texture.

VISCOSITY

Viscosity is probably the first property to master with acrylic painting. The nature of acrylic is such that it is not quite as opaque as some other mediums, and if the aim is to get a solid look there are a few techniques that can be used to achieve that result. It can of course be applied thickly with the inherent texture that will come with that style, but if a smoother painting is desired then understanding viscosity is a very useful skill.

Low viscosity paints are runnier and high viscosity paints are thicker. Think of viscosity as 'friction' between the paint, water and binder components, so very thick paint has a high friction state and watery paint a low friction and a low viscosity state. It does not refer to the transparency of the paint as you can have two mixes of paint with the same viscosity but different transparencies depending on the strength of the paint's pigment. So viscosity in this book's context means how thick or thin the paint is diluted, and I describe it with the analogy of a familiar subject, from milk to butter.

There are various types of acrylics available featuring thinner or thicker paints than the ones used here, but all are usable with each other to create all sorts of wonderful effects and textures. The techniques in this book feature artist's grade, medium viscosity, soft-bodied acrylic paints which are the most commonly used for smooth finishes of artwork.

VISCOSITY TIPS

The big advantage with acrylics is that they are really good for layering. A good habit to start with is to paint too thin rather than too thick when rendering representational images in a smooth finish style. Resist trying to get to the finished result in one go.

With smooth washes it's very important to mix up your water and paint to a consistent watery (low viscosity) dilution, otherwise the pigment will not run from the brush leaving a uniform area or an area of gradation.

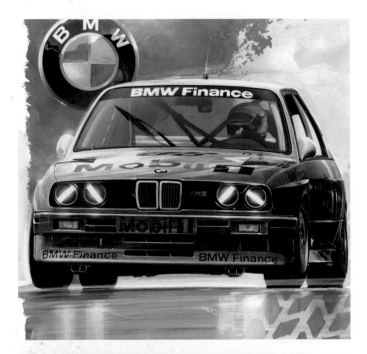

Fig. 1.13 BMW car illustration. In this illustration all the viscosity ranges are applied, from super low very transparent tints, to medium straight-from-the-tube brush work, and high viscosity thick gesso texturing.

LAYERING

Layering is a fabulous quality and acrylics excel at it, and it is this ability that so excited me when I started painting with acrylics. The realization that I could fine tune tonal values by strengthening every layer just by using a thin wash over and over again meant that I could bring subtlety into my acrylic images. So it is best to under paint and do a few weak layers than to go in too heavy if your style is representational and detailed (as an example see the shark illustration at the end of Chapter 12) – and I might say this a few times throughout the book.

For bold, heavy applications in a very stylized or abstract work, layering works just as brilliantly. There are no rules about going from 'fat to lean' or dark to light in acrylics: anything goes depending on the style of the painting. Tinting with watery layers on top of thick paint is fine, and vice versa.

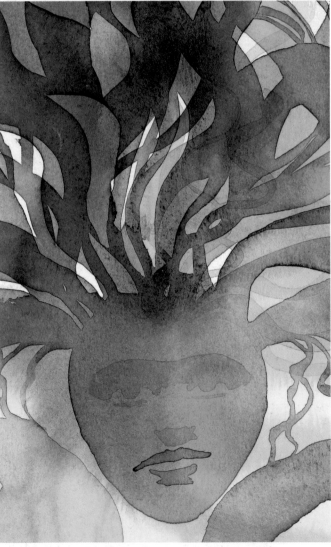

Fig. 1.14 Medusa head. Layer upon layer of watery colour applied on top of wet watercolour board and multiple dry layers.

BRUSH SKILLS

All the paintings in this book feature to some extent an element of detailed brush work, either brush drawing, highlighting or shadow marking.

The workhorse of those brushes is the Winsor & Newton No. 6 222 designer brush, or any similar brush by other makes. This is a brush with slightly longer hair than the standard length, but not as long as a rigger brush. It has a perfect tension for making thin and thick lines by increasing pressure on the brush and then releasing it. It becomes a pencil substitute for adding details, outlines and small shading areas.

Once you know how to make these lines it's surprising how often they become part of a painting.

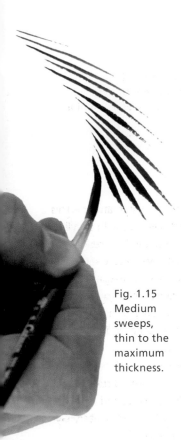

Fig. 1.15 Medium sweeps, thin to the maximum thickness.

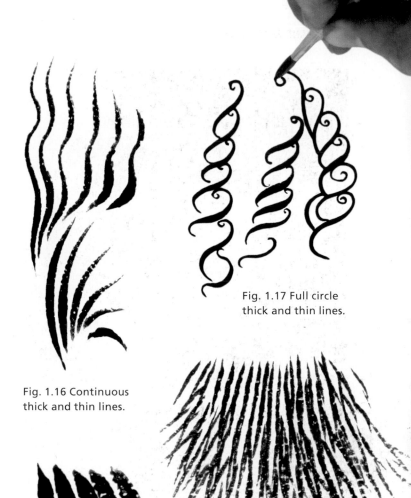

Fig. 1.16 Continuous thick and thin lines.

Fig. 1.17 Full circle thick and thin lines.

Fig. 1.18 Short fat lines on canvas.

Fig. 1.19 Fur lines on canvas.

Thick and Thin Lines

With a mixing brush, make a pool of fluid Mars black with a consistency of pouring cream. Rotate the designer brush in it so that it fills the whole brush, then flatten off the excess, and shape to a small blade.

Use your little finger straight as a support to help control height in either thick and thin brush marks or same thickness marks. Here is a typical variety of line types to practise in any colour.

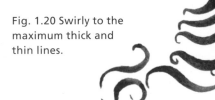

Fig. 1.20 Swirly to the maximum thick and thin lines.

Fig. 1.21 Cut out a variety of cardboard curves to act as a template for repetitive lines.

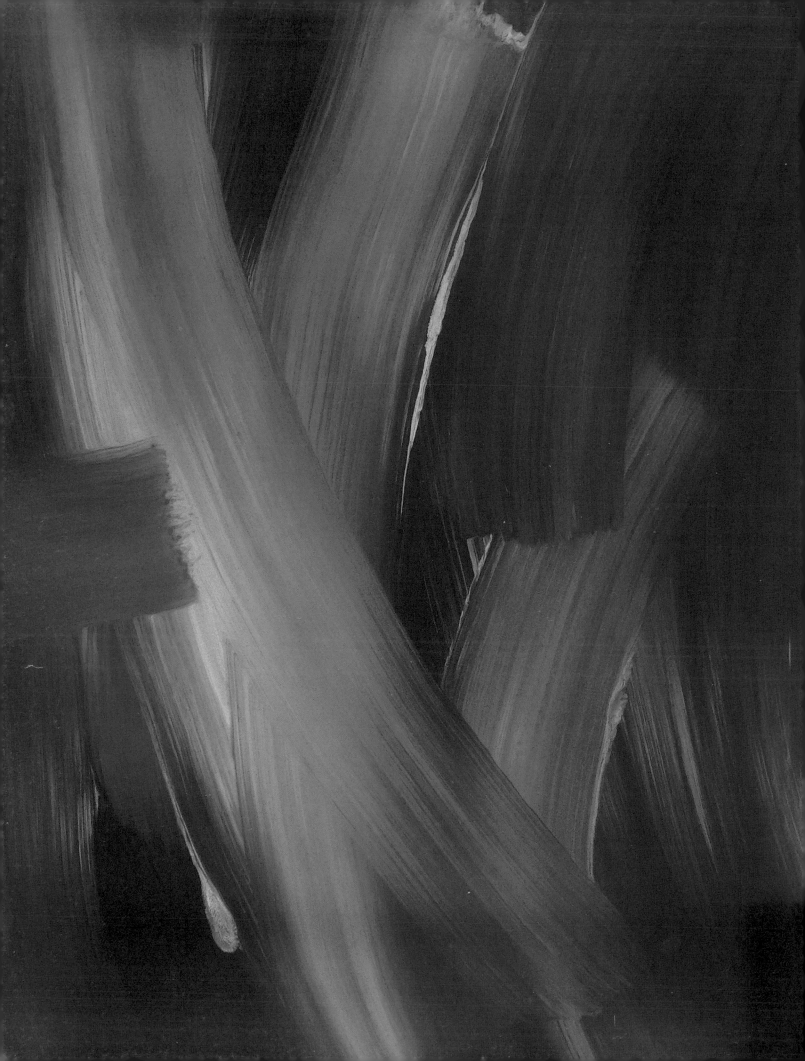

CHAPTER 2

SHADING AND BLENDING

Blending is probably the main challenge that most of us have with acrylics, as their fast-drying property can make them become too dry, too quickly.

Blending wet acrylic colours into each other becomes a time-limited exercise, unlike oils, and requires a little planning. To make successful blends in this context you need to make sure there is enough paint on your palette to match the area to be done, along with a brush of an appropriate size. This may require a retarder to be added to the mix, or a little water. However, in this book I've kept to using acrylics in their natural form.

Most paintings will have blended areas using different techniques: these may involve tints, washes or dry layers as well as the wet-in-wet technique.

Depending on the style of the painting, we sometimes have to create an illusion of blending because the area or style does not lend itself to the wet-in-wet approach. This is where 'dry-brush' and 'stippling' techniques create the blend.

I have created four ways to demonstrate blending colours and tones together with these reflective spheres. I have kept each strictly within the technique, but another great quality of acrylics is that we can also put them together. For example, the wet-in-wet technique can have a tint laid over, or a dry layer applied when it's dry. Each technique results in a particular look.

The blending approaches described here differ in the following way: the 'wet in wet' technique (Fig. 2.1) is quick and generally gives a rougher result. The 'dry brush' technique (Fig. 2.2) gives a slightly more refined blend with an illusion of blending, and the 'wash' technique (Fig. 2.3) an even more refined finish. The ultimate refined technique is a 'dry stippling' (Fig. 2.4) approach, which uses a combination of stippling and tints until a photographic quality is achieved. This technique takes the longest due to the amount of mark making required.

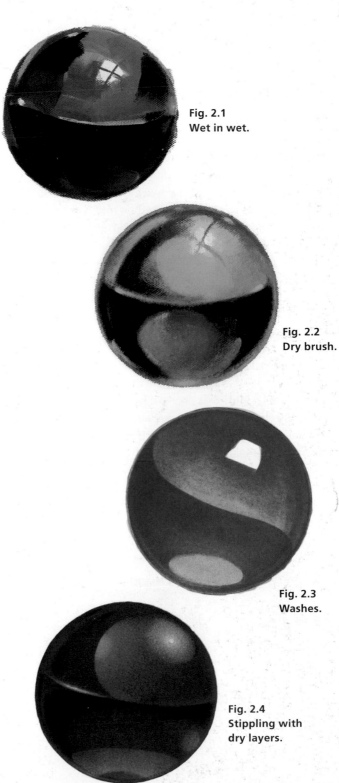

Fig. 2.1
Wet in wet.

Fig. 2.2
Dry brush.

Fig. 2.3
Washes.

Fig. 2.4
Stippling with
dry layers.

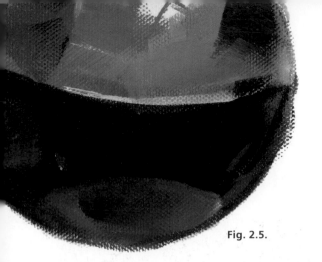

Fig. 2.5.

Wet in Wet

Wet in wet is probably the most popular way of painting in thick paint and is quite similar to oil painting, the major difference being the fast drying time of acrylics. With that in mind I tend to paint small areas at a time, blending as I go so that the paints fold into each other, rather than dry layering one on top of the other.

Applying the paint using this method results in a more painterly style to your work. In this example we are using a flat brush which is fairly large compared to the scale of the ball. This is deliberate for two reasons: it covers quickly, and we want to see the brush marks which give it a painterly style using a combination of the brush corner and the blade tip.

The ball is 4in in diameter so the canvas weave does not become too noticeable and provides a rough resistance, stopping the paint from skidding about.

I call it 'wet in wet' because we are applying paint into the previous wet layer and the aim is not to let any of it dry unless you are happy with that area. From start to finish we will be mixing the colour on the painting and not on our palette – that is, picking up the colour with our brush from our palette and mixing it into the painting.

Judging the amount to pick up with our brush takes a little practice if we are to obtain a uniform opaque covering, so to start with it is better to be mean with the paint than too generous: too much and it's difficult to get the tones to show, as it all blends together and you end up with deep ridges of excess paint.

Have a plan where shades are going to go (Fig. 2.6). A good place to start is to do a tonal sketch in either a pen or pencil so you have a rough idea of where you're going.

Fig. 2.6 Tonal sketch.

Wet-in-Wet Technique

MATERIALS NEEDED

- ½in synthetic flat brush with a nice 'blade' tip – that is, not splaying out too much

- A4-sized real canvas, either canvas board, or stretched or loose canvas

- Tubed acrylics: Dioxazine Purple, Titanium White or White Gesso

The paint used in this example is Titanium White for the light tone (you can use white gesso), and Dioxazine Purple (Fig. 2.7). Have a blob of each colour spaced out from each other ready on your palette.

Remember you need to do this with a sense of urgency throughout as acrylics dry quickly.

Draw a rough circle about 4in in diameter (Fig. 2.8). It needs to be big enough so the scale of the canvas weave does not interfere with the image.

Load up your flat brush and paint in the lower half of the ball with Dioxazine Purple neat from the tube, and with speed and a consistent thickness (Fig. 2.9).

Make sure it's not too thick because more paint is to be added and white will be blended in whilst it is still wet.

TIP: Use the minimum of strokes because the more you fuss and dab, the muddier and more overworked it looks. It's nice to see brush strokes with this style.

Dip into your white (Fig. 2.10) without cleaning your brush. We want random mixing effects.

Start around your highlight with your white paint and it will turn mid-purple (Fig. 2.11); then work your way round into the still-wet bottom half.

If it's too light, dip back into your purple and blend back and forth, varying your direction of strokes to avoid repeated parallel marks.

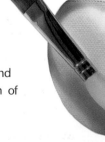

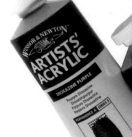

Fig. 2.7.

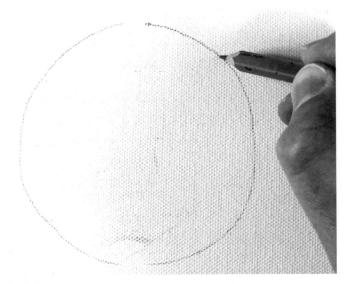

Fig. 2.8.

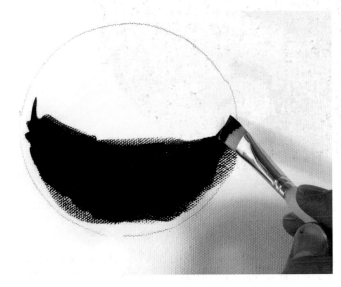

Fig. 2.9.

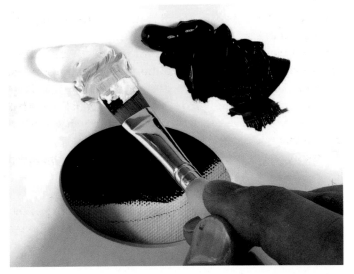

Fig. 2.10.

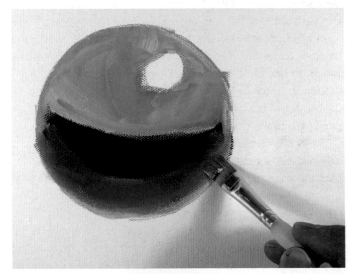

Fig. 2.11.

WET-IN-WET TIPS

Viscosity: Try to keep all your colours the same thickness and viscosity. Adding watery paint into thick paint will make it difficult to blend and it will become transparent. Here we are using paint straight from the tube with no water added.

Too much or too little: Using too much paint with each colour might diminish the effect, while too little will result in dry marks and ridges.

Don't let any areas dry: Unless you are happy with it.

Add a little water: If it's drying too quickly in hot conditions.

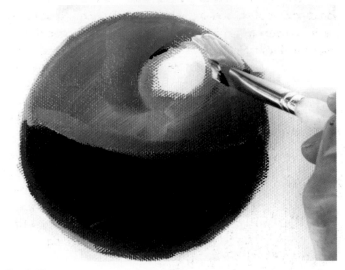

Fig. 2.12.

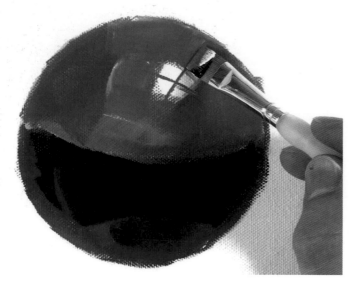

Fig. 2.13.

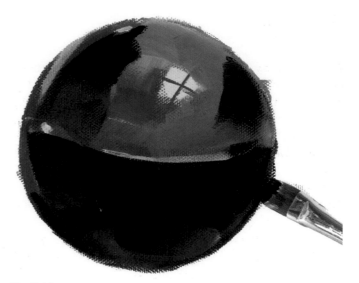

Fig. 2.14.

Add a little more white around the highlight (Fig. 2.12), and brush in where you feel there isn't enough contrast. You are aiming to have a whiter mix radiating away from the highlight.

Use the 'blade' of the brush to add your 'window' detail with mid-purple, and also to tidy up the edges with it (Fig. 2.13).

Finally dip back into the purple and add some purple 'reflections' (Fig. 2.14). Then clean your brush in water, dry it and add some white 'glints' here and there.

Hopefully you have ended up with a 'painterly' ball, and we can use this as a warm-up for Chapter 7 Thick Paint which takes this technique further, in the 'Victoria sponge cake' project.

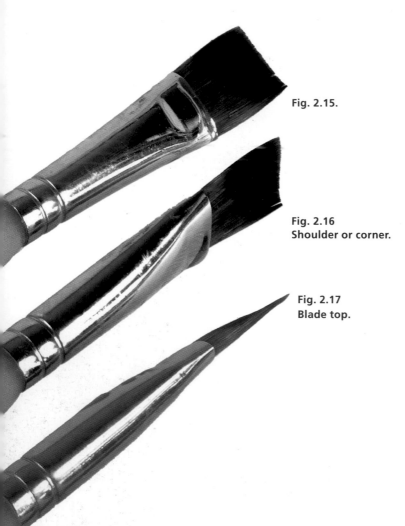

Fig. 2.15.

Fig. 2.16
Shoulder or corner.

Fig. 2.17
Blade top.

BRUSH TIPS

- Keep turning your brush over now and then to use the paint collecting on the other side, and to maintain a flat blade. Hold the brush ranging from about 45 degrees up to the vertical on this technique. Use the shoulder of the brush for smaller marks.

- Acrylic paint loves destroying brushes so try not to let it dry at the top of the hairs. Wipe the brush dry with kitchen cloth or towel in your fingers and not on a flat table as you can remove more paint thoroughly and not damage the brush.

Dry Brush

This is a classic way of creating an illusion of blending tones. I like to think of it as an alternative to shading with a pencil (Fig. 2.19), except we are using neat paint at just the right viscosity to create a similar effect. This exercise is a good practice run for the dry brush 'Egyptian Head' example described in Chapter 11, where we take the technique further into a variety of colours and smaller marks.

Quite often in a painting there will be small areas that need shading, and instead of blending wet colours together this dry-brush technique will do the task. It is especially effective when applying lighter tones and highlights on top of darker tones.

Don't be afraid of the 'big brush–small painting' concept. As you can see in Fig. 2.20, the brush used is a large hog-hair brush, because we want a wide area of uniform marks. The paint has no water added and feels like clotted cream.

The mannerism of brush strokes is one of small 'drags' slightly criss-crossing each other. The brush angle is low as· if you were 'cleaning' your brush of paint across the rough canvas surface, and bit by bit the paint will appear and build up. You will need to switch sides of the brush now and then before a re-load. Practise getting the right amount of paint on your brush: it needs less than you think.

(Fig.2.20) To start with, make sure your paint is mixed thoroughly to a mid tone using Phthalo Green with a little white.

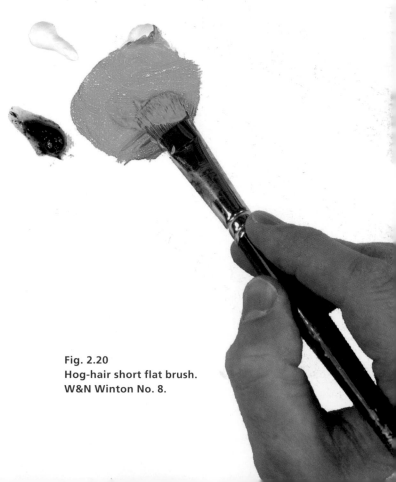

Fig. 2.18.

Fig. 2.19
Tonal sketch.

Fig. 2.20
Hog-hair short flat brush.
W&N Winton No. 8.

DRY-BRUSH TIPS

Rotate the board: Always rotate your work to suit your brush-stroke preference.

Low angle brush: Dragging the brush at a low angle uses the canvas weave to pick up the paint and create shading effects.

Choose the right canvas: If the canvas has imperfections or a very open weave, this will stand out.

Dry Brush Technique

MATERIALS NEEDED

- No. 8 Winsor & Newton short flat Hog Brush

- A4-sized real canvas, either canvas board, or stretched or loose canvas

- Tubed acrylics: Phthalo Green, Payne's Gray, Titanium White or White Gesso

---

(Fig. 2.21) Load up the brush and spread the paint evenly and thinly using a variety of brush directions. Paint a smooth, thin coat without ridges and just thick enough to cover.

(Fig.2.22) Finish the edges by rotating the board with an all-over, even tone.

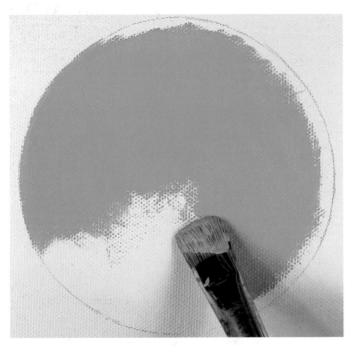

Fig. 2.21.

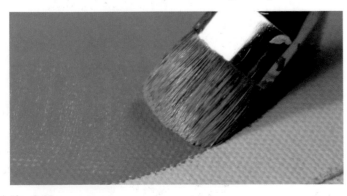

Fig. 2.22.

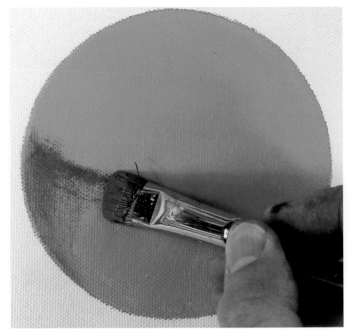

Fig. 2.23.

(Fig. 2.23) Add a bit more green to your lighter mix to make it darker to give a mid-tone. Thoroughly mix and load up. Tap your brush flat and remove any excess paint from high in the bristles, as this has a habit of 'blobbing' down unexpectedly.

(Fig. 2.24) Once the lower half has a darker mid-tone coat let it dry for a moment: if it is even slightly damp the next coat will bring away the layer before.

(Fig. 2.25) Again add a little more green to make an even darker green, and apply like before, shading areas from the outside of the ball.

(Fig. 2.26) After adding dark tones to the top half of the ball it's time to add the highlights. Mix up a light green by adding a little Phthalo green to white.

This is the stage where it takes on a more '3D' look. Start with the centre section in the top half, adding a lighter tone where it's needed.

(Fig. 2.27) Now with a very light tone but not quite white, add the window 'shine' and some lighter reflections in various places.

(Fig. 2.28) Turning the board round to suit your brush-stroke direction makes it easier to make marks accurately.

(Fig. 2.29) Finally add the white window highlight and darker cross bar.

This example has a relatively rough result with blending tones because the paint was applied thickly and the canvas has a medium tightness of weave. A smoother canvas and a dryer brush would allow a finer result.

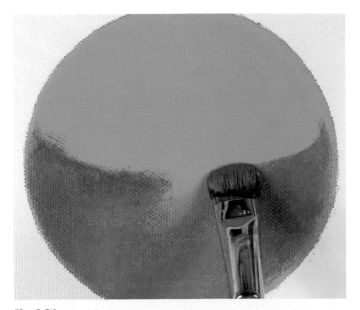

Fig. 2.24.

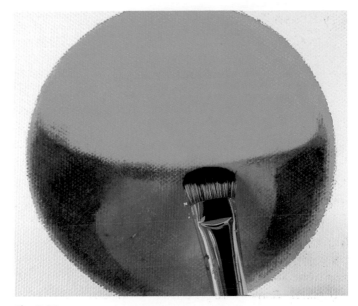

Fig. 2.25.

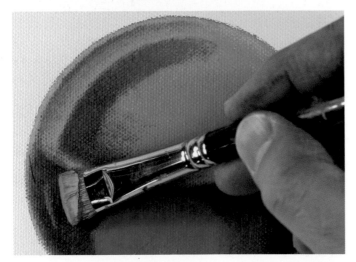

Fig. 2.26.

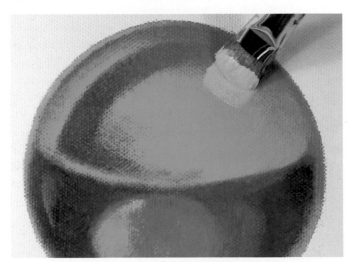

Fig. 2.27.

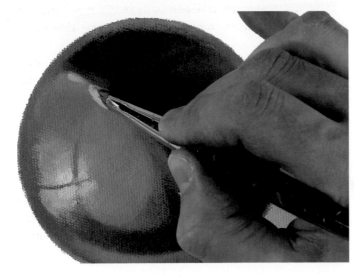

Fig. 2.28.

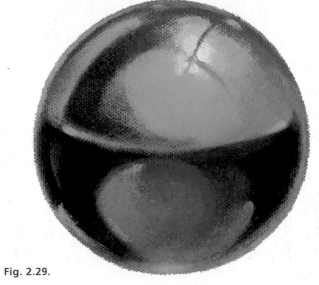

Fig. 2.29.

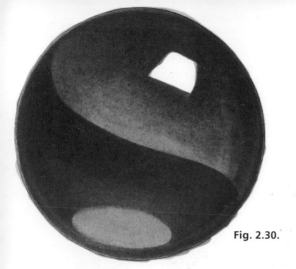

Fig. 2.30.

Washes

Washes are another brilliant property of acrylics. There are no limits to how many times you can layer another wash – in fact in the end the colour becomes solid.

In a 'watercolour' style painting transparency is the key principle, but with acrylics you have the option of adding a little opacity to the mix with either white or any other opaque colour (for opaque colours, see Chapter 1, Opacity, Viscosity and Layering). This will help to give a smoother and flatter result, and eliminates those tiny pigment marks that settle in the board texture, as seen in this example. Ultramarine Blue is a colour that often creates this effect.

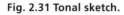

In this example Ultramarine Blue is the only paint used to show a basic principle of graduating washes. This could be taken further by using another transparent colour, or adding a tiny amount of white.

A full step-by-step example takes this exercise further in the street scene in Chapter 6 'Line and Wash'.

Fig. 2.31 Tonal sketch.

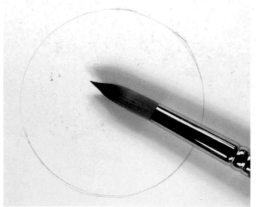

Fig. 2.32.

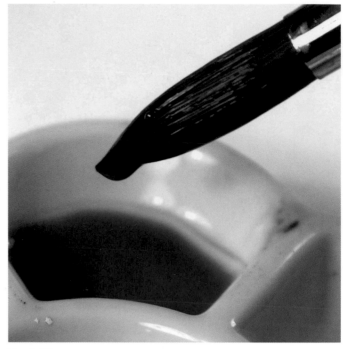

Fig. 2.33.

Washes Technique

MATERIALS NEEDED

- A large wash brush. Here I use a Winsor & Newton Cotman No. 14 Wash Brush 111

- Smooth watercolour board, or gummed and stretched watercolour paper

- Tubed acrylics: Ultramarine Blue, Titanium White

THE FIRST LAYER
(Fig. 2.31) First sketch a tonal drawing of the subject so that in your mind's eye you already know where the lightest and darkest areas will be.

(Fig. 2.32) On the smooth watercolour board draw a rough circle using a compass, jam-jar lid or even freehand!

(Fig. 2.33) Mix enough liquid to do at least five layers. Make sure the brush is loaded with watery colour almost to the point that it is dripping out of the brush.

(Fig. 2.34) With your board on a slight slope, paint your circle from the top to bottom in zig-zag strokes, leaving a little square-ish window. As long as the bottom edge of the wash is not allowed to dry no 'tide marks' will appear.

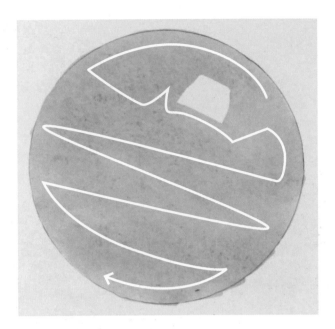

Fig. 2.34.

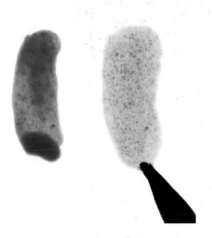

Fig. 2.36.

TWO IMPORTANT WASH SKILLS

The 'soak up' skill – removing wet paint:
After a coat of colour is laid down, rinse your brush and pinch it dry so you can now use it to 'soak up' an area of colour you would like lighter (Fig. 2.35). It's important not to 'fuss' the surface, but just dab once or twice, or slowly sweep the surface.

This can be done with successive layers and helps graduate tones in small, irregular and fiddly areas.

and drag the brush around the edges in long sweeps. The amount of softening will be influenced by a few variables: the amount of water on the surface, the amount of clean water in the brush, and the gradient of your board. See Fig. 2.40 and Fig. 2.41.

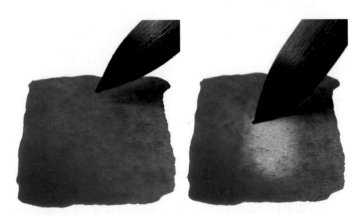

Fig. 2.35.

The 'soften the edge' skill:
This is best done with the board level. Before the edges of the colour have time to dry, apply a damp, clean brush along the outside edges at a low angle and encourage the paint to flow into your brush (Fig. 2.36). It's important not to fuss here too,

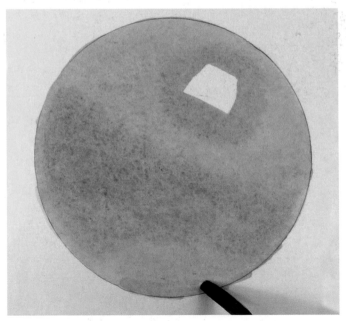

Fig. 2.37.

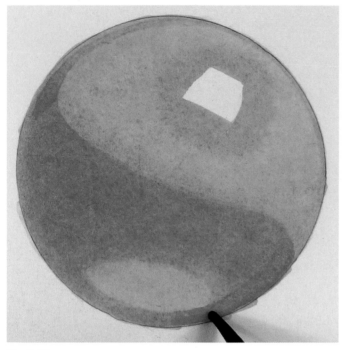

Fig. 2.38.

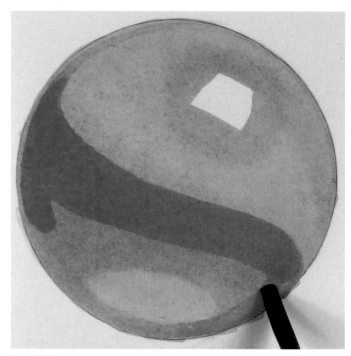

Fig. 2.39.

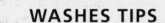

WASHES TIPS

Use thin dilutions: Use watery mixes first, building up to thicker ones.

Mix enough colour: It's easy to run out of colour with many layers.

Position the board on a slight slope: Let gravity do some of the wash.

Use a big brush that holds lots of colour: Less dipping, smoother shades.

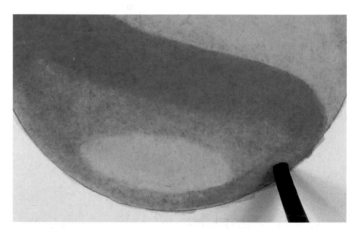

Fig. 2.40.

THE SECOND AND THIRD LAYERS

(Fig. 2.37) After the first layer is dry in approximately five minutes, load up the brush again and put on a second coat all over and let it dry.

(Fig. 2.38) With the third layer, leave a sharp edge across the middle of the ball and soften the edge of the light blue oval at the bottom.

THE FOURTH LAYER

(Fig. 2.39) Now with the fourth layer the colours can be stronger and lay in a strong band across the middle with the board on a slight slope. (Fig. 2.40) Then soften the lower edge with the brush cleaned and damp.

(Fig. 2.41) Using the same technique, now apply the darker blue to the top and soften the lower edge and allow it to dry.

It's always a good idea to underplay the strength of colour until you become familiar with it. This allows you to maintain the lightest areas until later on, and if you decide they need darkening it's a lot easier to do.

(Fig. 2.42) To build up the tones, keep adding more layers and softening on the bottom edges. This may require two or more washes to build up strength.

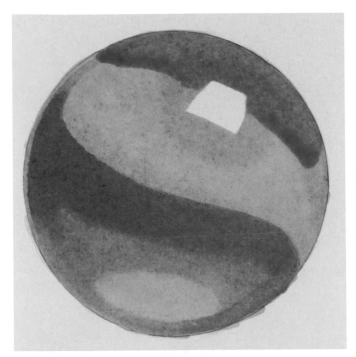

Fig. 2.41.

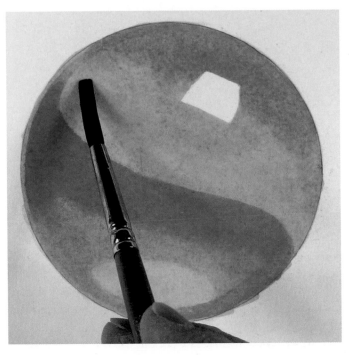

Fig. 2.42.

(Fig. 2.43) Build up more layers until the final strength of tone is achieved.

All that's left to do is to add a few highlights here and there in white and pale blue. If it's to be on a white background the circle edge could be cleaned up with a few thin layers of white gesso. Or if it were in a scene with a background, the surrounding

paint would cover up the rough edges; then a final circle edge of opaque light blue would be painted on the ball to sharpen it up further.

(Fig. 2.44) The final ball in its basic form. From here it could be made into an opaque painting with thin layers of extra shading and detail until it becomes almost photographic.

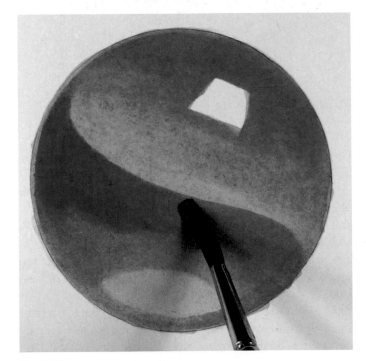

Fig. 2.43.

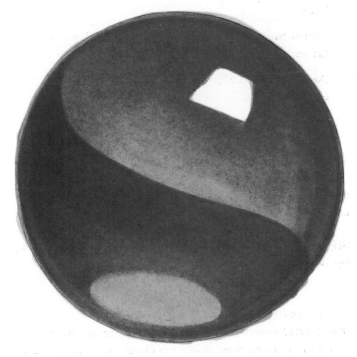

Fig. 2.44.

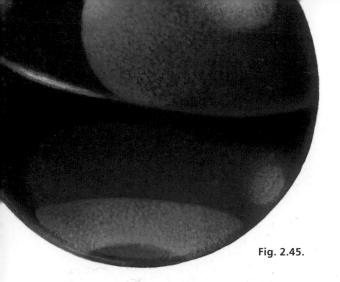

Fig. 2.45.

Stippling with Dry Layers

This red ball demonstrates acrylics' particularly brilliant quality: their ability to be painted in thin layers so that you can create an illusion of a blend or vignette or graduation. They can be applied transparently or opaquely, but the key is 'building up' the strengths of tone. Chapter 12 – Puppies – takes this further.

In this example it's an opaque finish in contrast to the transparent 'Washes' example described previously. Cadmium Red in this case is already opaque in nature straight from the tube. So we will use it thinly. White mixed with Cadmium Red will create our lighter tones, and Titanium White our highlights. Payne's Grey with Cadmium Red Deep will give the dark tones as on the tonal sketch (Fig. 2.46).

This could be done on gessoed canvas or gessoed MDF or hardboard, but this example is done on illustration board for a smoother finish. The key technique is to mix the paint thinly (Fig. 2.47) as if it were a watercolour on all the layers with the exception of the first coat: this is the blocking-in coat of mid tone, Cadmium Red (Fig. 2.48)

FIRST COAT – BLOCKING IN

Draw a light circle in pencil with either a jam-jar lid or compass. (Fig. 2.47) Mix the paint from the tube with water until it's both runny but still fairly opaque. (Fig. 2.48) Too thin and it will leave brush marks of different tones, and too thick will leave ridges of paint. It's not necessary to have your board on a slope, but it is helpful if you can rotate it to suit your painting directions. Don't leave any paint-stroke edges unless you are happy with them.

Fig. 2.46 Tonal sketch.

Stippling with Dry Layers Technique

MATERIALS NEEDED

- A ½in flat synthetic brush for blocking in

- A detail brush: Winsor & Newton Designer 222 round synthetic brush

- Smooth watercolour board or gummed and stretched watercolour paper

- Tubed acrylics: Cadmium Red medium, Deep Cadmium Red, Payne's Grey, Titanium White

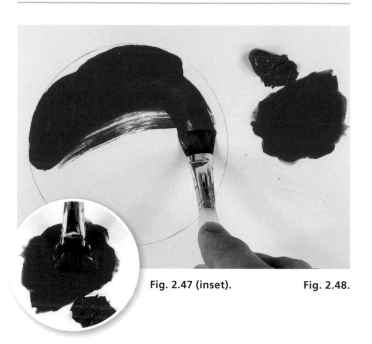

Fig. 2.47 (inset). **Fig. 2.48.**

(Fig. 2.49) Block in methodically, brushing the paint to a smooth and consistent finish.

MID-TONES

(Fig. 2.50) Using Cadmium Red Deep, mix with a little water until you have a thin consistency. Your brush marks should be like watercolour marks. Load your brush by rolling it in the colour at a low angle to a point, and test it so you are left with a nice mark. To complete this exercise the brush may need re-loading a dozen times so there needs to be enough liquid pre-mixed paint available.

(Fig. 2.51) Starting across the middle, work your way across the ball. The marks should be faint because in a moment you will go back over them filling any gaps. Think of it as shading with a stipple mannerism. Towards the outer edges it will be darker, and this will consequently have more layers, as indicated in the tonal sketch.

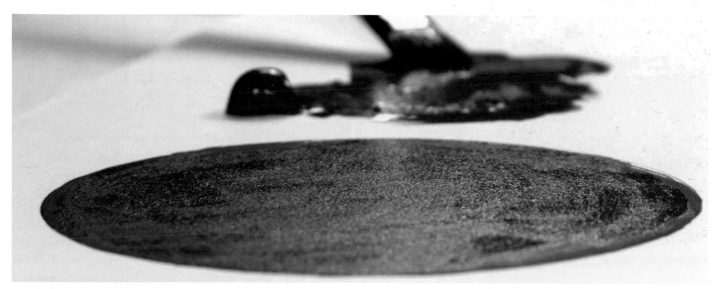

Fig. 2.49.

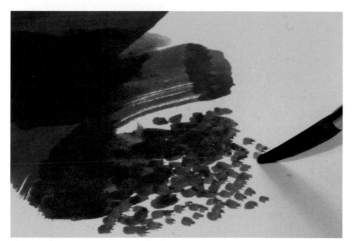

Fig. 2.50.

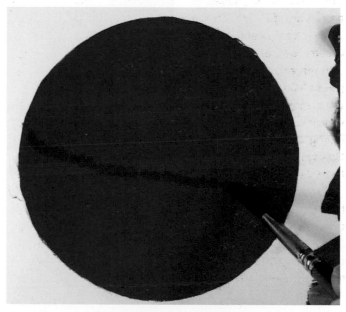

Fig. 2.51.

(Fig. 2.52) Once the mid tones are stippled in, it's an opportunity to refine any graduations you are not happy with, or add another reflective element.

(Fig. 2.53) Do this by stippling with the original Cadmium Red.

Now all that's remaining are to paint in two tones, an even darker tone and a lighter tone, before the highlights go in. So we will start with the light tones.

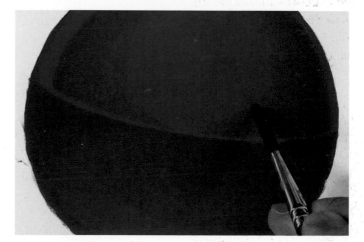

Fig. 2.52.

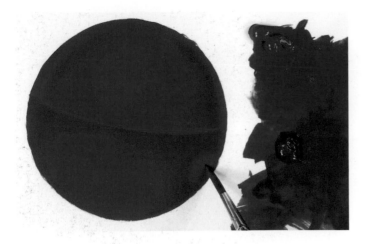

Fig. 2.53.

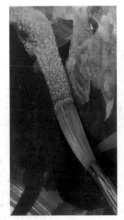 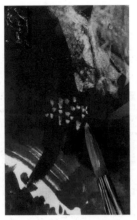

Fig. 2.54.   **Fig. 2.55.**

STIPPLING TIPS

Brush makes a nice point: Roll to a point or small flat tip after loading the brush.

Thin to medium viscosity: Too thick will leave strong marks.

Marks dry weaker and may need a second coat: Lighter tones often need a second layer.

LIGHT TONES

Mix pure white with water so it looks like milk (Fig. 2.54) and dab off enough liquid from your loaded brush until you get clean stipple marks (Fig. 2.55) like the dark red stipple marks done before.

(Fig. 2.56) Using the white stipple marks, start at the point where the white will be strongest, and work your way out, increasing the spacing of the marks.

As the weakest marks want to be on the outer edge it's possible to time those areas with the last marks available from the brush as it becomes drier.

(Fig. 2.57) When the brush is first loaded the paint will be making wetter marks and therefore slightly whiter in this case. Also as they dry they become weaker and less obvious. This allows you to make subtle marks, and the next layer will double the strength and so you build up an area of tonal gradation. Keep building the light stipples at the bottom of the ball, too, and put a little highlight across the middle.

DARK TONES

(Fig. 2.58) Mix a little Payne's Grey with Deep Cadmium Red to create the deepest tones on the underside of the ball. Keep the strength weak otherwise it'll look too dotty! Remember if you go too strong you can go over it again with Cadmium Red dots to soften it again.

THE HIGHLIGHTS

(Fig. 2.59) Take a little neat white and add a pin-point highlight.

(Fig. 2.60) Mix a milky consistency of white with water and radiate dots away from the central dot. For extra subtlety the mix could be weaker towards the outer edges.

This is our basic stipple illusion of blending. Added to this can be tint washes and other brush-mark stippling to add further realism and content.

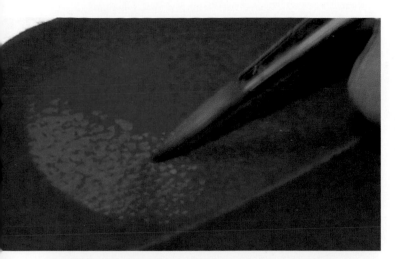

Fig. 2.56.

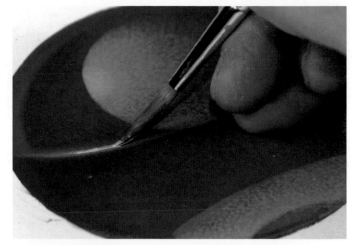

Fig. 2.57.

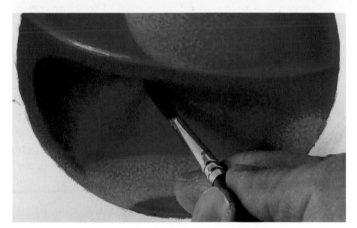

Fig. 2.58.

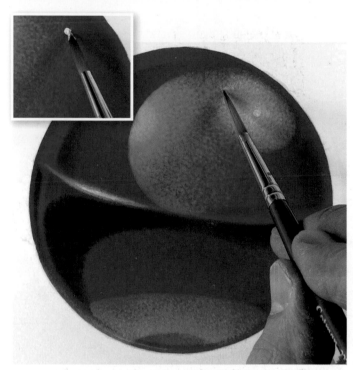

Fig. 2.59 (inset). Fig. 2.60.

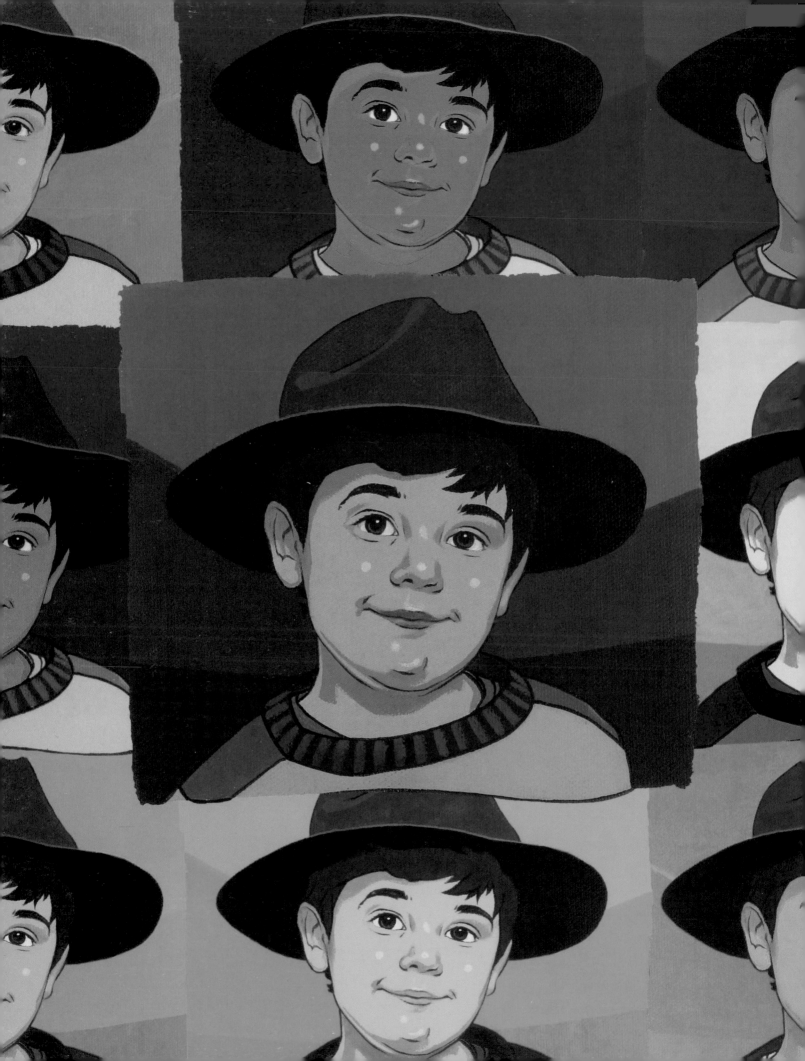

CHAPTER 3

FLAT COLOUR

This is the technique of applying opaque layers to form a flat, uniform tone.

Introduction

Obtaining areas of flat colour is easy if you take a little time over it, by letting each thin opaque layer dry before applying another one. This is a useful effect if the painting or illustration has a graphic quality, so that areas of flat tone with a thin uniform surface may be created without any brush marks.

This project takes a photograph and reduces it to flat colours like a cartoon or a piece of pop art. This example has been applied on canvas to give it an 'arty' feel rather than an illustration which would be traditionally done on HP or CP illustration board or watercolour paper. (HP Hot Pressed board has a smooth finish, whereas CP Cold Pressed Illustration board has a slightly textured finish.) Gessoed canvas is also a great surface which has been chosen in this example.

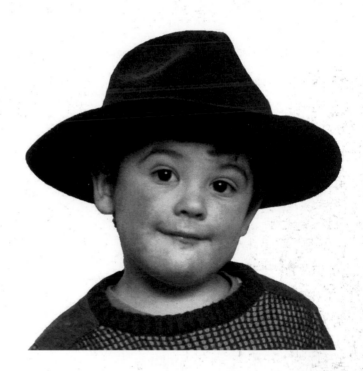

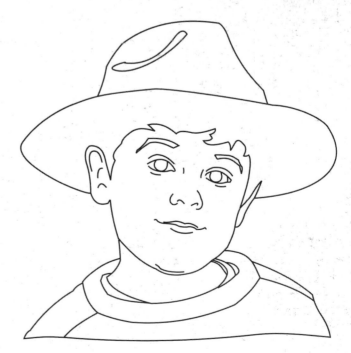

TOP RIGHT: Fig. 3.1
Photocopy the photo to 200 per cent, if you would like to do your own line drawing. Tape tracing paper over the copy.

BOTTOM RIGHT: Fig. 3.2
Photocopy the line drawing guide to 200 per cent on to tracing paper, cut it square from the A4 paper and tape into place along the top on the front of the canvas board.

Preparation

MATERIALS NEEDED

- Brushes (see image below)

- A photo reference and line drawing

- Tracing paper

- Pencil, line pen or fine line brush

- Imagetrace® paper for tracing down or a 6B soft pencil for using on the back of the photocopy or trace

- A tracing pen or sharp 2H pencil

- Canvas board or illustration board

- A flat synthetic brush for applying the paint

- A round detail brush for the outlines

- A mixing brush, for creating pools of reusable colour

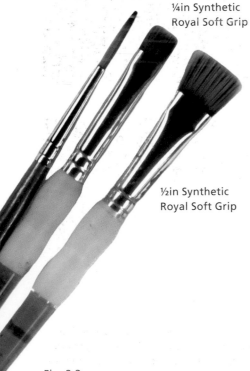

Synthetic Cotman
Winsor & Newton No.4
222 Designer Brush

¼in Synthetic
Royal Soft Grip

½in Synthetic
Royal Soft Grip

Fig. 3.3.

First coat

Second coat

Third coat

Fig. 3.4.

Paints

The exact tones and colours in this exercise are not important. For example, when using browns and blues it can be either Cobalt or Ultramarine, the browns can either be Burnt Sienna, Burnt Umber or Vandyke Brown. In this image the following have been used:

Titanium White or Gesso
Burnt Umber (hat)
Burnt Sienna (skin shadow, background)
Cobalt Blue (jumper, hat)
Ultramarine Blue (jumper)
Dioxine Purple (skin shadow)
Cadmium Yellow (background)
Cadmium Red (background)
Payne's Grey (hat, jumper)
Pale Terracotta (skin)
Mars Black (line work)

Using the Supplied Line Drawing

When trying this example on canvas use the supplied line drawing, enlarging it by 200 per cent or more on a photocopier. Most photocopiers will accept an A4 sheet of tracing paper which is ideal, but normal white copy paper will work too.

The advantage of tracing paper is that it allows you to see instantly where you need to make adjustments avoiding having to lift the copy paper up and down many times to get an idea of which bits need amending. Painting it at 200 per cent will make the details clearer.

The Shortcut Using No Line Drawing

It's possible to miss out the line drawing by tracing straight through the photo, which is on photocopy paper. The down side is it may not be as clear and as clean as the version that has had the finer points of line work resolved.

Using Your Own Line Drawing

(Fig. 3.5) Print out to size a photo and tape a piece of tracing paper over it and tape it in position. Using a pencil, fine black marker or a brush with acrylic paint, trace the outlines. Here a brush has been used.

(Fig. 3.6) An important point to make when doing any tracing is to be focused on consistent 'centre of line' tracing. In other words, when drawing a circle around the pupil of the eye, keep on the very edge, not on the inside of one pupil and the outside edge on the other pupil. It's these little details which appear exaggerated in the line drawing. It's very easy to 'wander' either side of the real edge. This can get compounded like a Chinese whisper when tracing through for the second time.

(Fig.3.7) The carbon paper tracing will leave a carbon line which ideally is just faint enough to be seen. Too much pressure can result in a heavy dark line, which can be difficult to obscure with paint.

The Three Painting Stages

The first stage is to complete all the flat colours on the face and hat and then the background. The second stage is to add the shadow flat colours around the face, and the third stage is all the line work and any paint tweaking, like the corner of the eyes, for example.

Painting the Face

Make sure the trace is taped securely in position, as re-tracing may be needed in some areas later.

(Figs 3.8 and 3.9) Squirt neat Pale Terracotta into a palette well, or a mixed-up flesh colour using yellow, red and white neat from the tubes. This is already opaque and thick enough to use as it is, and there is no need to add water, which would make it too transparent.

(Figs 3.10 and 3.11) Load up the brush and apply the paint in short strokes, making sure to connect with the previous stroke, keeping the paint fluid and not allowing any edges to dry as this will leave marks.

(Fig. 3.12) The aim is to spread the paint uniformly and thin-ly with no paint edges being left. Keep the direction of brush strokes random so no parallel or repeat marks are made.

(Fig.3.13) The first coat will leave a semi-transparent result with a few dark and light patches.

(Fig. 3.14) After three coats the result will be flat and opaque.

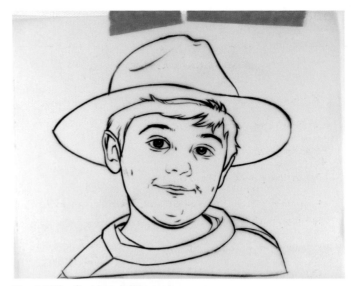

Fig. 3.5 The first brush line trace.

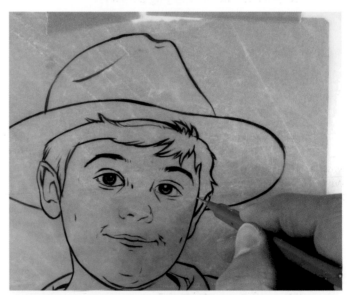

Fig. 3.6.

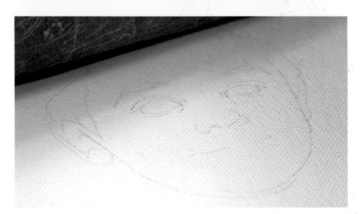

Fig. 3.7 The Imagetrace® paper tracing will leave a carbon line which ideally is just faint enough to be seen. Too much pressure can result in a heavy dark line, which can be difficult to obscure with paint.

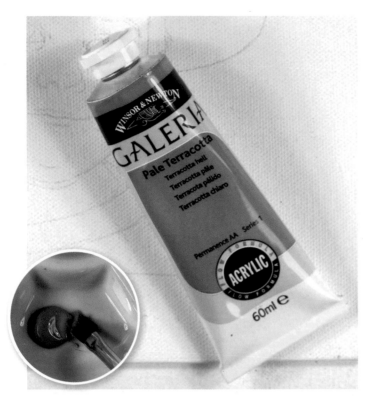

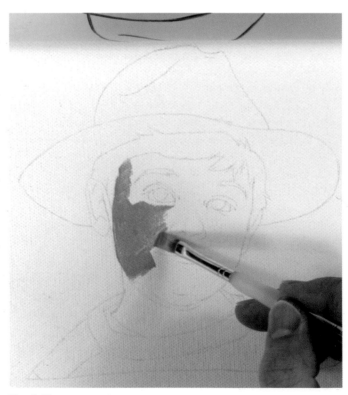

CHECK YOUR EDGES

Check with your tracing that all the flesh tones in the areas required have been completed. In this picture (Fig. 3.16) the neck is not yet done.

FLAT COLOUR TIPS

- Mix enough colour at the beginning for successive layers.

- Vary the brush angles to avoid parrallel marks.

- Four thin coats are better than two thick ones.

- Keep the trace in position until the end.

- Adding a little white to the mix helps create an opaque finish.

Fig. 3.8.   Fig. 3.9.

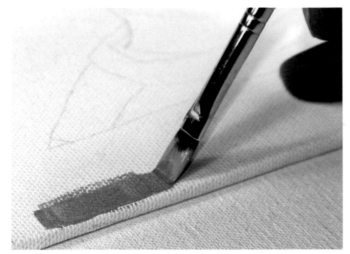

Fig. 3.10. Thinly applied.

Fig. 3.11 Use random brush angles and overlap them.

Fig. 3.12.

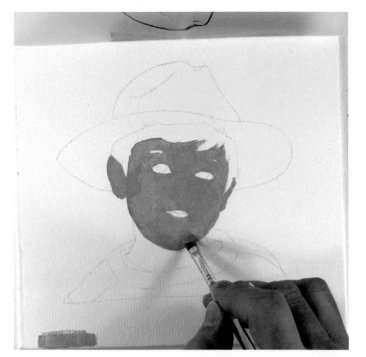

Fig. 3.13.

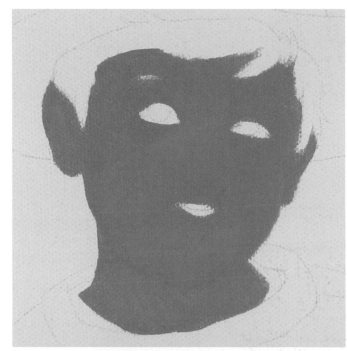

Fig. 3.14 After three coats.

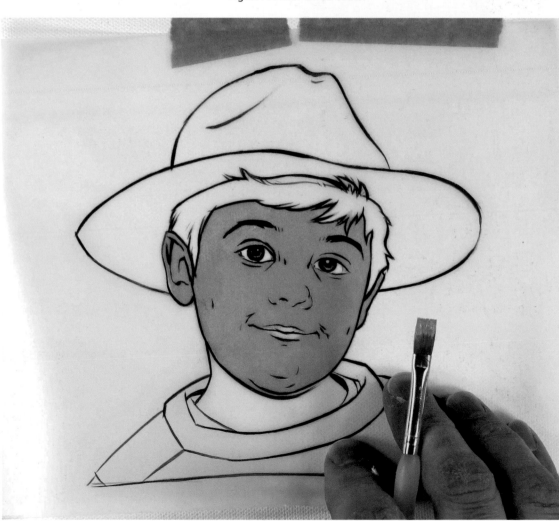

Fig. 3.15
Checking your areas
of colour.

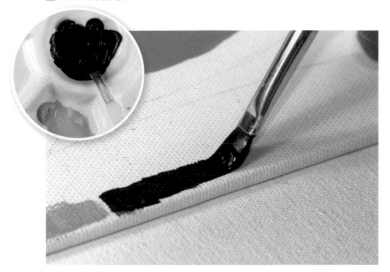

Fig. 3.16 (inset).   Fig. 3.17.

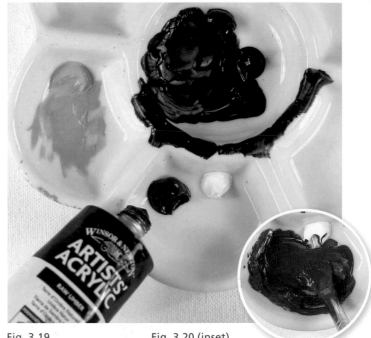

Fig. 3.19.   Fig. 3.20 (inset).

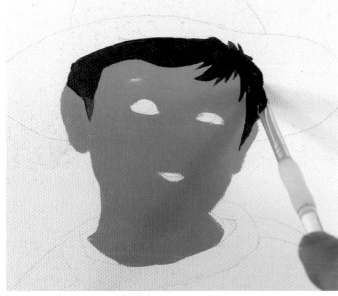

Fig. 3.18.

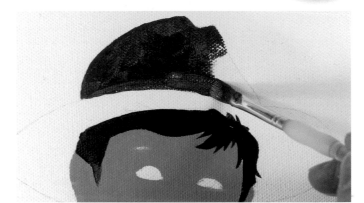

Fig. 3.21.

The Hair and Hat

Mix thoroughly the hair colour, which in this case is Burnt Umber and Black, and again apply thinly (Figs 3.16, 3.17 and 3.18).

Use Raw Umber and White again for the hat. White is a very strong colour and only a little is needed to create a lighter and more opaque Raw Umber. (Figs 3.19–3.22).

The next couple of pages demonstrate altering the colour to enhance the effect. After painting the brim of the hat, lighten the top part.

For the rim, mix enough paint to do three layers. A little Cobalt Blue and Burnt Umber and a little white have been used here (Figs 3.23–3.25).

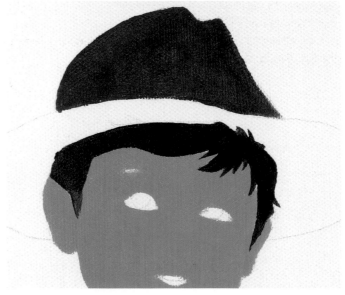

Fig. 3.22.

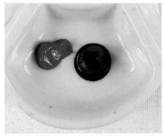

Fig. 3.23.

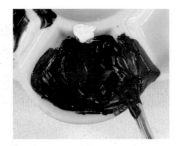

Fig. 3.24.

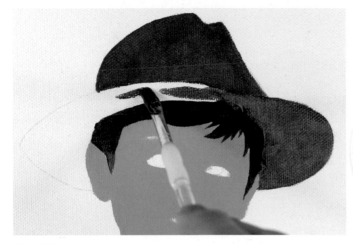

Fig. 3.25.

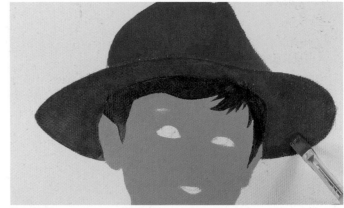

Fig. 3.26.

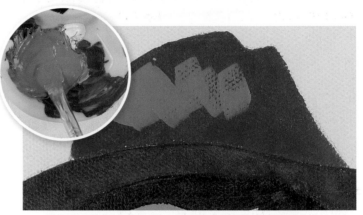

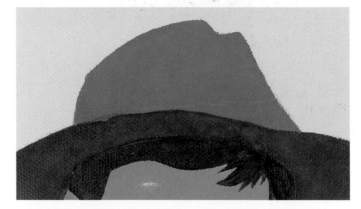

Fig. 3.27 (inset).   Fig. 3.28.

Making Changes is Easy

After the second coat on the top part of the hat (Fig. 3.26) try changing the colour and tone when the paint is dry.

Raw Umber and White have been used (Figs 3.27–Fig.3.29), giving a yellower and lighter finish. The more white that's in the mix, the more opaque the result.

A third layer can be added to the rim, and another layer to the hair (Fig. 3.30).

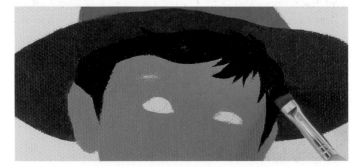

Fig. 3.29.

Fig. 3.30.

The Jumper

Ultramarine and Payne's Grey have been used to give a dark blue. Due to the lack of white this will need three coats (Fig. 3.31).

The mix is not too runny but just thick enough to spread thinly.

Check with your tracing guide where the boundaries are (Fig. 3.32).

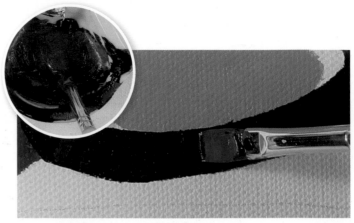

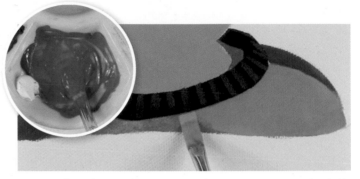

Fig. 3.35 (inset).   Fig. 3.36.

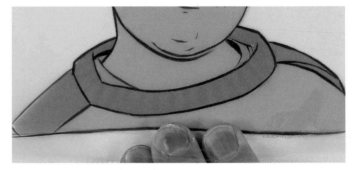

Fig. 3.37 (inset).   Fig. 3.38.

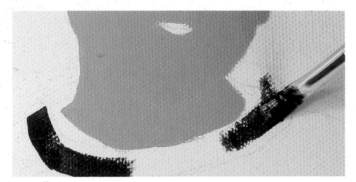

Fig. 3.31.

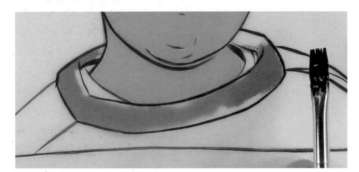

Fig. 3.32.

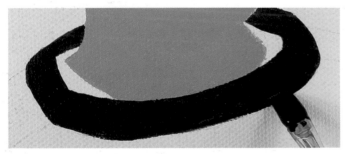

Fig. 3.33.

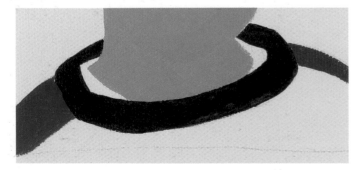

Fig. 3.34.

Fig. 3.39.

Use the blade of the brush to make corners and edges (Fig. 3.33).

For the shoulders, add a little white into the blue collar mix, making sure you still have enough for another coat on the collar (Fig. 3.34).

Using a bit more of the shoulder colour, add the detail marks around the collar. As it's a more generous dab of colour, once may be enough (Fig. 3.35 and Fig. 3.36).

Mixing Cobalt Blue with White, add two coats on the main jumper front, and add a darker mix of those two colours for the T-Shirt (Fig. 3.37 and Fig. 3.38).

Make a final check with the tracing before adding the details (Fig. 3.39).

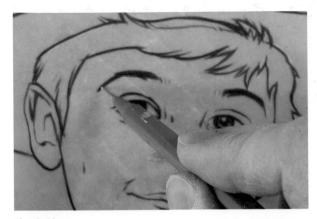

Fig. 3.40.

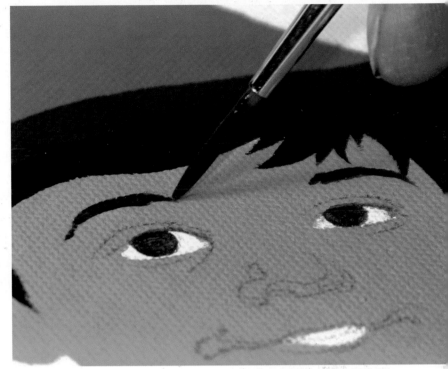

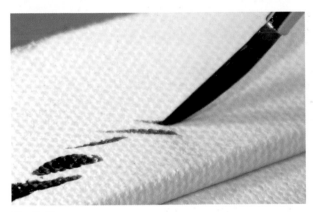

Fig. 3.41.

Fig. 3.42.

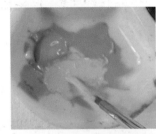

Fig. 3.43.

The Details

(Fig. 3.40) With Imagetrace® paper, trace down the face details. Mix a little water into neat Burnt Umber so that it is runny enough to flow from the brush, and paint in the eyebrows and pupils.

(Fig. 3.41) Use a soft long brush like the one pictured, which has a nice blade and tip. This will need a few coats as there is no white in the mix.

Using our brush skills learnt in the 'Brush skills' chapter, make delicate thin and thick lines on the eyebrows. The canvas has a rough surface which can disrupt the line a little so it may need two or three strokes (Fig. 3.41 and Fig. 3.42).

The Highlights

(Fig. 3.43) There are only a few highlights on the face in this style of painting, so a tiny mix of white and Terracotta is all that's needed.

(Fig. 3.44) Light colours like white tend to fade as they dry, so top up the effect with another coat.

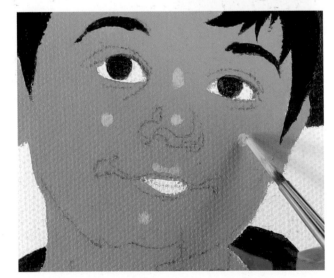

Fig. 3.44.

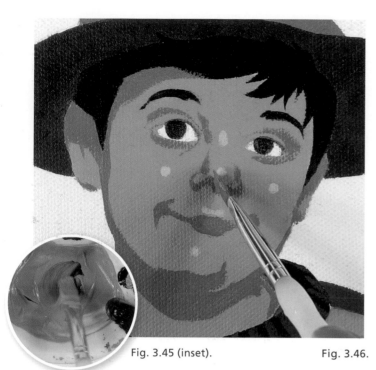

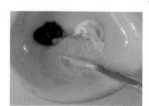

Fig. 3.45 (inset).   Fig. 3.46.

The Shadows

The shadow colour is a white base with a small amount of Burnt Sienna and Dioxine Purple (Figs 3.45 and 3.46).

There's no line to follow for the shadow so it's a case of squinting at the photo and judging where the natural edge of the shadow will end.

There's a wider area of shadow colour under the chin, so a wider soft brush was chosen to add in these shadows. The two corners and blade of the brush usually give the required detail.

Eye Colour

Depending on the lighting, eyes are very rarely white in paintings. When the white highlight is added, the contrast against the pale grey or blue of the eye can be seen. (Fig. 3.47) Add a tiny amount of Ultramarine Blue to White, and use the detail brush to add the blue (Fig. 3.48).

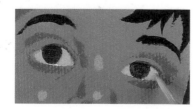

Fig. 3.47.   Fig. 3.48.

The Background

(Fig. 3.49) With our mixing brush, make up enough dark red to cover the area three times. Cadmium Red and Burnt Umber have been used here to create a duller red (Fig. 3.50 and Fig. 3.51). It is useful to paint a large area with a mixing brush.

(Fig. 3.52) Use Cadmium Yellow and Cadmium Red for the orange upper background area. Thoroughly mix the two colours before applying (Fig. 3.53). It's tempting to do it one coat, but if you do it in two it'll have a smoother finish by making sure the coats are not too thick.

(Fig. 3.54) With the background finished and the trace taped securely in position, the line work can be started.

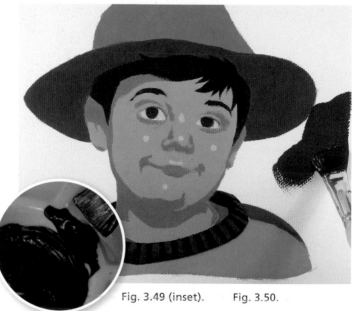

Fig. 3.49 (inset).   Fig. 3.50.

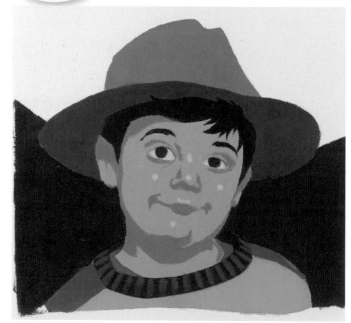

Fig. 3.51.

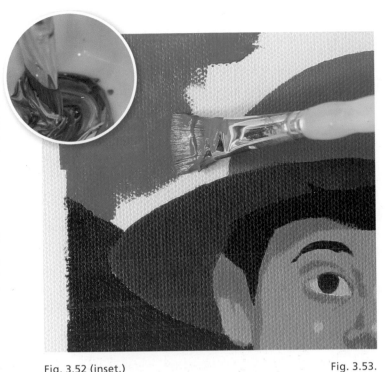

Fig. 3.52 (inset.)

Fig. 3.53.

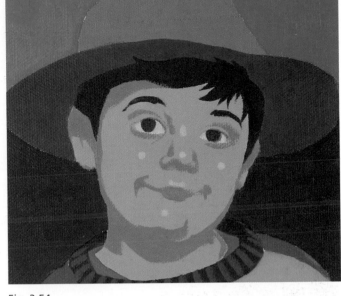

Fig. 3.54.

The Black Outlines

This is the final stage and it's a good idea to have an area to prac-tise line making before the final line (Fig. 3.55 and Fig. 3.56).

Mix the black with a little water until it's like single cream, fluid enough to be drawn out of your brush but not to drip out.

(Fig. 3.57) Load the brush by rotating it in the mix and then squash it slightly into a blade. It's the blade that's making the fine line and not a round 'point'. It is useful to use the little finger as a support to get either thick or thin lines or uniform lines.

(Fig. 3.58) Check the lines and re-trace them as a guide for your brush. However, do them as lightly as possible.

(Fig. 3.59) After the black lines are completed, the last bit of tweaking makes all the difference. Dab the white highlight on the eyes and the light brown around the iris (Fig. 3.60). Little areas in the ears might need sharpening up and the bottom lip might need a lighter colour.

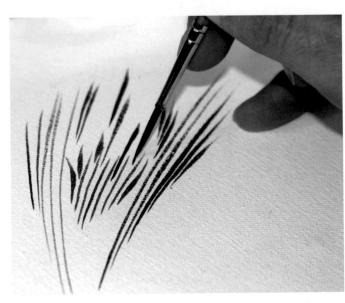

Fig. 3.55.

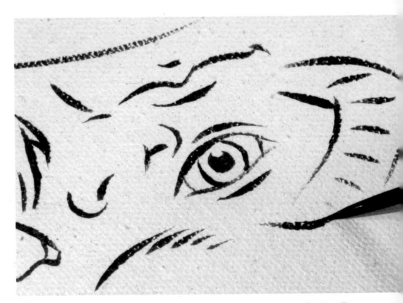

Fig. 3.56.

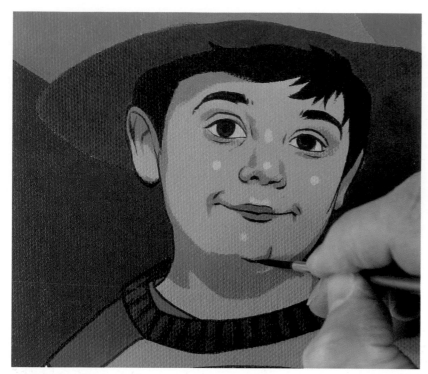

Fig. 3.57.

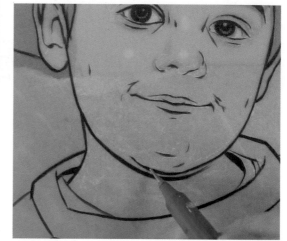

Fig. 3.58.

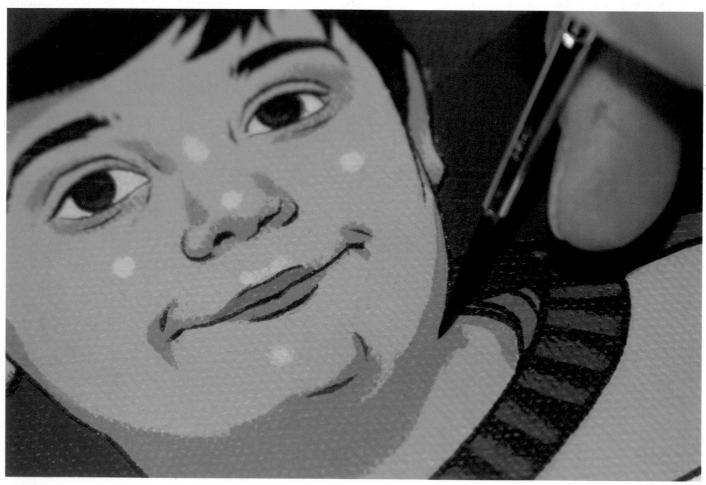

Fig. 3.59.

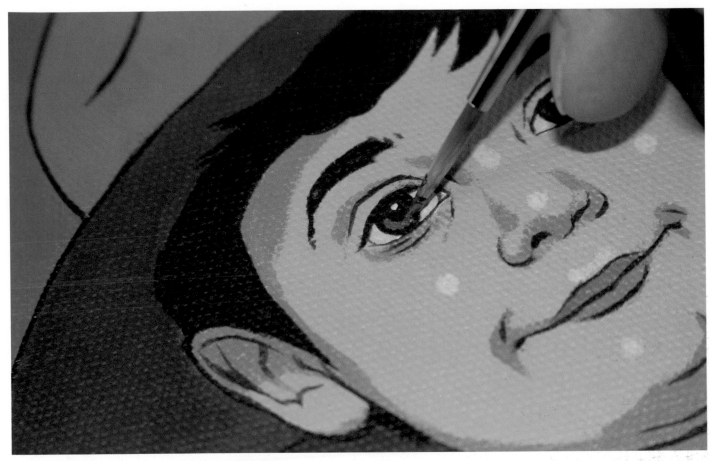

Fig. 3.60.

Alterations

HAT TOP

(Fig. 3.61) One alteration on the hat to make it darker again. The tone before was quite light and was competing with the face and background. The face will stand out by darkening the hat.

As before, mix up Burnt Umber and Payne's Grey, enough for three more coats. As all the coats are thin the total thickness still looks uniform and smooth.

HAIR

(Fig. 3.62) This is another alteration with the boy's hair to a lighter brown so it stands out from the hat rim. Use Burnt Umber and Yellow and apply two coats.

(Fig. 3.63) A highlight can be added to the rim of the hat by mixing Raw Umber with a small amount of white.

(Fig. 3.64) A middle band of background colour can be used to soften the edge crossing the hat.

In conclusion, if the wrong colour is applied, corrections can be made easily due to the forgiving nature of acrylics.

The technique used in these examples of flat colour takes a conventional approach but can be varied in so many ways. Instead of black lines, coloured lines can be used, as well as a range of muted or even brighter colours.

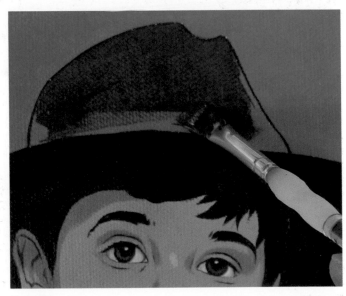

Fig. 3.61.

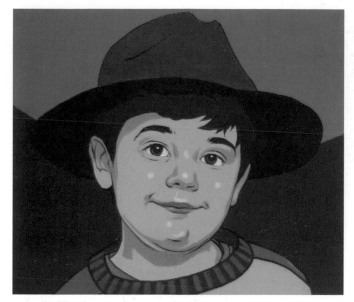

Fig. 3.62.

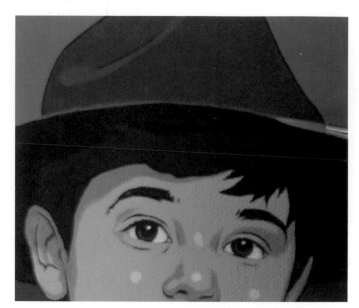

Fig. 3.63.

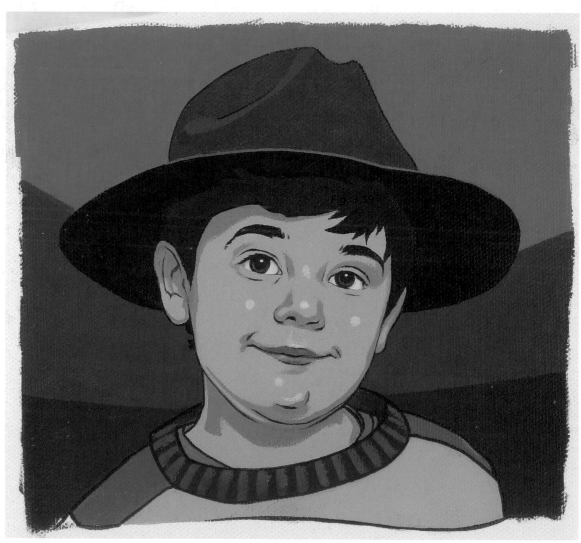

Fig. 3.64 The finished painting.

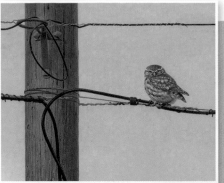

Fig. 3.65.

FLAT COLOUR

Here are some examples using thin layers of flat colour in paintings and illustrations. The principle shown here is the same as the boy's portrait using one mix of colour.

The owl's background has two or three layers of grey blue applied thinly on gessoed canvas, with a final coat mixed with a little more white, creating a hint of something like mist or fog. In this instance a pure flat colour may not look as aesthetically appealing as the 'patina' of brush marks.

The sky in the lamb painting below has the same process of three or four layers of an opaque ultramarine mid-blue. Another two to three layers of an opaque cobalt mid-blue are graduated, thinning towards the horizon before adding the clouds on top.

Flat colour illustrations can be done without leaving brush marks like this fox example. Different surfaces will have an impact of the 'flatness'. Here it shows the effect done on a rough watercolour board.

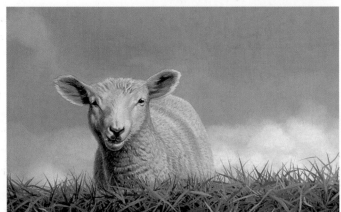

Fig. 3.66.

Fig. 3.67.

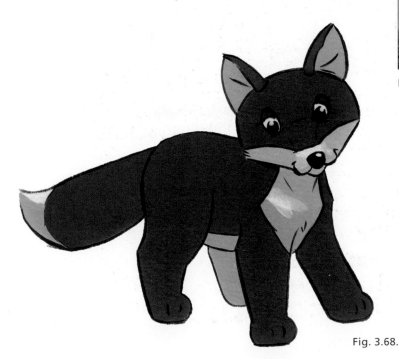

Fig. 3.68.

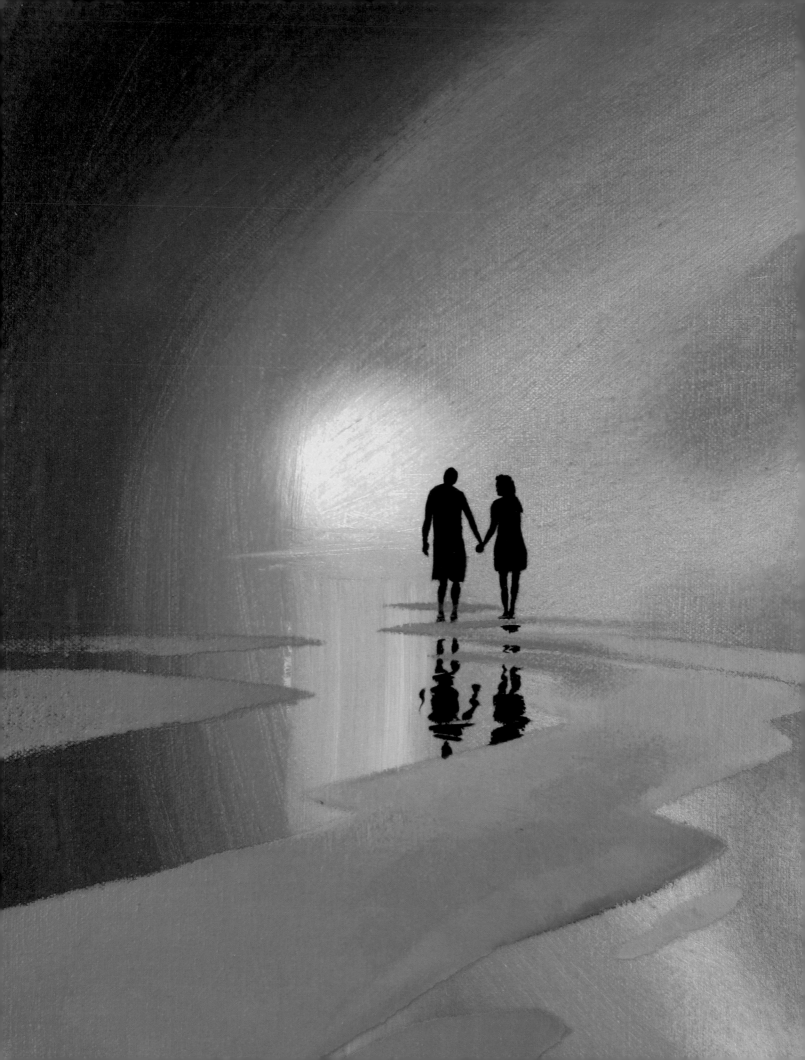

CHAPTER 4

FAN BRUSH

Blending on Canvas

MATERIALS NEEDED

- 1. A fan brush Winsor & Newton hog hair between Nos 5 and 8

- 2. A hog short flat brush No. 8 or equivalent

- 3. A detail brush, soft flat synthetic brush. Royal No. 6

- Winsor & Newton Artist's Acrylics: Cadmium Yellow medium, Cadmium Red medium, Quinacridone violet, Dioxazine purple, and Titanium white acrylic

- 14 × 10in canvas, either a secured loose sheet, a canvas board, or a stretched canvas

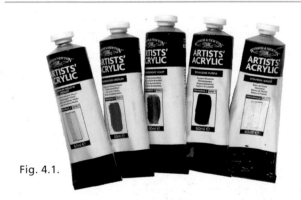

Fig. 4.1.

Royal Soft Grip Synthetic No. 6

Winsor & Newton Hog Short Flat No. 8

Winsor & Newton Hog Fan No. 8

Fig. 4.2.

This exercise is a lot of fun as you don't have to be precise. You can play with blending the colours for a while, as long as you keep moving the paint.

The fan brush is a perfect choice for delicate blending and softening harsh wet marks. It is great at blocking in skies and clouds, out-of-focus-effect backgrounds, fog or mist, long wavy grasses or any areas that require two or more colours subtly running into each other.

In this example I've chosen a simple sunset scene with conventional colours to illustrate the effect. However, if you don't have the colours I've used, try any colours (Figs 4.3 and 4. 4): there's no hard and fast rule, as this image borders on the abstract.

The choice of a bristle fan as opposed to a soft synthetic fan brush is important. The paint will be used initially straight from the tube and on canvas, therefore it's so thick it requires a stiff brush to drag it back and forth.

PREPARATION

Tape the canvas down if you are working with loose sheets. I find it's easiest to work with the canvas flat on a desk so you can stand over it. If you prefer to work with the canvas upright, the paint should not be so runny that it dribbles downwards.

New canvas boards or stretched canvases that have been wrapped in shrink wrap or cellophane may need a light sponge scrub with soap and water to remove an oily film.

Have your line guide ready for the second stage. It's not necessary to trace the drawing down as you may end up with the sun higher up than mid-way.

You will need some kitchen towel to wipe off excess paint as you go along because you may feel there is too much colour on your brush running into the lighter colour. Have a pot of clean water to hand, so you can add a tiny amount here and there if the paint is too thick or getting too tacky.

That's it: we are ready to block in this background!

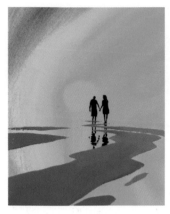

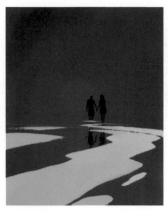

Fig. 4.3.   Fig. 4.4.
There are no colour rules! Try any three colours.

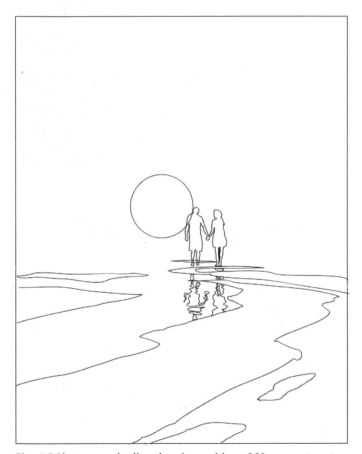

Fig. 4.5 Photocopy the line drawing guide at 260 per cent on to tracing paper.

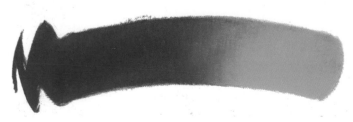

Fig. 4.6.

FAN BRUSH TIPS

Rotate your painting: Brush at angles that are comfortable for better mark making.

Not too much water: Add just a little water at a time if the paint is too thick or dry.

Remove excess paint often: Excess paint creates lines and ridges.

Re-splay the brush hairs: The brush will get clogged and the hairs will need readjusting to a uniform spread.

Tacky = smooth blend time: As the paint becomes tacky, slightly criss-cross diagonally with a clean damp brush.

BLOCKING IN THE BACKGROUND

Ignore the figures and sand ripples, and don't put the sun in until the end of this stage. Bear in mind that you need to keep the paint moving, otherwise the drying process will start and hard lines will form.

(Fig. 4.7) Place one pea-size blob of paint in the areas shown, which will be in the middle of each sweep of colour. With a 14 × 10in canvas this should be enough to cover it, but most importantly it's better to put on too little than too much. You can add more later if needed.

(Fig. 4.8) Dip your fan brush in water and start sweeping back and forth with the darkest colour first, in this case Magenta. Add a drop of more colour if it's not covering.

Vary the direction slightly with each stroke in a criss-cross manner. This helps to blend and avoid parallel lines. Hold the brush almost vertically and near the end, using a combination of the wrist and arm which will produce delicate long sweeps. We tend not to use our wrist if holding the brush lower down the handle.

(Fig. 4.9) Once all the red areas are done, start blending into the orange. You may need to add a tiny amount of water if it's getting too dry. (Fig. 4.10) Finish blending the red and orange before going on to blend the yellow.

(Figs 4.11, 4.12 and 4.13) Once you have finished blending the orange with the red, clean your brush and dry it touch dry. In the next minute or so the paint will become slightly tacky.

(Fig. 4.14) This is a good time to give it a gentle blend all over again, starting with the brightest area. The hog brush is only just touching but is enough to 'fine tune' any hard brush lines that may be left.

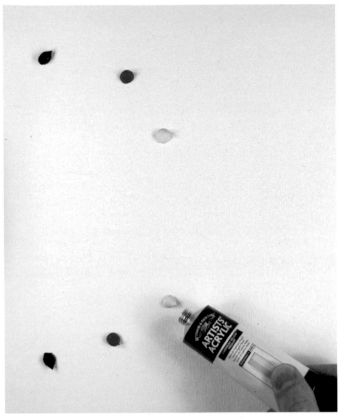

Fig. 4.7 Important: the whole background blend is done quickly so the first colour does not have time to dry.

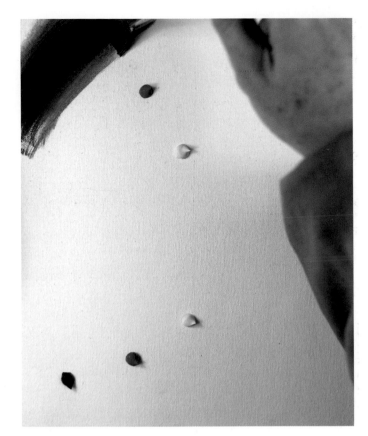

Fig. 4.8.

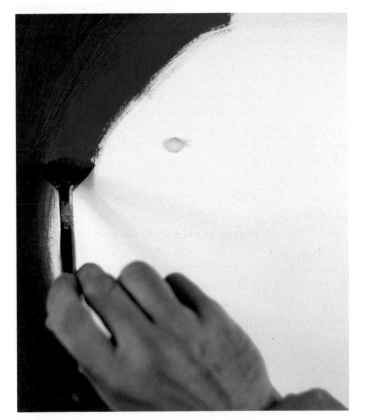

Fig. 4.9.

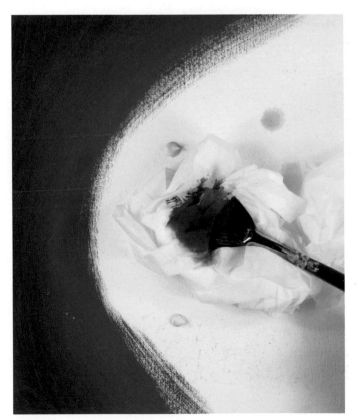

Fig. 4.10.

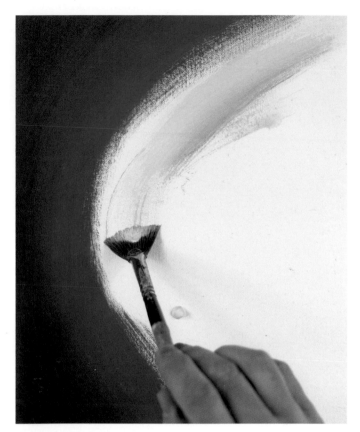

Fig. 4.11 Still wet!

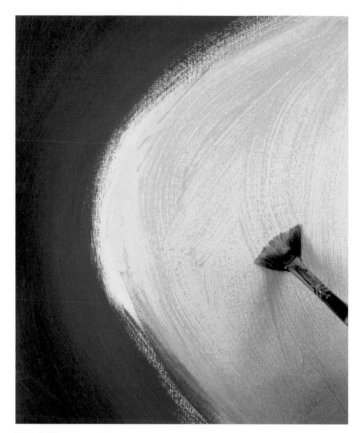

Fig. 4.12.

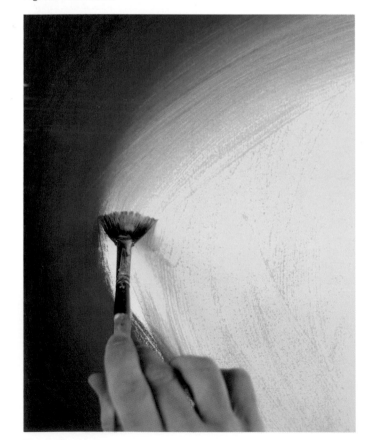

Fig. 4.13.

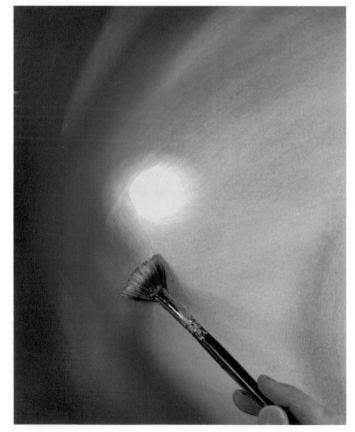

Fig. 4.14 Still wet!

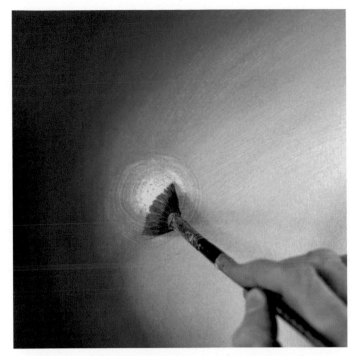

Fig. 4.15 Tip: when the paint begins to get tacky it's easier to blend smoothly.

The Sun

(Fig. 4.15) Have a piece of kitchen towel handy, and a blob of yellow on a palette. Clean your brush. Dampen it with some water and make a round sun by rotating your brush and diluting the colour. Remove the paint off your brush with a kitchen towel, and repeat until you have the white of the canvas again. Add a nice blob of yellow back in the centre, and soften out to the edges of the deep yellow or orange.

(Fig. 4.16) Dip your brush into a blob of yellow off canvas, and create the reflection by making a swift vertical mark with a shimmy zig-zag at the bottom. Once done we need to leave it to dry for 30min.

(Fig. 4.17) When it's dry, lay the line guide over to remind yourself where the sand bars go. Try doing it by visualization, or trace them through with the Imagetrace® paper, or with the traditional soft pencil rubbed on the underside.

THE FOREGROUND

(Fig. 4.19) With the hog bristle detail brush, mix up a mid purple by adding Dioxazine Purple to Titanium White straight from the tube. No water is needed. Load the brush and wipe the excess off the sides.

(Fig. 4.20) Using the blade of the brush, start from under the sun and zig-zag your way down with gentle strokes. Your marks may not be completely opaque so let those strokes dry for a minute before repeating with a new layer. Allow to dry for 15min.

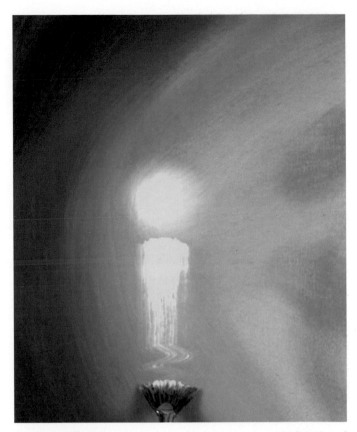

Fig. 4.16 Still wet!

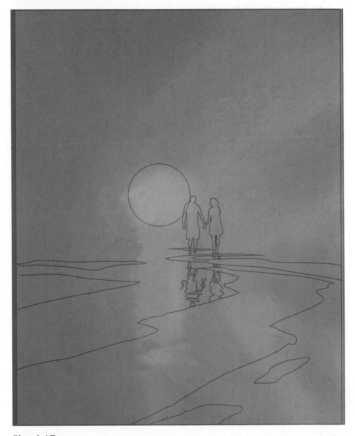

Fig. 4.17.

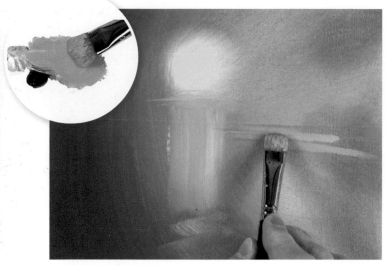

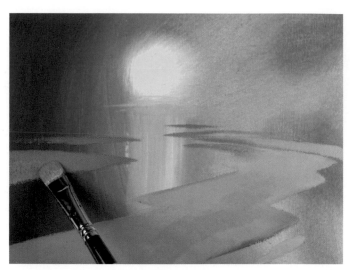

Fig. 4.18 No water in the mix (inset). Fig. 4.19 Dry background.

Fig. 4.20 Remember, the mid-purple sand banks may need a few layers to create an opaque finish.

The Figures

(Fig. 4.22) Trace down the outlines of your figures, making sure the mark is fractionally on the inside of the silhouettes so the paint will hide them.

Finally with the small flat synthetic brush load the brush evenly with the Dioxazine Purple. Again, use no water.

Use the brushes' corners and block in the figures which may need two layers to achieve a solid colour.

(Fig. 4.23) That's it, and I hope you have something similar which will inspire you to try larger versions with larger fan brushes on a wild abstract!

The key is to notice when the paint starts to become tacky to get smoother blends. Try thicker and thinner amounts of paint and you'll soon get to know what works for you.

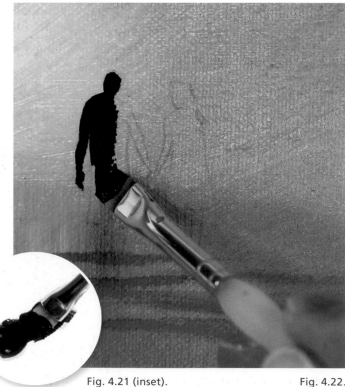

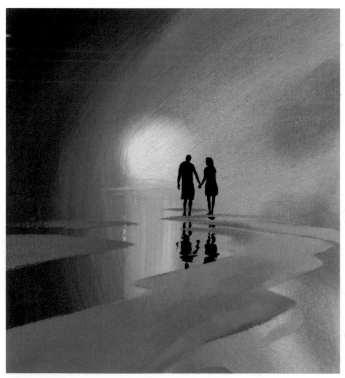

Fig. 4.21 (inset). Fig. 4.22.

Fig. 4.23 The finished painting.

FAN BRUSH TECHNIQUE

Here are a few more simple examples using only the fan brush. These are at a stage where marks could be created by removing the paint whilst it's wet, and then softened again with the fan brush.

When it's dry, new layers of tints, semi-opaque and heavy paint can be put on top without disturbing the original coat.

Canvas, gessoed plyboard and MDF board make great surfaces to use the fan brush.

Adding a tiny amount of white into pigments will create a lighter but smoother finish. The image 'Foggy Coastline' (Fig. 4.24) has white in the darker blue area, whereas 'Green Swirl' (Fig. 4.25) uses purely transparent greens. The green brush marks could be softened by gentle cross hatching with an almost dry fan brush when it's at the tacky stage.

'Yellow Sunset' (Fig. 4.26) has the added thick paint brush marks of yellow and dark red.

Grab a board and a fan brush and have a go! The hours fly by doing these!

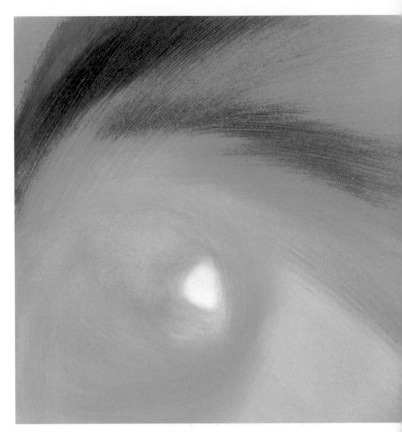

Fig. 4.25 *Green Swirl*, acrylic on canvas board, 30×30cm.

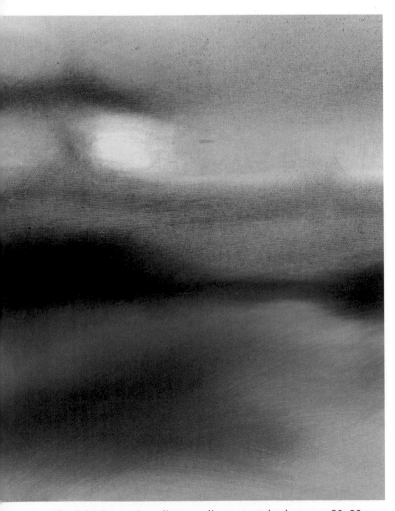

Fig. 4.24 *Foggy Coastline*, acrylic on stretched canvas, 30×20cm.

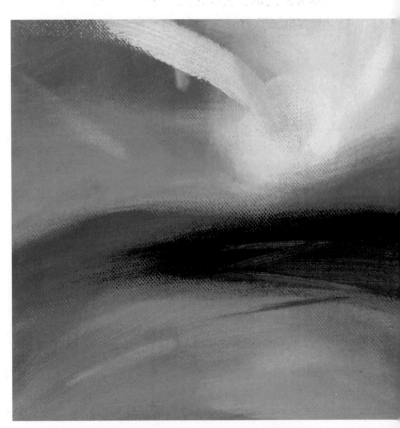

Fig. 4.26 *Yellow Sunset*, acrylic on canvas board, 20×20cm.

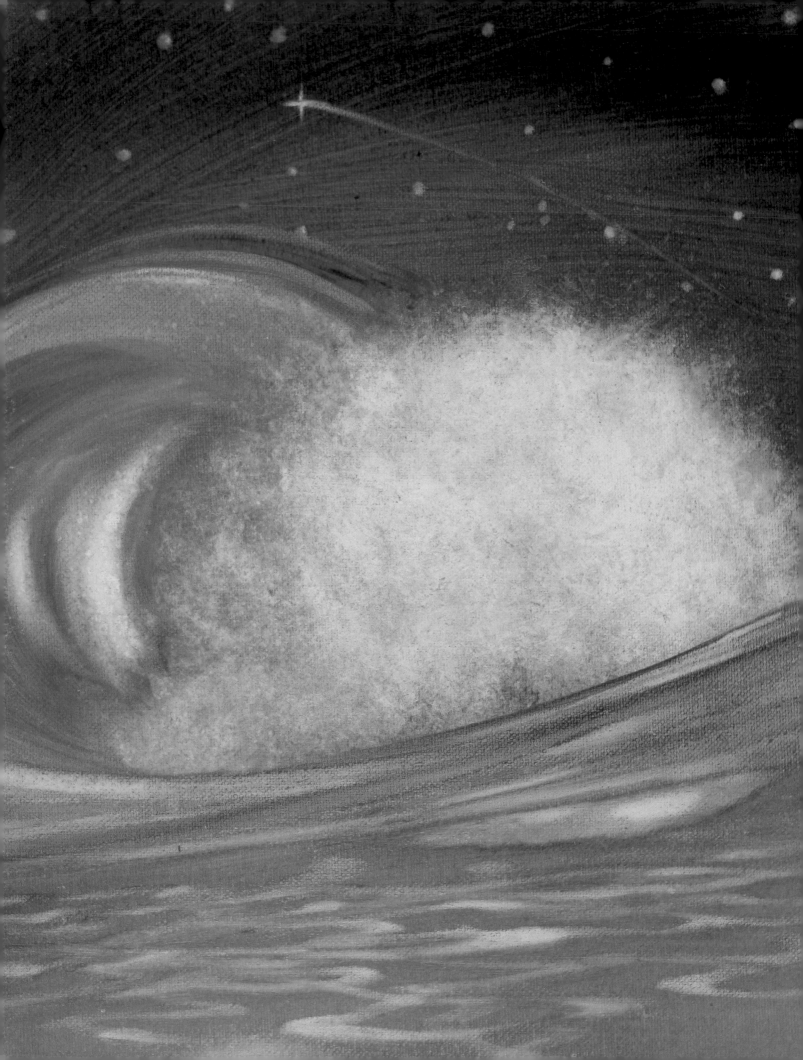

CHAPTER 5

ON AND OFF

Removing wet pigment as a way of creating form

This painting takes about thirty minutes before it becomes too dry, so speed is of the essence.

Removing paint in a painting as it's been worked on is just as important as putting it on. With that in mind, here is a technique where all the details and form are created by various levels of removing the paint by suction.

Sucking up really wet washes with a dry or damp brush in a watercolour painting is one way to create lighter areas; this example differs slightly in that, for the most part, the paint needs to be a little tacky.

This example has been done on canvas board at 180 × 220mm – canvas board primarily because pressing on to the canvas to remove the paint is a little more predictable. However, the technique will still be suitable for stretched canvases and gessoed boards such as hardboard and MDF.

MATERIALS NEEDED

- 12 × 10in canvas board

For putting on the paint:
- No. 8 Bristle Hog Fan Brush
- Azanta 1in long flat Hog Brush

For taking off the paint:
- Winsor & Newton No. 8 ½in flat Hog Brush
- Detail Brush Winsor & Newton 222 No. 6
- Tubed acrylics: Payne's Grey, Dioxazine Purple, Ultramarine Violet, Cadmium Yellow Medium, Phthalo Blue Green shade, Phthalo Turquoise
- Kitchen towel or cloth

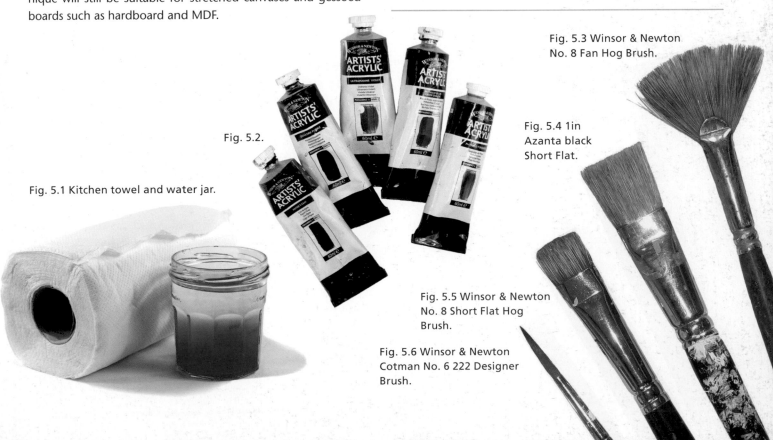

Fig. 5.3 Winsor & Newton No. 8 Fan Hog Brush.

Fig. 5.4 1in Azanta black Short Flat.

Fig. 5.2.

Fig. 5.1 Kitchen towel and water jar.

Fig. 5.5 Winsor & Newton No. 8 Short Flat Hog Brush.

Fig. 5.6 Winsor & Newton Cotman No. 6 222 Designer Brush.

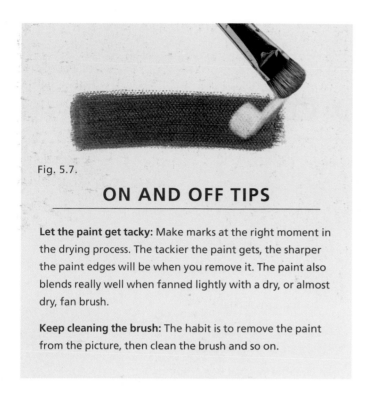

Fig. 5.7.

ON AND OFF TIPS

Let the paint get tacky: Make marks at the right moment in the drying process. The tackier the paint gets, the sharper the paint edges will be when you remove it. The paint also blends really well when fanned lightly with a dry, or almost dry, fan brush.

Keep cleaning the brush: The habit is to remove the paint from the picture, then clean the brush and so on.

ON AND OFF TECHNIQUE

Fig. 5.8 is a rough and ready sketch with the general idea for areas that can have paint removed. The exact shape of the wave and general composition is not necessary as things might change in all the sweeping of colour. Experiment and keep the paint on the move until you are ready to let it go tacky and start taking it off.

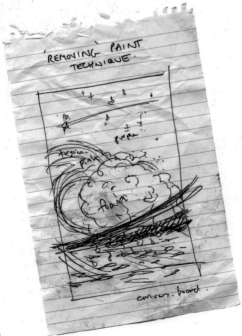

Fig. 5.8.

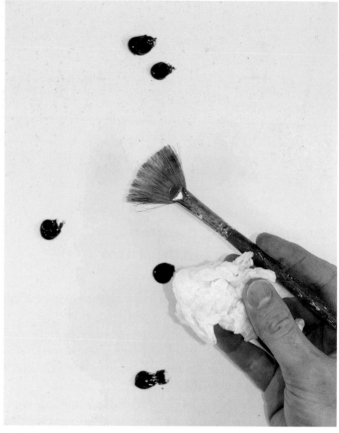

Fig. 5.9.

(Fig. 5.9) Place pea-sized paint blobs directly on to the canvas. Dip the Fan Brush in water and have a damp kitchen towel ready to clean the brush for the next colour.

(Fig. 5.10) Starting at the top, do long back and forth sweeps which slightly criss-cross over each other, blending as you go. Use water sparingly if you need to keep it fluid.

(Fig. 5.11) Give the brush a wipe to take off most of the violet, then dip it in water and continue with the blue-green shade. The aim is to use just enough water to create a uniform spread of paint; it's easy to get it too wet and thin. Brush the wave in curved sweeps as the next picture shows.

(Fig. 5.12) Use a final sweep to suggest the wave surface, and then clean and re-dip with water before sweeping across the Payne's Gray.

(Fig. 5.13) Clean and dry the brush, which may need the hairs re-spacing occasionally.

(Fig. 5.14) The whole area is now wet, with the top part going slightly tacky. Don't worry if it looks darker or lighter than this. If it's darker, a damp fan brush will remove it, and if it's too light add another pea of paint.

(Figs 5.15 and 5.16) With a damp scrunched-up kitchen towel, remove areas with a mixture of twisting and dabbing to get a

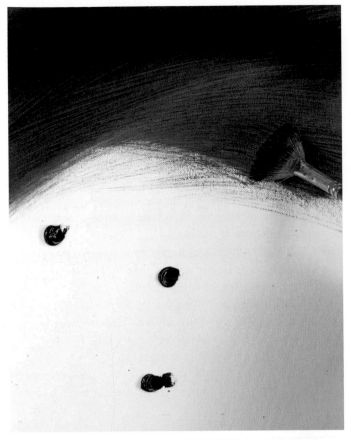

Fig. 5.10.

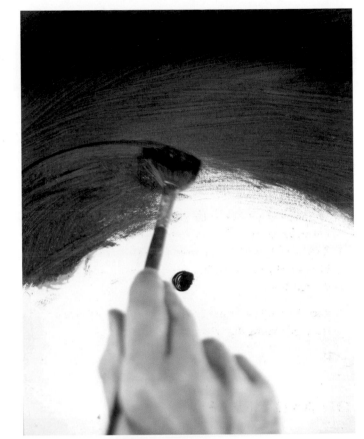

Fig. 5.11.

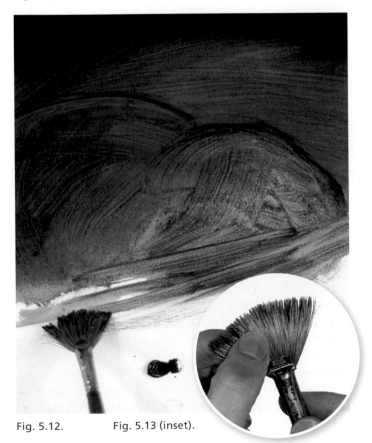

Fig. 5.12.   Fig. 5.13 (inset).

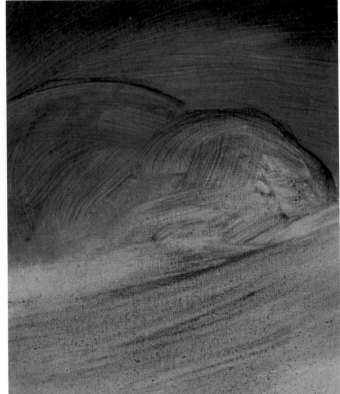

Fig. 5.14.

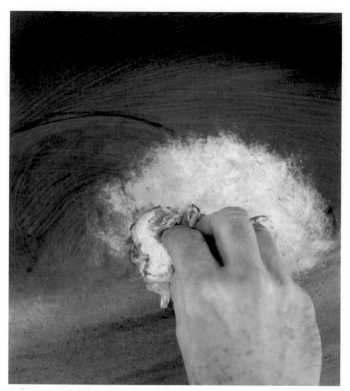

Fig. 5.15 Everywhere still wet!

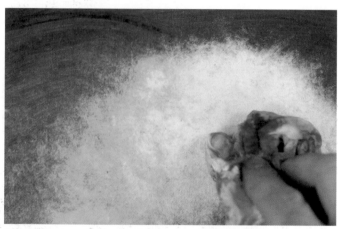

Fig. 5.16.

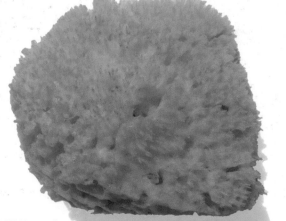

Fig. 5.17 Natural sponge makes good water spray marks too.

lighter blue. To get it back to almost white, use a wet kitchen towel and try to use the folded areas to get sharper white marks.

Fig. 5.19 shows wave forms with Hog brush marks. The long-haired Hog has a little more give than the Short Flat, which is better for sweeping a wet area and moving the pigment around. Pigment tends to collect at the edge of the brush strokes, thereby creating the wave form.

Dampen the brush and create the wave edges. Sharper marks are made if the surface is tacky, and softer marks if it's still wet. Choose the right moment to make the desired marks.

(Fig. 5.20) Use all the edges of the brush to create marks. Keep removing the excess liquid from the brush with kitchen towel. Once the wave is done, re-dab the outer edge of the foam to bring it back in front of the wave.

(Fig. 5.21) With the blade of the brush, sweep left and right to make lighter lines on the surface, leaving the bottom fifth of the painting empty for the sand ripples.

(Fig. 5.22) Sand ripples: Switch to the Short Flat Hog because here, sharper-edged marks are required and the paint may be almost dry. If the paint is touch dry it can still be removed if it's thin enough, especially with a damp brush.

(Fig. 5.25 and Fig. 5.26) Star making: The sky will now be tacky or touch dry. Use a wet Designer 222 detail brush to gently

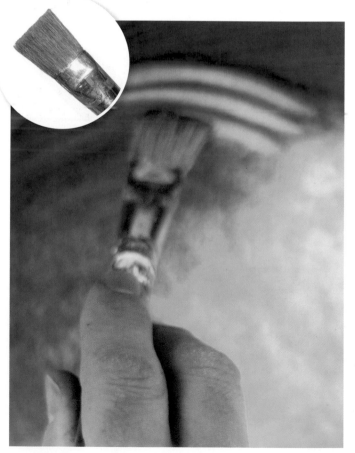

Fig. 5.18 1in Azanta black Short Flat (inset).   Fig. 5.19.

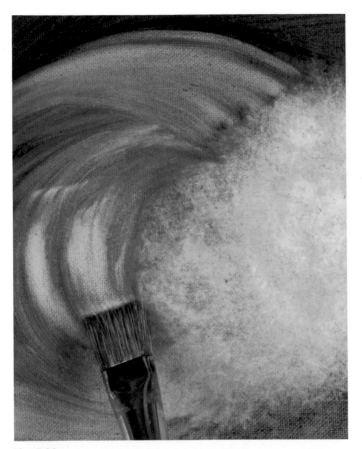

Fig. 5.20.

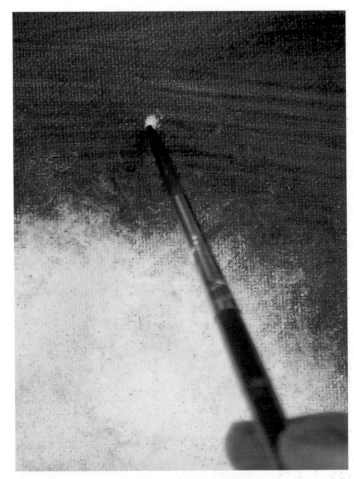

Fig. 5.24.

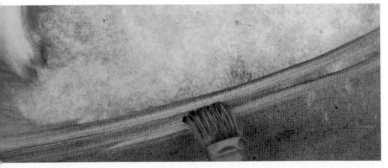

Fig. 5.21.

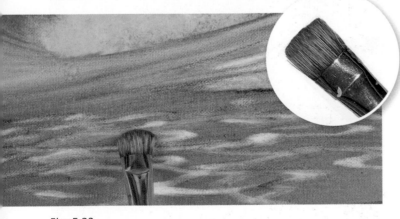

Fig. 5.22
Fig. 5.23 Winsor & Newton No. 8 Short Flat Hog Brush (inset).

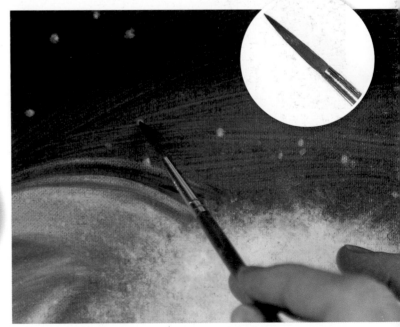

Fig. 5.25.
Fig. 5.26 Winsor & Newton Cotman No. 6 222 Designer Brush (inset).

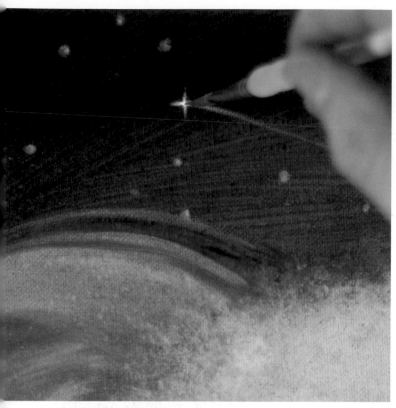

Fig. 5.27 Sky almost dry!

agitate the paint loose, then wipe the brush dry to soak up the colour and create a star. Repeat if it's not light enough.

(Fig. 5.27) Adding long white lines requires a short flat synthetic brush, as hog hair brushes at this scale are not good at soaking up pigment.

(Fig. 5.28) Semi-opaque paint can also be removed with a stiff brush, so long as it hasn't reached a tipping point of being too thick. A single-cream-like consistency of mixed turquoise and white is added over the bottom half with the long bristle flat brush. Softly blend using criss-cross strokes as it gets tacky.

(Fig. 5.29) Finally, before the paint dries use a damp short-haired bristle brush to rub and soak up the paint to leave light highlights at the intersections of the light ripples.

(Fig. 5.30 and Fig. 5.31) This technique can make fun abstracts which evolve into something else as the paint keeps getting pushed around. Any highlighting that is soaked and rubbed off can be softened again with the fan brush.

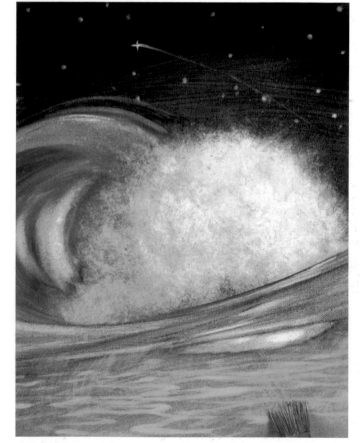

Fig. 5.28.

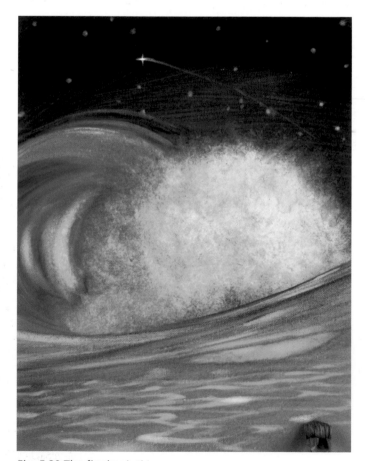

Fig. 5.29 The final painting.

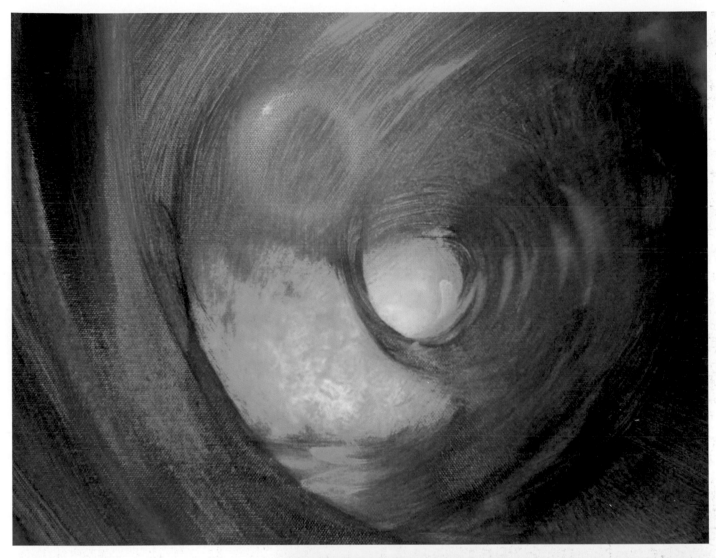

Fig. 5.30.

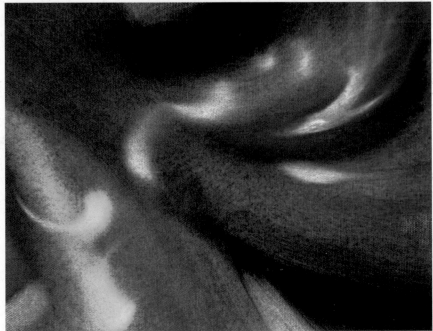

Fig. 5.31.

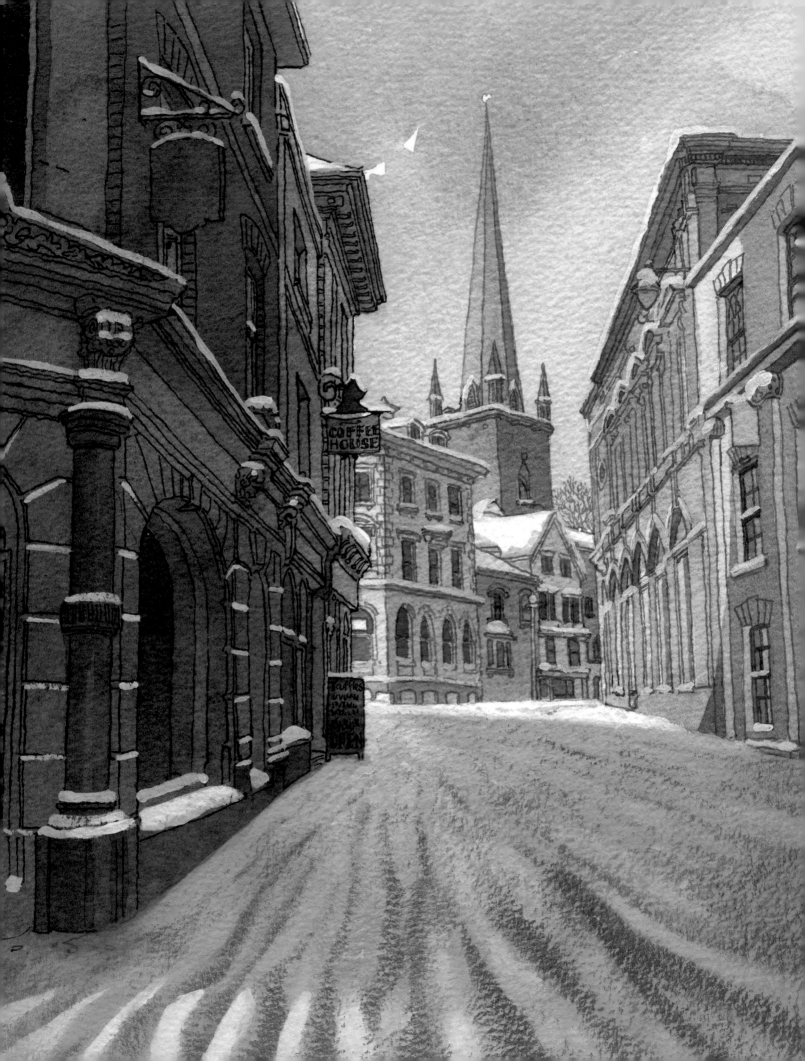

CHAPTER 6

LINE AND WASH

Including opaque dry brushing

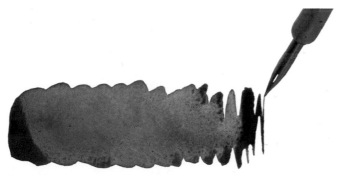

Fig. 6.1.

In this chapter the following topics are explored:

* Stretching watercolour paper
* Applying ink lines
* Wash layers
* Opaque dry brushing

THE TECHNIQUE

The idea is to use transparent washes that run into each other creating a variety of tones within and over a line drawing. As the colours are transparent and the ink lines waterproof there's no bleeding, and it allows further tint washes.

The medium is watercolour paper and there is a wide variety of smooth to rough papers in different weights which will all give a different quality to the end result. This example is on St Cuthbert's 300lb Bockingford CP (NOT) watercolour paper, readily available on spiral pads.

The line work can be any variety of waterproof line. An exception to that rule for example could be watercolour pencils which run when wet, but this can create interesting effects too, as some line work will run more than other areas. However, the most popular choices are the classic Indian ink line made with a dipping nib or coloured permanent marker, or 2B pencil, to name but a couple. I've chosen four coloured acrylic inks to match receding tones over distance.

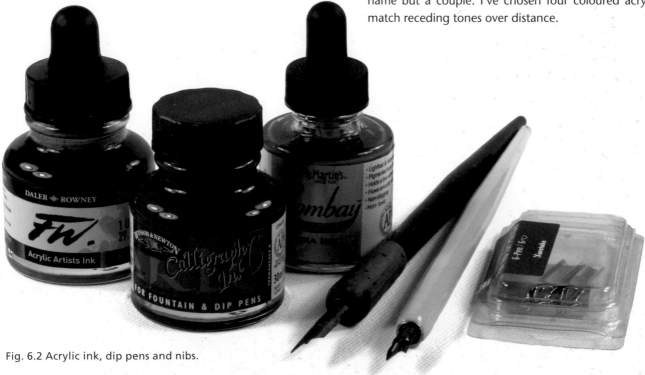

Fig. 6.2 Acrylic ink, dip pens and nibs.

MATERIALS NEEDED

Preparation:

• MDF or similar board to stretch the paper on

• 2in wide gum tape

• Kitchen towel

• 10 × 14in 300lb Bockingford CP (NOT) watercolour paper

Painting stage:

• Acrylic inks or Indian ink

• Ink pen

• Winsor & Newton No. 14 Wash brush

• Synthetic mixing brush

• Winsor & Newton Designer 222 No. 6 Detail brush

• Line drawing supplied; enlarge to size

• (Tracing paper if creating your own line drawing)

• Tracing pen or 6H pencil

• Imagetrace® paper

• Colours: Ultramarine Blue, Burnt Sienna, Raw Sienna, Cadmium Yellow, Payne's Grey, Ultramarine Violet, White Gesso

STRETCHING PAPER

Watercolour paper, no matter how thick and heavy, is prone to buckling if enough water is applied in any one coat. This creates two headaches: the first is that the paper buckles, and the second is that it's harder to do line work. The buckling that forms then influences where the pigment flows and settles, producing unintentional effects. So there's a method to avoid these effects, which is stretching the paper by soaking it.

The following steps explain the easy process of stretching the paper.

Have a piece of MDF or hardboard board to tape it to. The board may need to be rotated during the painting so it only needs to be a couple of inches bigger than the paper.

(Fig. 6.8) After marking in the corner which side is up, run the paper slowly through water. There's no rush to tape the paper either, as the fibres need to expand over a minute or so.

(Fig. 6.9) Let the paper drip for a moment, and make sure which side to lay it down.

(Fig. 6.10) Lay the paper down on the board, carefully avoiding drips from fingers which may appear later.

(Fig. 6.11) Pull the gum tape sticky side down under your fingers through the water to ensure all areas of the tape are wet. Let the excess drip off for a moment.

(Fig. 6.12) Lay the tape half on the paper and half on the board. Any less than half on the paper runs the risk of it pulling loose on shrinking.

(Fig. 6.13) Wipe dry the excess water off the tape, making sure not to touch the paper as this may result in marks in the colour washes.

Leave at an angle to dry to prevent pooling of any water. Depending on temperature and air movement the paper will be flat and dry between four to six hours and ready to use.

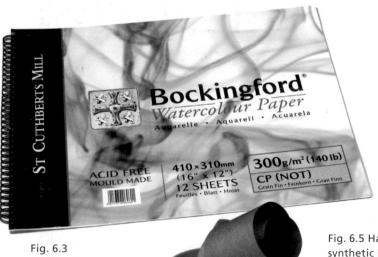

Fig. 6.3
Watercolour paper.

Fig. 6.4 Gum tape.

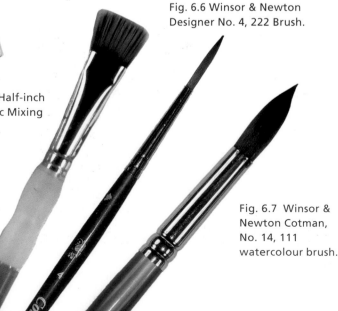

Fig. 6.5 Half-inch synthetic Mixing Brush.

Fig. 6.6 Winsor & Newton Designer No. 4, 222 Brush.

Fig. 6.7 Winsor & Newton Cotman, No. 14, 111 watercolour brush.

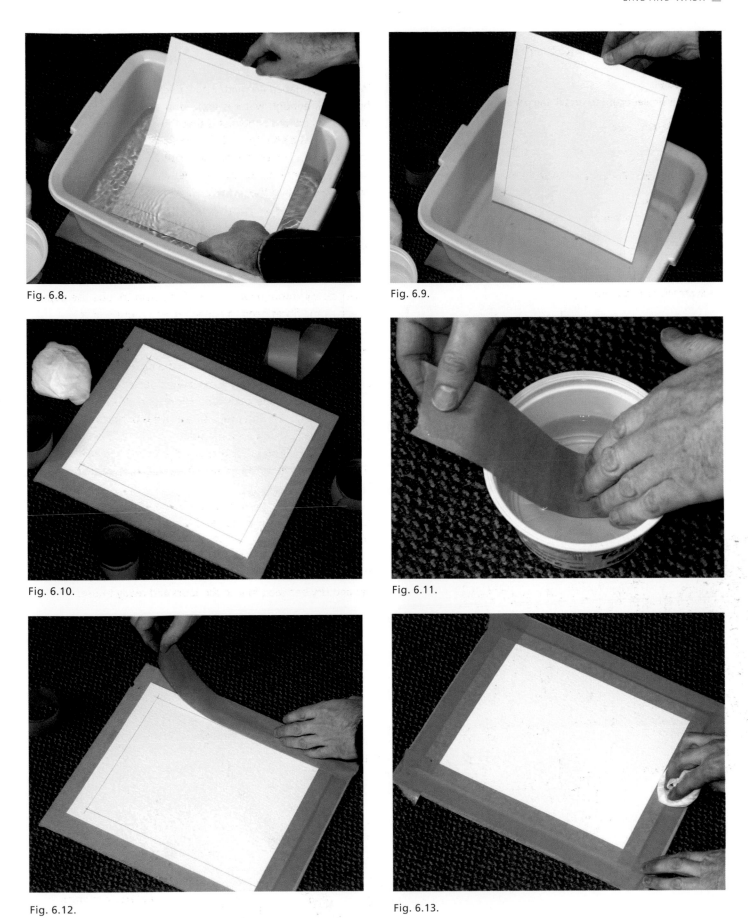

Fig. 6.8.

Fig. 6.9.

Fig. 6.10.

Fig. 6.11.

Fig. 6.12.

Fig. 6.13.

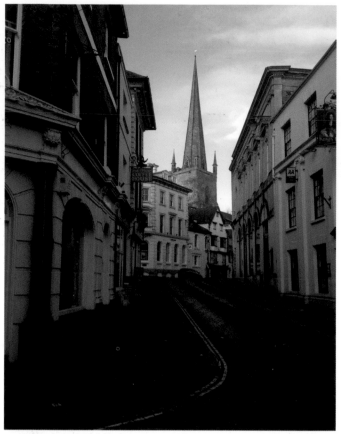

Fig. 6.14 Enlarge the photo to 350 per cent to create your own line drawing on tracing paper, or enlarge the line drawing, right, by 350 per cent.

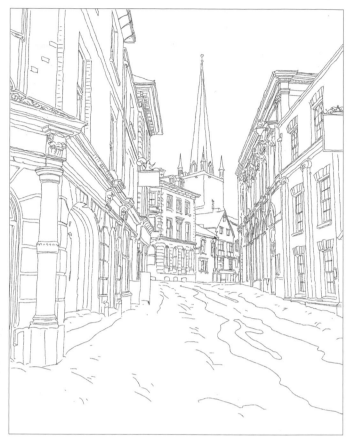

Fig. 6.15.

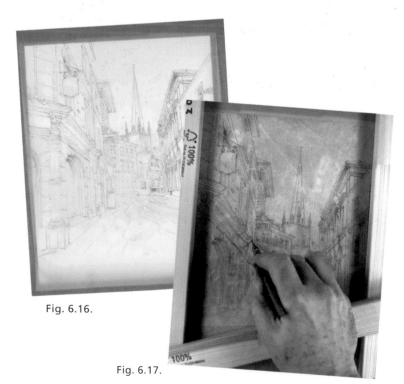

Fig. 6.16.

Fig. 6.17.

THE DRAWING

Line Tracing

(Fig. 6.16) Attach the line drawing to the board and slide under the Imagetrace® paper ready to trace through the line work with either a 6H pencil or a tracing pen.

(Fig. 6.17) Support your wrist on a piece of wood which is propped on two more supports to prevent any pressure from the hand making unintentional marks. With this kind of work it's important not to get any marks that need rubbing off and might potentially damage the paper.

Line Painting

(Fig. 6.18) This is an ink pen with a fine nib which will give a variety of lines from thin, thick, broken and occasionally blobs. The first colour is sepia, the darkest tone for the nearest building.

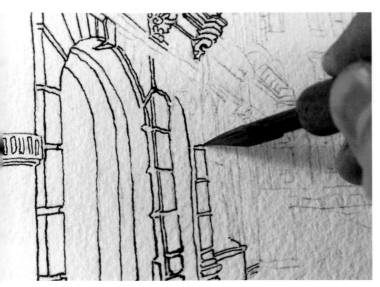

Fig. 6.18.

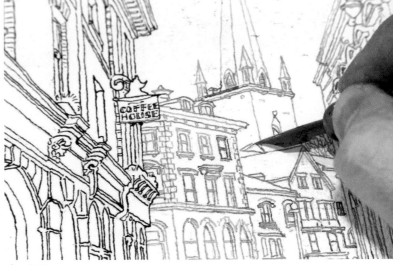

Fig. 6.19.

(Fig. 6.19) Each building is inked in a different colour, suggesting a diminishing tone to represent distance. The right-hand side building is completed in brown and the centre buildings in mauve, and finally the church in blue.

(Fig. 6.20) Let the ink dry for ten minutes. Now the final line drawing is ready to have colour washes.

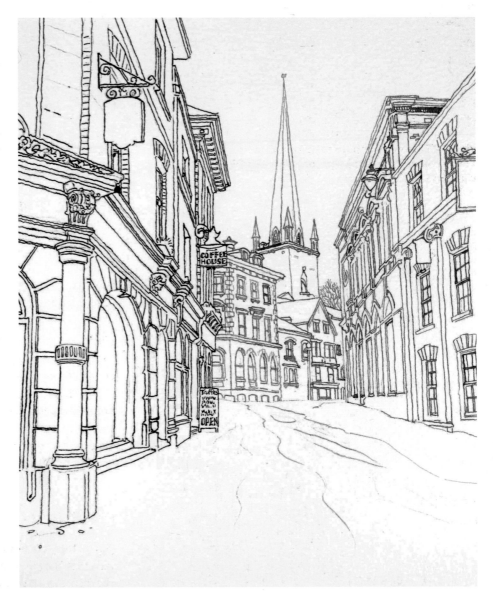

Fig. 6.20.

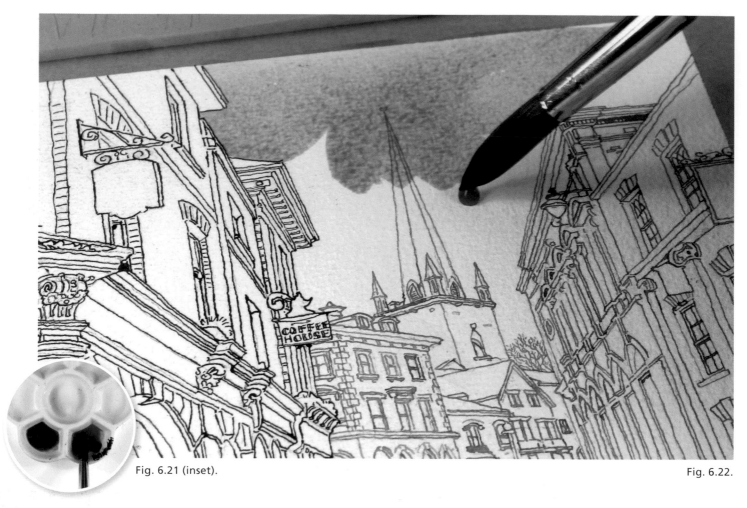

Fig. 6.21 (inset).

Fig. 6.22.

LINE AND WASH TIPS

Be generous with water: Let colours flow into each other with full brush loads of watery pigment.

Alter the board levels: Change the angle of the surface to match the desired colour flows.

Use a good brush: A large, round wash brush with a perfect tip can paint tiny detailed areas.

Drop in clean water: Deliberate, interesting 'tide edges' can be created by adding a drop of clean water into a drying area of colour.

ADDING THE COLOUR

(Fig. 6.21) It's important to have tablespoons of mixed colour ready to drop in. Use a non-painting, old synthetic mixing brush to mix the colours thoroughly and to prolong the life of the wash painting brush. Load up the wash brush to dripping point.

(Fig. 6.22) With the board on a slight slope and when the paper is dry, start methodically from the top down with the sky. The pigment wants to flow with gravity to the bottom but must be guided by the tip of your brush. Go over the church.

(Figs 6.23 and 6.24) Continue down the left building with a lighter mix and without joining the sky. Once filled in, load up the brush with purple and drop it in on the wet blue and let it mix. Lay the board flat if you prefer the spread of paint to stay locally.

(Fig. 6.25) Using the same purple wash, fill across the road and up the nearside right building all the way down to the bottom. With the same wash fill in the shadow areas of the background buildings.

(Fig. 6.26) Using the detail Designer 222 brush, begin to fill in the sunlit building on the right with a pool of raw sienna.

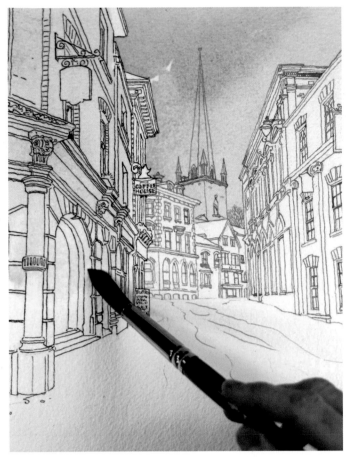

Fig. 6.23.

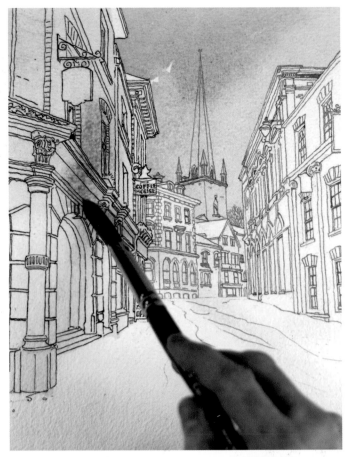

Fig. 6.24.

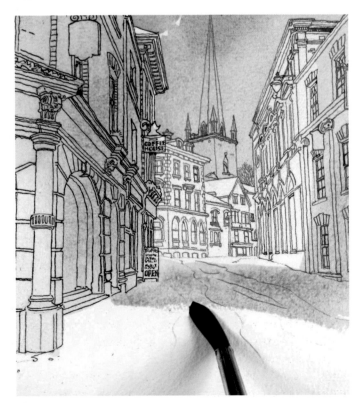

Fig. 6.25.

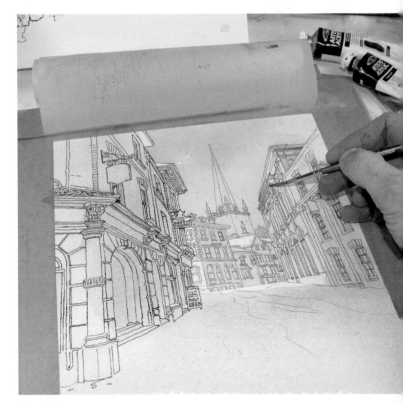

Fig. 6.26.

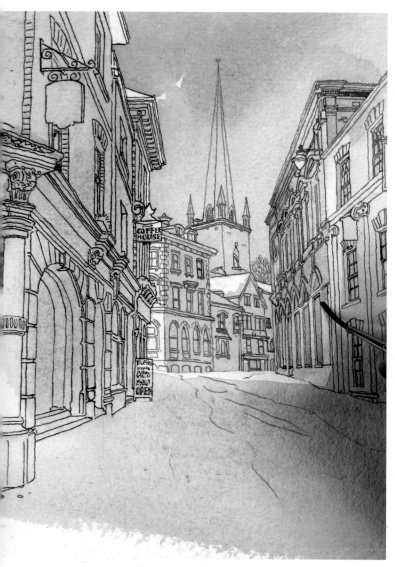

Fig. 6.27.

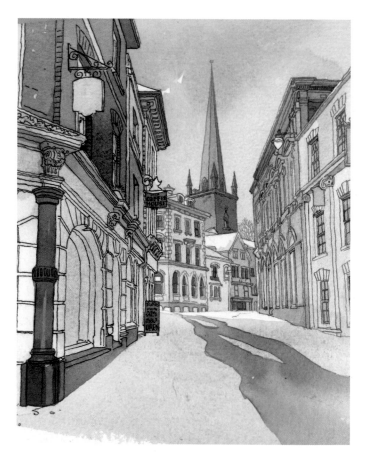

Fig. 6.28.

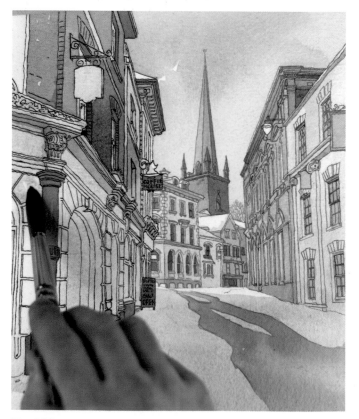

Fig. 6.29.

(Fig. 6.27) With a mixture of Raw Sienna and Burnt Sienna washes, paint in all the warm, coloured areas, including the church and the left-hand side building. Have purple ready to add in afterwards to create blends of colour.

(Figs 6.28 and 6.29) Washes don't have to be thorough: sometimes leaving speckles of the previous colour adds interest. See the nearest top wall and clouds. Add the cream walls in the foreground with diluted Raw Sienna and a purple track in the centre of the road; also the details of the shop signs, the background purple window glass, and the green paintwork to the centre building.

The Shadow Tint

Now add a dramatic wash of shadow over the whole mid-ground to foreground using Payne's Gray. Use plenty of water and spread quickly. The first brush strokes ignore the detailed irregular edges of the building tops as they can be touched in with the smaller detail brush accurately.

(Fig. 6.30) Using a broad synthetic flat brush, the shadow area is washed in on the left and bottom. (Fig. 6.31) Before it dries tweak in the edges of the building with the same colour using the detail brush.

(Figs 6.32 and 6.33) The droplet effect: Whilst the shadow area is wet, drop in a few droplets of clean water and the pig-ment will be sent to the outer edges of the water drop. This can be most effective in loose botanical and nature paintings.

(Fig. 6.34) Details: The tonal strength of the middle building might need making darker, and it's easy to put on another layer of blue or purple.

(Fig. 6.35) The windows are made darker with two colours of deep purple and Burnt Sienna.

(Fig. 6.36) When the paint is dry, add another large tint of shadow. It is now dark enough to apply the lighter, dry brush opaque snow with the ½in flat synthetic brush, using a dry brush technique.

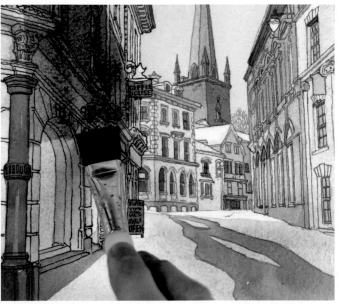

Fig. 6.30.

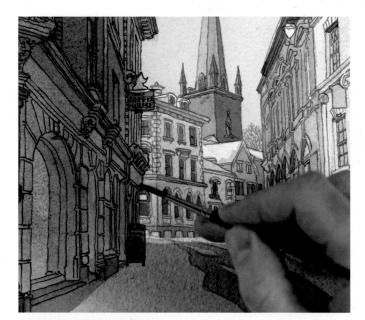

Fig. 6.31.

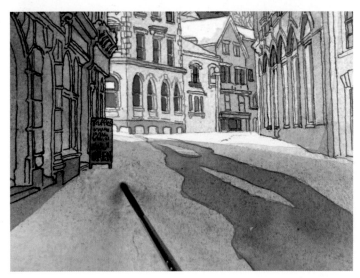

Fig. 6.32.

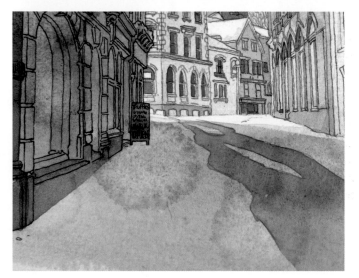

Fig. 6.33.

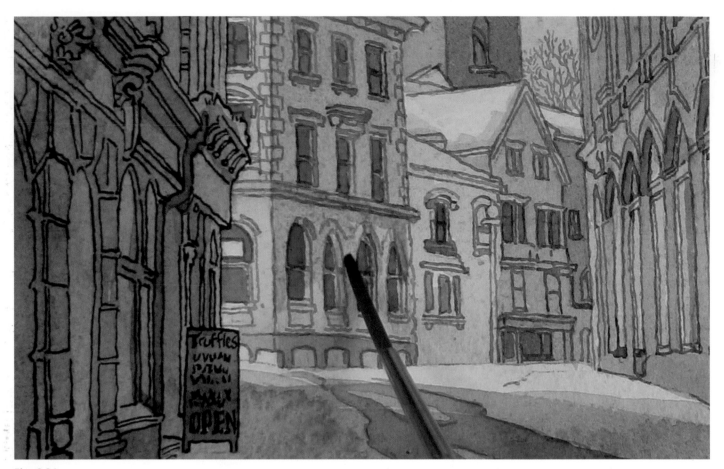

Fig. 6.34.

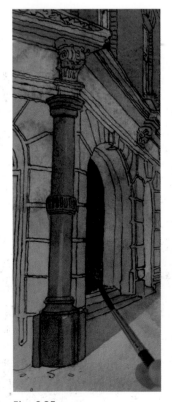

Fig. 6.35.

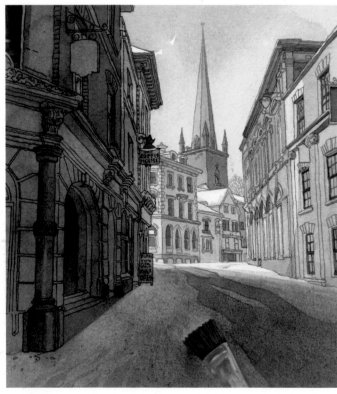

Fig. 6.36.

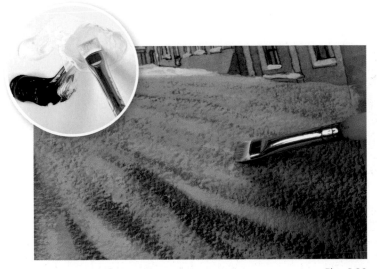

Fig. 6.37 (inset). Fig. 6.38

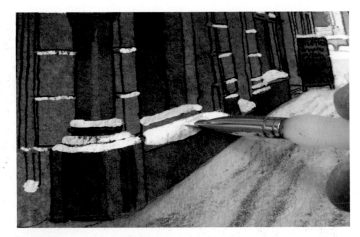

Fig. 6.39.

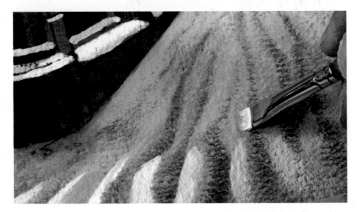

Fig. 6.40.

OPAQUE SNOW

The roughness of the paper lends itself to applying some dry brush snow (Fig. 6.37). Using the paint neat from the tube and with no water in the mix, blend a little Ultramarine Blue with White Gesso to achieve the main light blue colour. Use almost neat white for the highlights.

(Fig. 6.38) Drag the brush at low angles to remove the cream-like paint, with a ¼in flat synthetic brush.

(Fig. 6.39) Add highlights of pure white gesso on all the ledges.

(Fig. 6.40) Create highlights on the top of the snowdrifts with pure white gesso using gentle, low angle brush strokes.

(Fig. 6.41) Put in the final touches to the snow. The snow shading element to this picture is a technique similar to the dry brush technique on canvas described in Chapter 11, and could be applied as a style for a complete painting.

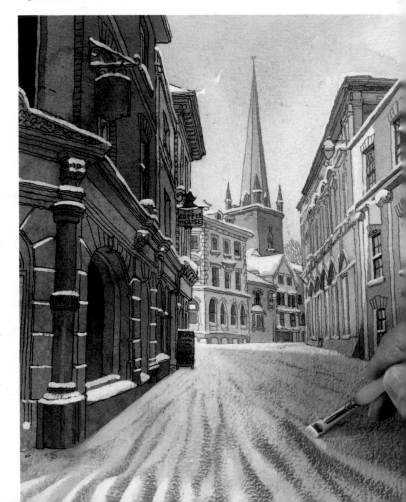

Fig. 6.41 The final painting.

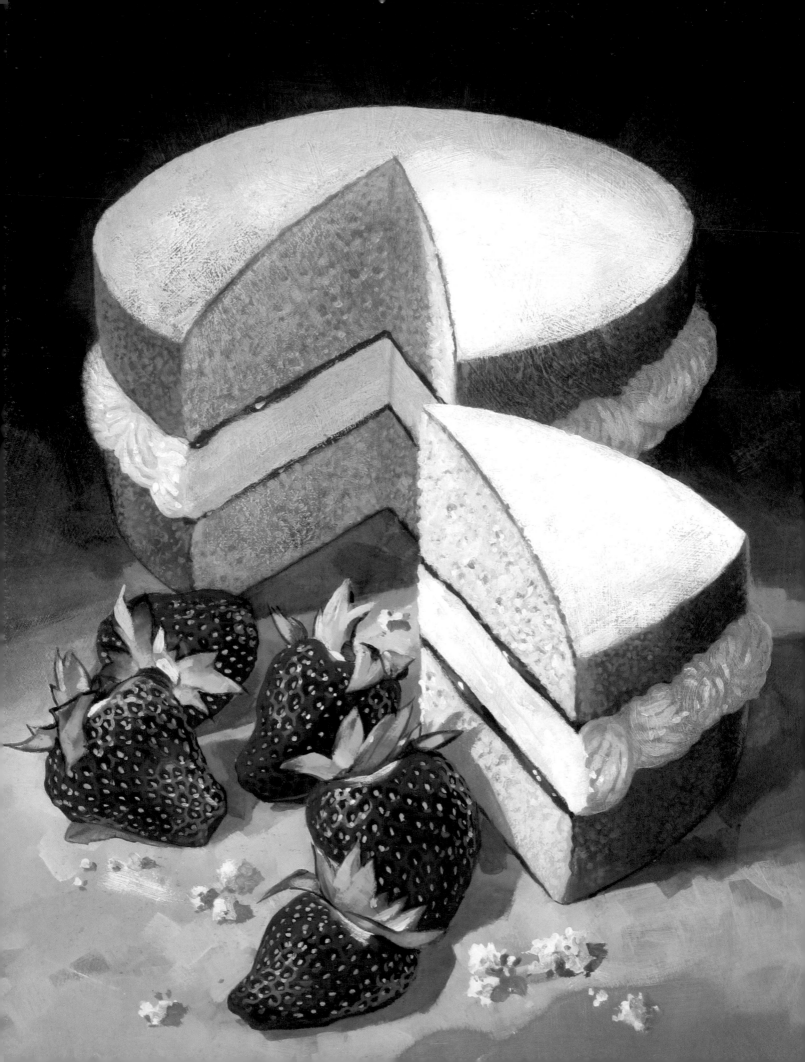

CHAPTER 7

THICK PAINT

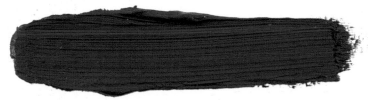

Fig. 7.1.

TECHNIQUE

This example is called 'Thick Paint' because it is painted with predominantly undiluted paint from the tube. It uses regular medium viscosity artist's grade paint without any thickening agent, and is a classic way of using paint. The technique is both wet in wet and wet on dry, resulting in a variety of mark making. The same painting could be achieved with the next level of thicker paints such as heavy-bodied paint or a thickening agent, resulting in a less detailed painting.

It is painted on MDF board without the interference of a canvas texture but with a smoother gesso priming effect instead, using the preparation advice in the next chapter, Rock Texture.

Paint is applied to one area at a time so the paint strokes run into each other and on top of each other whilst the paint is wet. The general colour is mixed on a palette first and blocked in, but each time the brush is re-filled, a little of the other colours used in the mixture is picked up on the brush to avoid a flat result. So for example if a mid blue-gray is mixed from white, blue and Payne's Grey, those colours are picked up randomly in small amounts.

The brush choice is wide for this type of painting, but

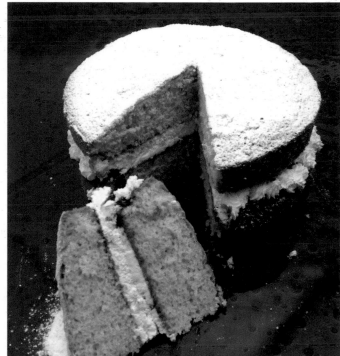

Fig. 7.3.

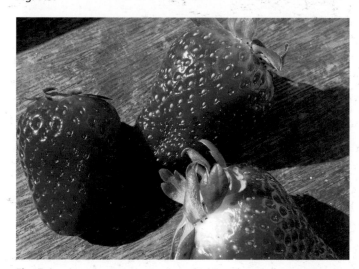

Fig. 7.4.

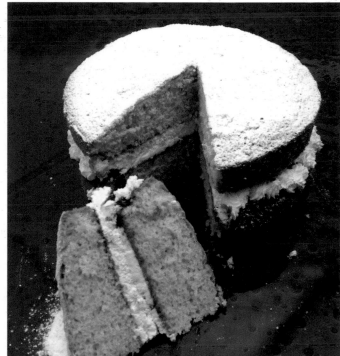

Fig. 7.2.

because thicker paint is being used, hog brushes are particularly good at applying larger amounts of paint. Two types of detail brushes are used, the 222 Designer brush and the very long-haired Rigger brush.

This example is painted at this book size of 220 × 280mm. The line art supplied (Fig. 7.5) is a guide based on the photo references, but feel free to create your own composition!

This uses the Shading techniques in Chapter 1, Wet in Wet.

THICK PAINT TECHNIQUE

MATERIALS NEEDED

- 35 × 30cm MDF board
- White gesso
- 3in wide bristle brush for gessoing
- Azanta ½in Hog long hair
- Winsor & Newton No. 8½in Hog
- Royal Soft Grip Synthetic flat ¼in brush for fiddly areas
- Winsor & Newton No. 6½in Filbert Hog long hair
- Winsor & Newton Designer 222 No. 6 Detail brush
- Winsor & Newton Designer No. 6 Rigger brush
- Kitchen towel
- Winsor & Newton Artists' Acrylics tubes: Yellow Ochre, Raw Sienna, Burnt Sienna, Dioxizine Purple, Payne's Grey, Cobalt Blue, Hooker's Green, Cadmium Red, Cadmium Yellow
- Imagetrace® paper

Gesso the Board

The cake painting has a smooth surface of gesso so it's primed with three layers of gesso applied uniformly thinly. (*See next Chapter 8 for detailed method.*)

Once dried, it is ready for a background all-over colour of Burnt Sienna. It can be raw Sienna or Burnt Umber or even red. This is to add another visual element to the final painting with the occasional area shining through untouched or glowing through semi-opaque areas.

(Figs 7.13 and 7.14) Using the Azanta long-haired bristle, mix a little bit of water into neat Burnt Sienna and scrub over all the gesso background.

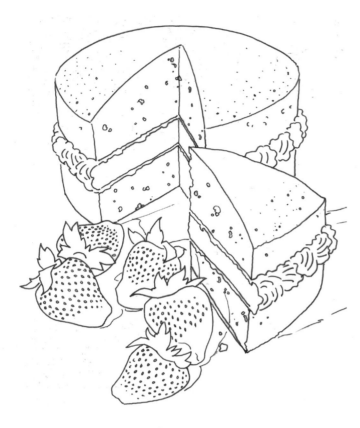

Fig. 7.5 Copy the line drawing 225 per cent on to tracing paper.

Fig. 7.6 Winsor & Newton Azanta ½in, medium-length hair hog brush.

Fig. 7.7 Winsor & Newton No. 8 short-haired flat hog brush.

Fig. 7.8 Royal Soft Grip No. 6 Synthetic Detail brush.

Fig. 7.9 Winsor & Newton No. 6 Filbert Fine Hog brush – longer bristles, rounder edges.

Fig. 7.10 Winsor & Newton Designer 222 No. 6 Detail brush.

Fig. 7.11 Winsor & Newton Designer No. 6 Rigger brush.

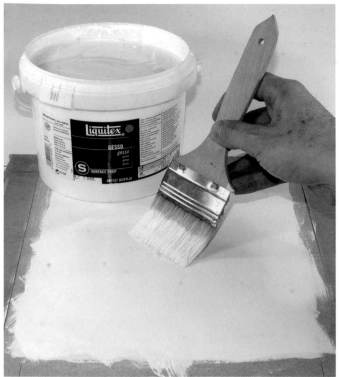

Fig. 7.12.

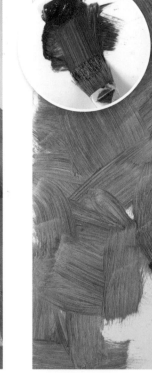
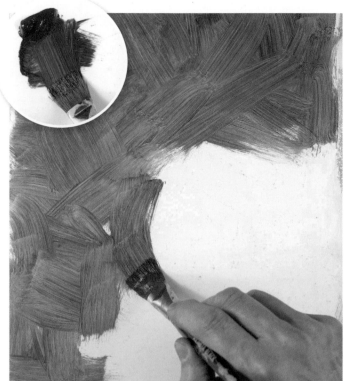

Fig. 7.13 (inset).   Fig. 7.14.

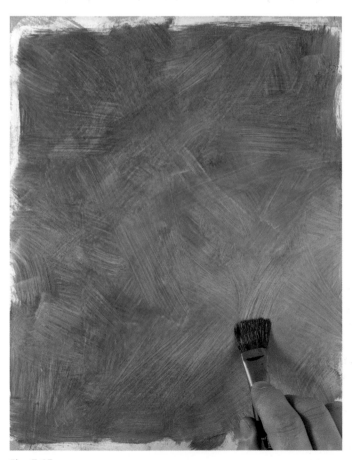

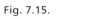
Fig. 7.15.

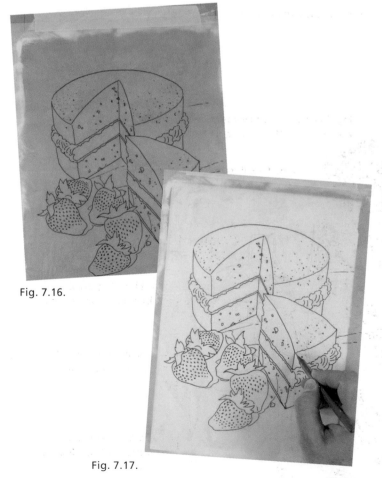

Fig. 7.16.

Fig. 7.17.

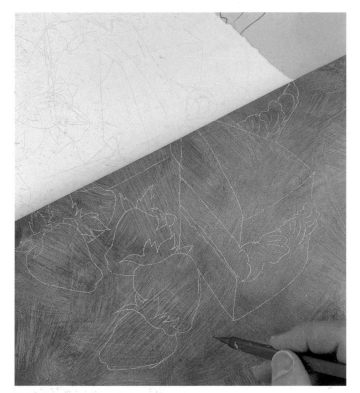

Fig. 7.18.

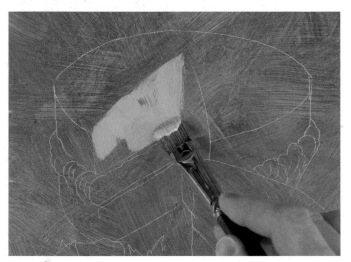

Fig. 7.19.

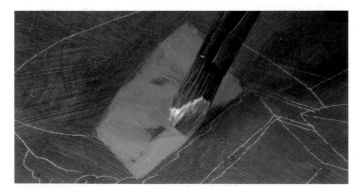

Fig. 7.20.

(Fig. 7.15) It doesn't need to be a uniform colour. Dark and lights all add to the effect.

(Figs 7.16 and 7.17) The drawing is taped into position and the Imagetrace® paper is placed underneath.

(Fig. 7.18) A white line should be visible after tracing through. As this picture is not photographic, exact outlines are less crucial so there's no need to keep the trace drawing taped to the board.

Painting In Sections

(Figs 7.19 and 7.20) Using the No. 10 Langnickel 400 Hog or similar, mix with no water, Raw Sienna and white with a little yellow for the cake middle. Note this is not the finished colour which is in shadow. The shadow is the last tint.

(Fig. 7.21) Finish the first coat on the cake middle, and leave it to dry whilst going on to the cream centre.

(Fig. 7.22) The cream: Mix a tiny amount of Raw Sienna into the white, and a tiny amount of yellow for a creamy colour. Brush in heavily and get swirls of brush marks.

(Figs 7.23 and 7.24) The outsides of the cake: Still neat from the tube, mix Burnt Sienna with a little Raw Sienna and White to give it opacity, and block in the cake sides, with a little more raw Sienna for a lighter top.

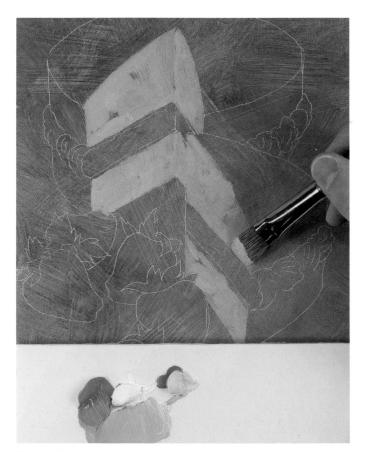

Fig. 7.21.

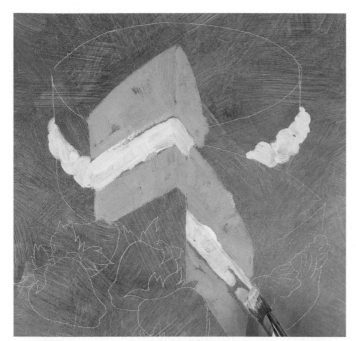

Fig. 7.22.

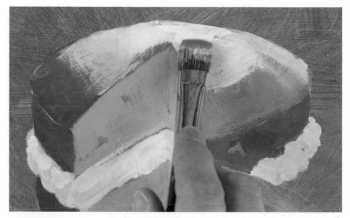

Fig. 7.25.

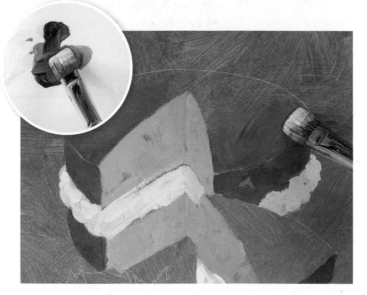

Fig. 7.23 (inset).   Fig. 7.24.

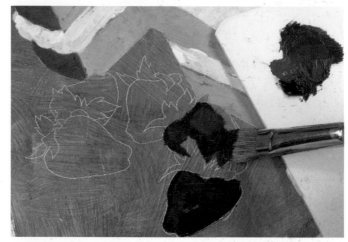

Fig. 7.26.

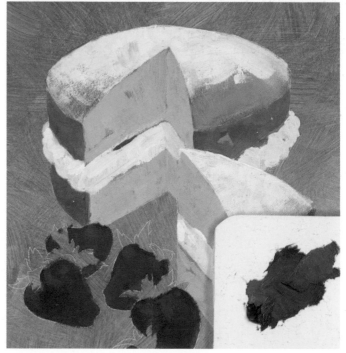

(Fig. 7.25) A quick dry wipe of the brush, and dip it into pure white for the icing. The colours will mix slightly as you are brushing, then paint a second coat when it's dry (Fig. 7.30).

(Fig 7.26 and 7.27) The strawberries: mix Cadmium Red with a little Payne's Grey to get a dark red, and block in with the short flat Hog brush.

(Fig. 7.28) Lighting: add pure Cadmium Red highlights to the strawberries with generous daubs.

Fig. 7.27.

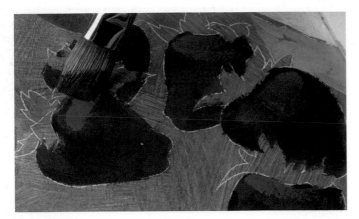

Fig. 7.28.

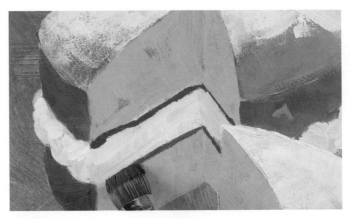

Fig. 7.29.

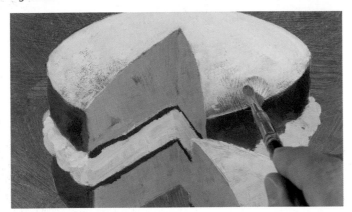

Fig. 7.30.

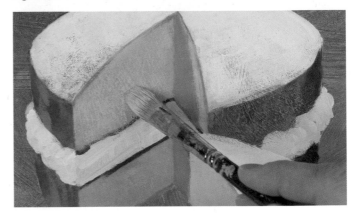

Fig. 7.31.

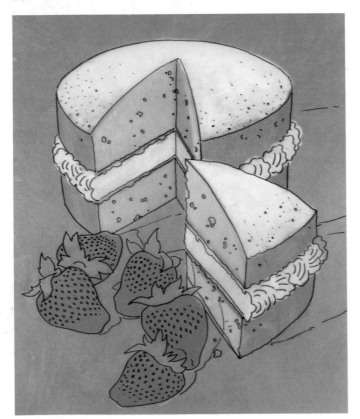

Fig. 7.32.

(Fig 7.29) Jam and the outsides again: With the tip and edge of the Hog brush, gently nudge in Cadmium Red.

Shade the outside of the cake with another coat of Burnt Sienna with a little Payne's Grey mix.

(Fig. 7.30) Icing: Add another layer of pure white with an emphasis on dragging the brush at a low angle to pick out the texture of the board to mimic the cake surface.

(Fig. 7.31) Inside texture: Using a light mix of white and Raw Sienna, drag the brush over the texture of the board allowing some of the darker tone to show through underneath.

(Fig. 7.32) Check the outlines every now and again. I'd left off some cream on the slice at far right for example.

(Fig. 7.33) Leaves: Using the small flat synthetic detail brush, mix a few greens, light green made with white, a brighter green made with yellow, and a dark green made with Hooker's Green and Payne's Grey. Paint one leaf at a time so the colours blend a little.

(Fig. 7.34) All the leaves are finished except at the edges, which can be tidied up with darker green edges.

(Figs 7.35 and 7.36) For this section use the Hog Azanta brush. Mix Cobalt Blue and Payne's Grey and White in various tonal strengths so it starts darkest at the top, working lighter towards the bottom. Leave little bits of the background showing through.

(Fig. 7.37) Use the little detail brush to get in around the leaves and strawberries.

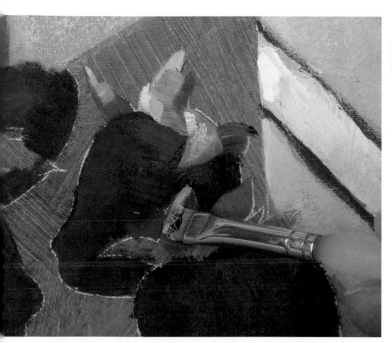

Fig. 7.33.

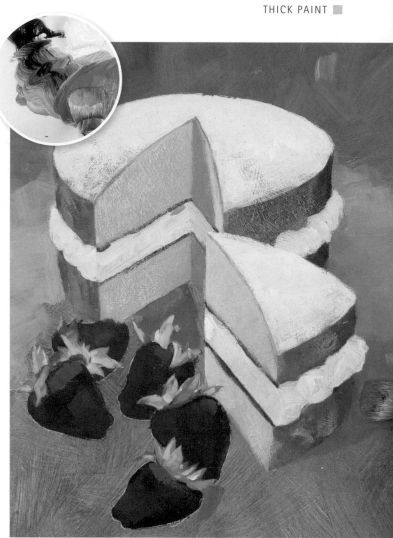

Fig. 7.35 (inset).   Fig. 7.36.

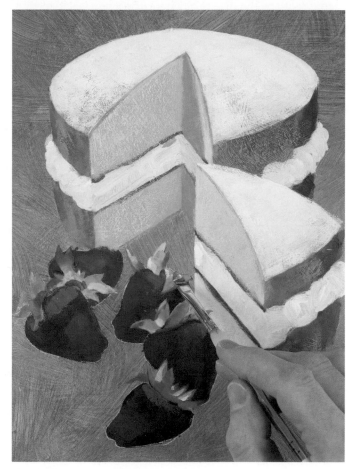

Fig. 7.34.

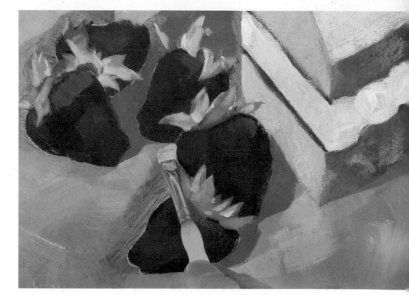

Fig. 7.37.

Turn the Work Upside Down!

Cake details: Quite often we forget and make marks that could have been that little bit more accurate if we just keep turning it to a more comfortable angle.

(Fig. 7.38) Edges: do not use water. With a little 50/50 mix of Burnt Sienna and Raw Sienna, tidy up the edges, rotating the painting to suit your brush strokes.

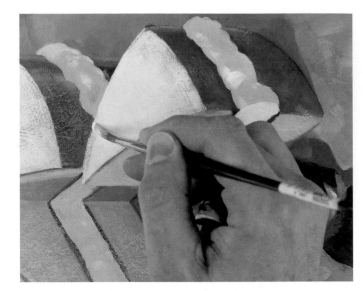

Fig. 7.40.

(Fig. 7.39) Now using the soft round 222 detail brush for finer marks, re-shape the cake to a better circle if you feel it needs it. I did, and mine was way off!

(Fig. 7.40) A bit more re-shaping is needed around the edges. Always paint up to, or over, edges when blocking in, as quite often they need defining accurately later.

(Fig. 7.41) A dark mix of Burnt Sienna with a little Dioxazine Violet is now added to shade the cake with thick paint and gentle sweeps. A good technique for this is to pull the brush tip towards your palm and not sweep either side.

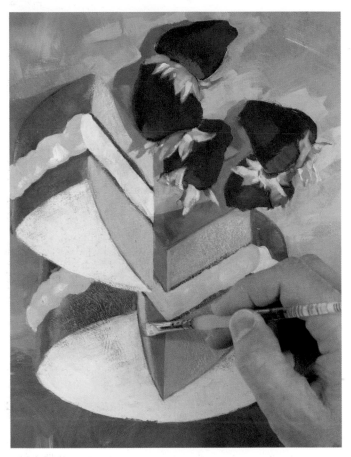

Fig. 7.38.

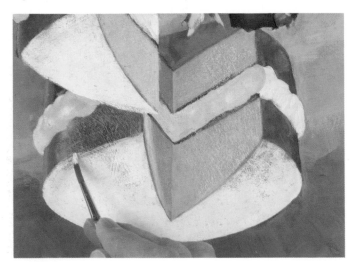

Fig. 7.39.

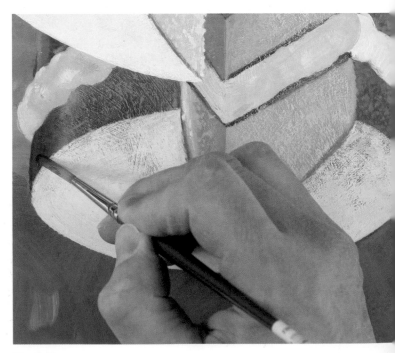

Fig. 7.41.

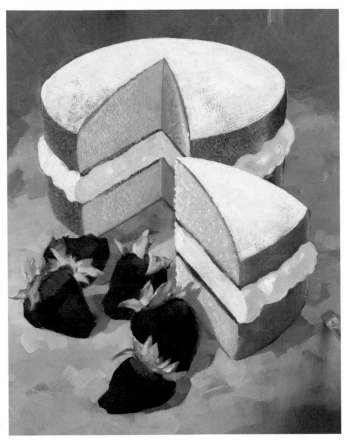

Fig. 7.42.

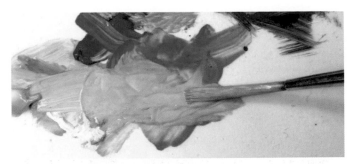

Fig. 7.43.

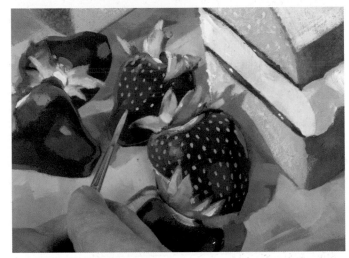

Fig. 7.44.

Back to the Normal Viewpoint

(Fig. 7.42) Background: adding darker shadows: use a little of the dark mixture that was used for the top of the painting to add brush marks surrounding the base of the cake.

(Figs 7.43 and 7.44) Strawberry details: using the Rigger Brush, mix up a deep yellow with a little Cadmium Red in the Cadmium yellow. Dab the brush to a point and make the seed marks. The viscosity needs to be just thin enough to run down the brush hairs.

(Fig. 7.45) Use a dark red mixed from Cadmium Red and Payne's Grey for the pip recesses.

(Fig. 7.46) Add reflections on the lit side of the strawberries with a mix of White and Dioxazine Violet in a semi-opaque dilution.

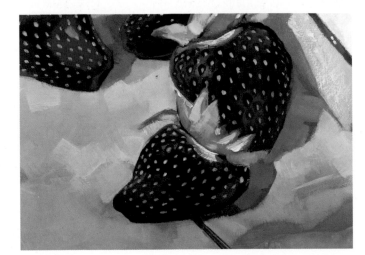

Fig. 7.45.

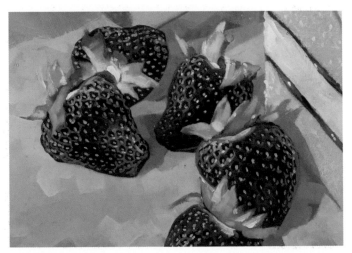

Fig. 7.46.

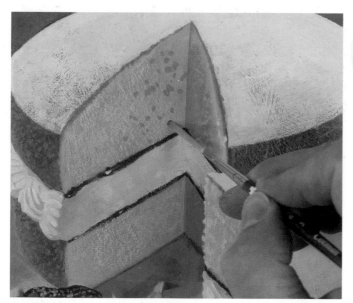

Fig. 7.47.

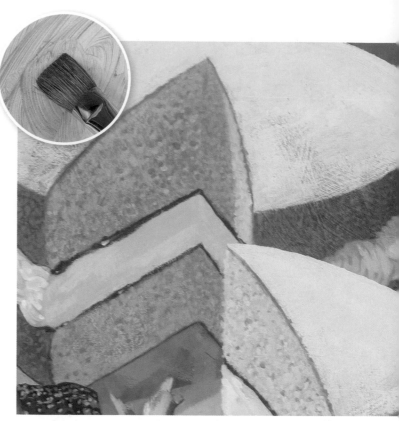

Fig. 7.49 (inset).   Fig. 7.50.

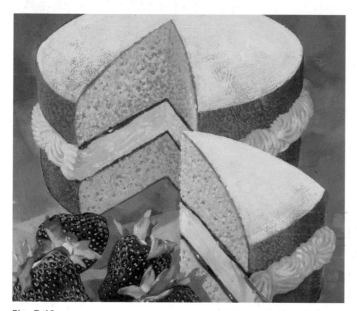

Fig. 7.48.

(Fig. 7.47) Cream, jam and sponge texturing. Add mid-tone 'holes' in the sponge with Raw Sienna and a little white mixed together.

(Fig. 7.48) Highlights of white on the wet jam and cream in the middle, and 'swirls' on the outsides. Shadow cream colours of Raw Sienna and a little Violet.

(Figs 7.49 and 7.50) Put in the tint shadow on the inside. With the Flat Hog as in the picture, use diluted Raw Sienna, brushing over the dry inside sponge area. Don't be too generous and keep spreading the small amount uniformly.

(Fig. 7.51) Darkening the background: To bring the cake forwards, the background is darkened to heighten the contrast. Our eye automatically goes to the point of the most contrast,

so shading is added around and on top of the cake to bring the focal point back to the top of cake slice.

Using a little water, mix Payne's Grey with a little Dioxazine Violet and a tiny amount of white. As you brush around the cake in short brush marks, dip every other dab into a little more of the white so there's a variety of subtle tones and not just one colour tone.

(Fig. 7.52) The final background tones are now complete.

(Fig. 7.53) Give a final dark green edge to the leaves with Payne's Grey and Hooker's Green.

(Fig. 7.54) Put in a little reflected light – a mix of Dioxazine Violet and white applied thickly to the cream with the rigger brush.

THICK PAINT TIPS

LIGHT PRESSURE: Too much pressure and the paint becomes semi-transparent.

WET IN WET: Explore the blending of colours with thick paint.

VERY LITTLE WATER: Most of the time paint is applied straight from the tube or via a mixing palette.

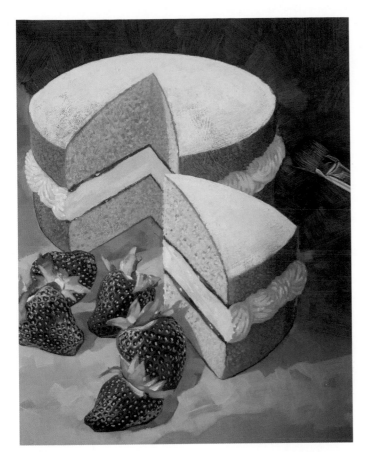

Fig. 7.51.

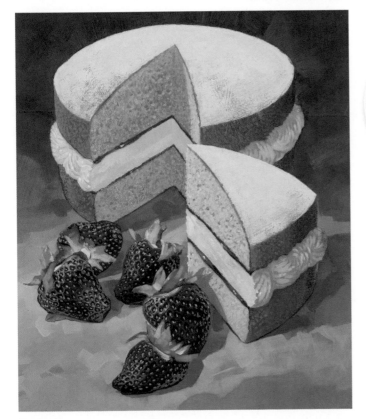

Fig. 7.52.

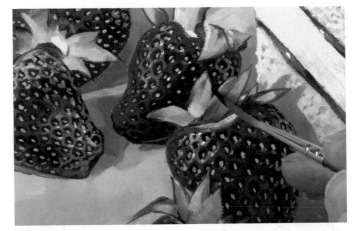

Fig. 7.53.

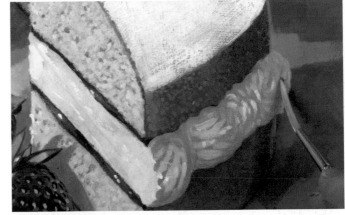

Fig. 7.54.

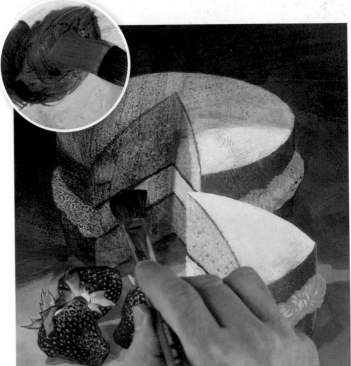

Fig. 7.55 (inset).

Fig. 7.56.

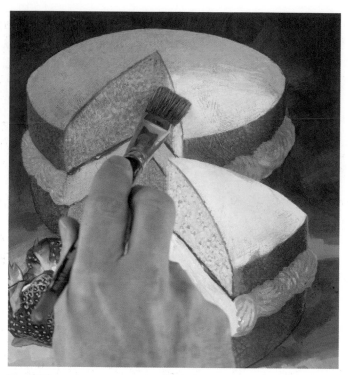

Fig. 7.57.

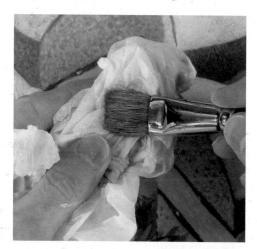

Fig. 7.58.

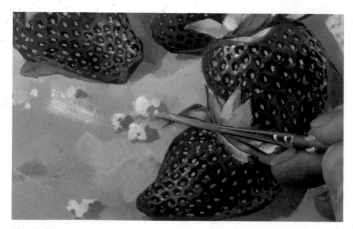

Fig. 7.59.

TINTING

(Fig. 7.55) Prepare a watery mix of Dioxazine Violet with a flat hog brush.

(Fig. 7.56) The paint will look dark at first. The knack is to keep it moving until it gets slightly tacky, and at the same time remove paint from your brush frequently until you reach the tone that looks best. If it's not coming off, dampen the brush slightly.

A light gentle criss-cross brushing at the end will uniform the brush marks. Keep an eye on the shadow border edges across the cake and floor: don't let those dry.

(Figs 7.57 and 7.58) As the tint dries you may need to 'scrub' the paint off with the damp hog bristle brush. If it's too wet the paint comes off completely. Dry your brush to the optimum level so it removes not too much.

(Fig. 7.59) Paint a final few crumbs with a mix of White and Yellow Ochre.

(Fig. 7.60) The final shadow is quite subtle over the icing. The great quality about acrylics is that another tint can be put over it again to make it a little stronger, and in that way dramatic moody lighting can be created.

This way of using acrylic paint is probably the most popular way of painting: it's a mix between loose and detailed, so the best of both worlds. This is painted with medium viscosity paints used at their thickest; the next alternative is to go even thicker with heavy bodied paints and have more texture in the brush strokes.

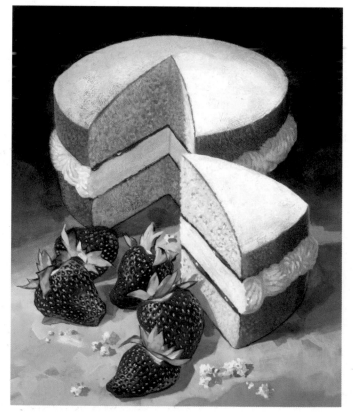

Fig. 7.60 The final painting.

MORE THICK PAINT EXAMPLES

(Figs 7.61 and 7.62) Both the images shown here use thick paint neat from the tube.

The rabbits have a textured gesso base applied with the palette knife in a similar manner to the one in Chapter 8, Rock Texture. The background was painted with a 1in bristle brush to get a looser feel with thick opaque colour mixes. The rabbits were done with a smaller hog brush and neat paint too.

The Shire horse was a more delicate technique, still with neat paint mixes using the Designer 222 brush for the hair. Neat paint hog brushwork was used on the hills, and semi-opaque layers of oranges and yellows with a synthetic flat brush for softer marks. Thin washes of semi-opaque blue were used for the clouds.

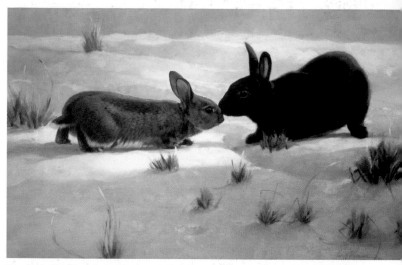

Fig. 7.61 *Rabbits Kissing* by Ian Coleman. Acrylic on MDF board. 30 × 20in.

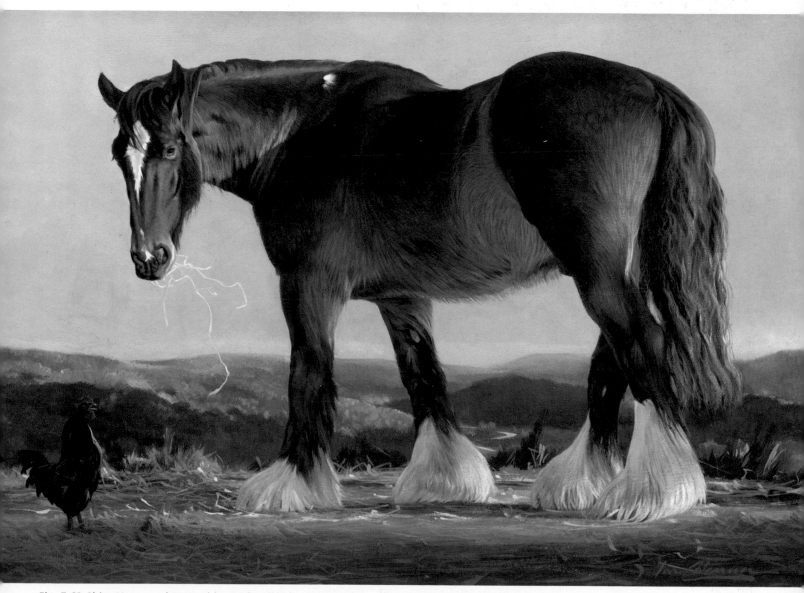

Fig. 7.62 *Shire Horse and Barnvelder Cockerel* by Ian Coleman. Acrylic on MDF board. 12 × 8in.

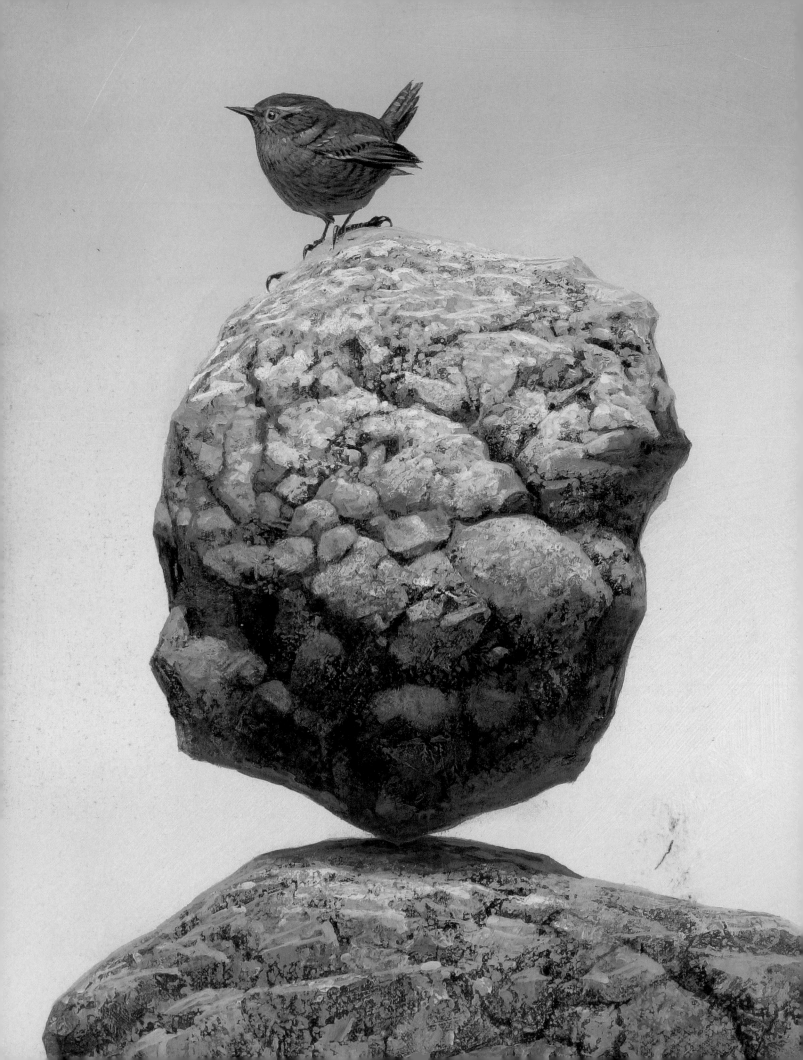

CHAPTER 8

ROCK TEXTURE
Gesso Texturing Technique

GESSO AND ITS USES

Gesso is mainly used for priming surfaces on board or canvas. Sometimes the art you are planning may benefit from the textural effect from another application of gesso to harmonize with the image above it. The pre-gessoed canvases can be primed again with your style of brush marks. When priming a board it's best to build up in a few thin layers, as detailed later in this chapter.

Gesso is also a great white paint substitute for a more opaque paint. I use it for fine lines such as whiskers and detail marks.

Acrylic can be mixed with gesso to create coloured primers and thicker paints. Like acrylics, it's a tough and versatile medium which gives another opportunity to create marks by sanding it with regular sandpaper or wet and dry paper. It's easy to get it so smooth that it's like glass. You can scrape it with scalpel blades and imprint it with objects as it becomes dry.

This is a simple technique to create a variety of rock-like textures. Every texture will depend on the amount of gesso used, the way in which the palette knife is moved, and how many layers are applied. It's also great for dirt and grit and wood-type textures. The secret is.... don't apply too much. If the aim is to create convincing texture that doesn't have a craft-like or 3D quality to it, then it's better to be frugal with the gesso. It's easy to get sculptural with it!

In the process of creating this rock example there are a few extra tips and tricks to give it form, which are described in the process. These are primarily using coloured gesso, removing paint, and tinting.

(Figs 8.1 and 8.2) Textural gesso effects are applied with a palette knife, and impressions made with various objects. When dry, colour can be applied and either rubbed in with a brush or cloth. In turn, those colours when dried can either be re-tinted with alternative colours (Fig. 8.1) or sanded to bring back the white highlights (Fig. 8.2).

(Fig. 8.3) This picture shows rock texture on canvas, pigment rubbed in, sanded lightly and tinted multiple times.

This example is painted at this book size of 220 × 280mm.

Gesso comes in a few colour varieties and qualities. Three brands that I use regularly are Winsor & Newton Artist's Acrylic

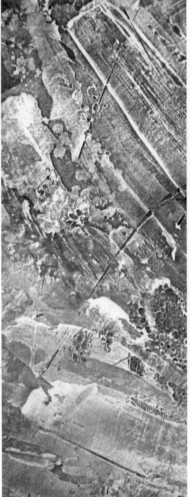

Fig. 8.1.   Fig. 8.2.

White Gesso, Liquitex White Gesso, and Golden White Gesso. All provide a solid, opaque white with a fine tooth.

Gesso in its various stages of drying out in its containers provides useful options according to whether a dryer or a runnier gesso is required. For these rock effects a medium to dry gesso is preferred. Old gesso can also come in handy!

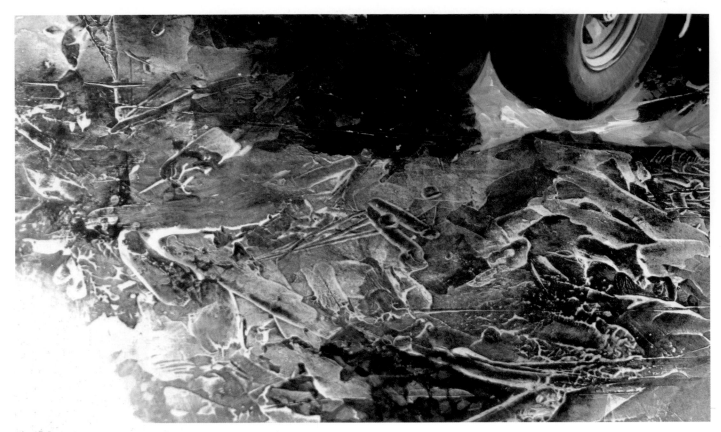

Fig. 8.3.

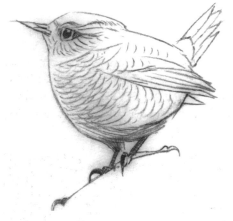

Fig. 8.4.

GESSO ROCK TIPS

KEEP THE BLADE PARALLEL: Get that suction of the gesso on the surface in small rotations with spaces.

FLATTEN THE GESSO AS IT'S ALMOST DRY: This will remove any peaks and create harder edges for a better effect.

LESS IS MORE: Build up the texture in subtle flattened layers by avoiding being too generous with wet gesso.

Fig. 8.5 shows a few of the gesso brushes I use in preparing surfaces for painting. They are all stiff bristle brushes used for a variety of purposes depending on the scale of the work or how textured the surface is to be. The main brush I use is the one illustrated centre left, a Winsor & Newton Series K Varnish brush. Synthetic brushes tend not to have the strength to push and pull thick gesso about.

Palette knives come in a variety of sizes and shapes, and the main knife I use is a 35mm diamond-shaped blade (Fig. 8.7). This knife allows small-scale texturing with high precision. Larger works tend to be done with larger knives, and depending on the type of painting, the choice of blade shape will have a significant effect on the style of the painting.

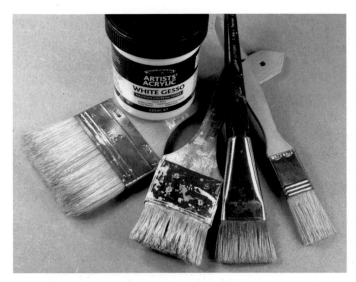

Fig. 8.5.

ROCK TECHNIQUE

MATERIALS NEEDED

- Winsor & Newton White Gesso

- Small palette knife 35mm, diamond shape

- 2in wide bristle brush for gesso

- Synthetic flat ½in brush for tinting

- Winsor & Newton Designer 222 No. 6 Detail Brush

- MDF board

Fig. 8.6 Winsor & Newton Designer 222 No. 6 Detail brush.

Fig. 8.7 Synthetic flat ½in brush.

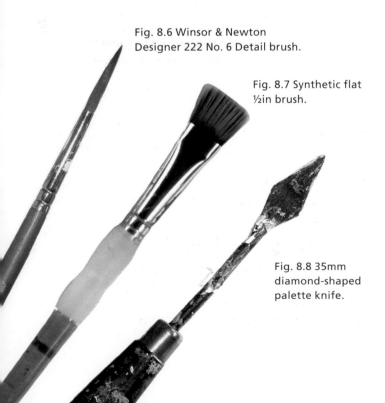

Fig. 8.8 35mm diamond-shaped palette knife.

Gesso the Board

Normally I apply between two or four coats of white gesso to obtain a completely solid base. For a rougher finish it might only be two coats, but for a smoother finish I thinly apply four coats with a gesso brush. When it's dry, a light sanding with wet and dry paper will flatten any ridges and give extra tooth.

(Fig. 8.9) A technique that produces a smooth finish is one of random directions with a loaded gesso brush, and then finishing with an empty brush and a light 'dusting' to flatten it off.

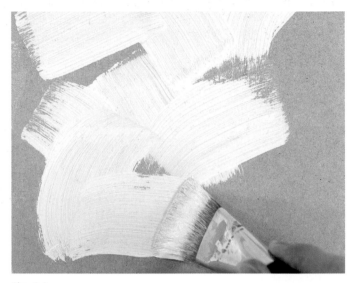

Fig. 8.9.

Colouring the Gesso

In this example the first coat is white gesso, but the next two are coloured with blue. Each coat must be dry, as any moisture in the previous coat will remove those areas that are still slightly damp.

(Fig. 8.10) Make sure you don't create ridges, as it's surprising how obvious it can appear in the finished piece.

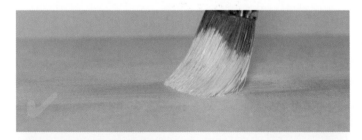

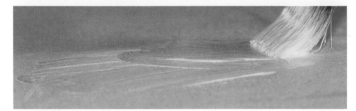

Fig. 8.10.

First Colour Coat of Two

(Fig. 8.11) With a blob of blue placed on the gessoed board neat from the tube, blend it in with a loaded gessoed brush (Fig. 8.12). This is, in effect, our base priming, and will achieve a solid covering of the board with the added benefit of being the sky (Fig. 8.13).

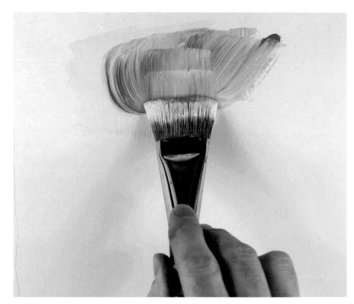

Fig. 8.14.

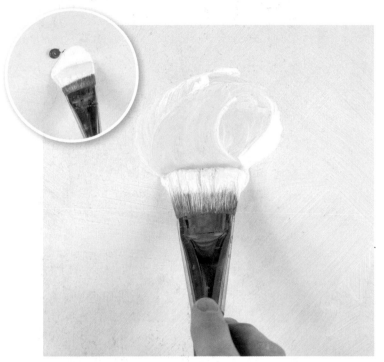

Fig. 8.11 (inset).   Fig. 8.12.

Fig. 8.15.

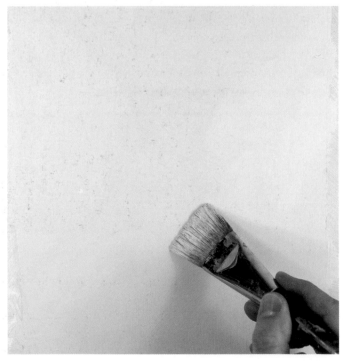

Fig. 8.13.

Second Colour Coat

(Fig. 8.14) Repeat the same procedure with a slightly more generous amount of blue.

(Fig. 8.15) Keep the blending on the move until you are happy with it. If it's slightly too thick and dry, add a little water to your brush.

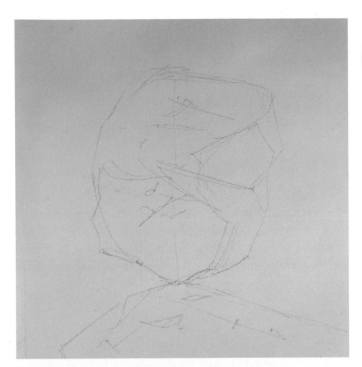

Fig. 8.16.

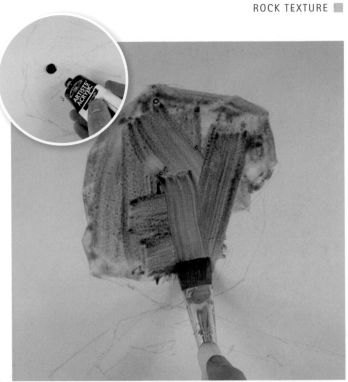

Fig. 8.17 (inset).   Fig. 8.18.

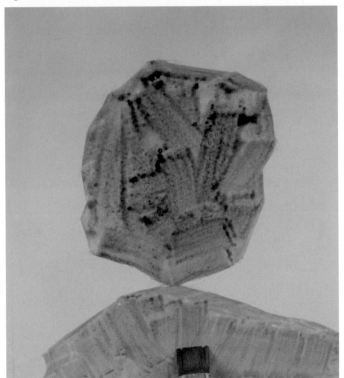

Fig. 8.19.

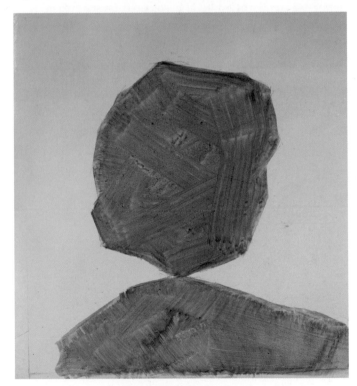

Fig. 8.20.

(Fig. 8.16) When it's dry, draw a few rough outlines of the rocks. Because the end result will be opaque, none of the lines will show through.

(Fig. 8.17) This coat needs to be thin. With a blob of Payne's Grey on the rock, dip the main painting brush into water and spread the colour about (Figs 8.18 and 8.19).

(Fig. 8.20) This is our base tone which will appear in the background of our rock colour.

After blocking in the grey colour, the paint will become nice and tacky in a minute or so, ready for smoothing. Using the same brush wiped dry, spread the paint about again and in the process it will become softer and more uniform.

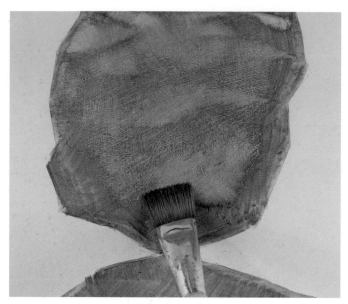

Fig. 8.21.

Removing with a Damp Brush

Before we apply the white and coloured gessoes, there is an opportunity to 'sculpt' with a damp brush, like the wave in Chapter 5. It's a style in itself without adding the gesso, but this technique of removing and reapplying thin colours creates a pleasant effect. I've shown here the basic technique, which could be taken a lot further using smaller and stiffer brushes.

(Fig. 8.21) It is best done when the paint is just drying, but not absolutely dry. With a damp brush it is possible to remove the thin layer of paint and pull the pigment around so you end

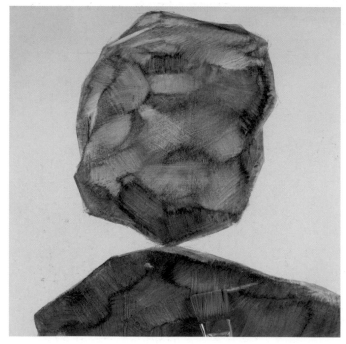

Fig. 8.22.

up with dark edges here and there. (This only works satisfactorily on gessoed MDF or canvas, not papers.)

(Fig. 8.22) As the brush loses its effect, re-dampen it. If you need to darken a whole area add more pigment and do a second coat.

Wide, flat brushes work best, either hog bristle, or new and used synthetic brushes as shown here.

Adding Gesso 'Rock'

Use a small 35mm diamond-shaped palette knife. Have white gesso ready on a palette so you can dip the bottom of the blade in it.

(Fig. 8.23) There is a knack to using the palette knife. Rotate it in small circles with the bottom of the blade parallel to the surface. 'Parallel' is important, as this creates a subtle and low-lying

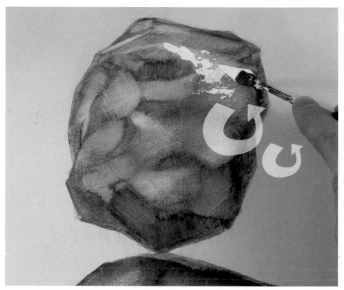

Fig. 8.23.

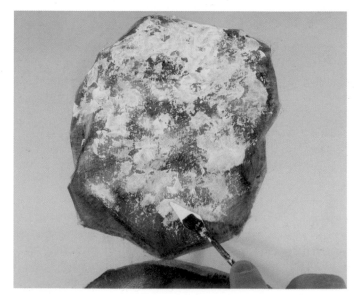

Fig. 8.24.

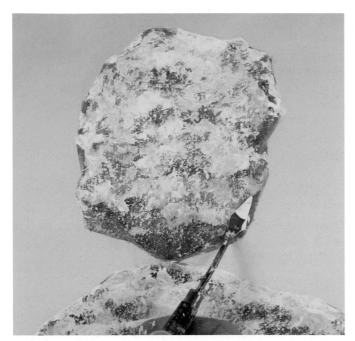

Fig. 8.25.

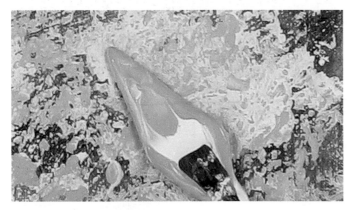

Fig. 8.26.

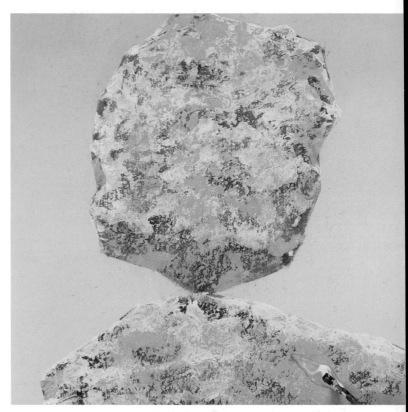

Fig. 8.27.

Detailing and Tinting Cracks and Holes

(Figs 8.29 and 8.30) The detail brush Winsor & Newton Designer 222 is used for both detail lines and small areas of tinting. The brush is dabbed flat for tinting areas and rolled round to a point for the line work.

effect, while 'stabbing' and 'digging' create too much texture. You need to feel that 'suction' of the blade on the board.

(Fig. 8.24) Make the paint marks sparse at first, moving to irregular spots and eventually joining up a few. Those areas where the light strikes the most, such as the top and a few areas on the side, can be more thoroughly covered.

(Fig. 8.25) The rock is now covered with the first layer of white gesso. If anything, underplay the coverage because another layer of grey gesso will now cover 25 per cent.

The Grey Gesso Layer

(Figs 8.26 and 8.27) Mix a mid-grey gesso colour with Payne's Grey and repeat sparingly with an emphasis on the shaded areas. This could be done with other colour tones and then another sprinkling of white to create an even more 3D effect.

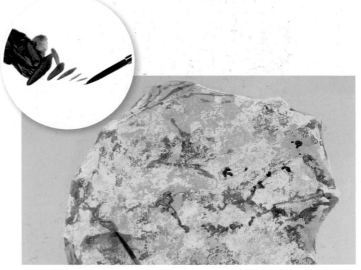

Fig. 8.28 (inset).   Fig. 8.29.

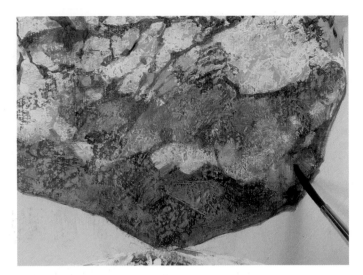

Fig. 8.30.

Large Area Tinting

(Fig. 8.31) For the lower rock use the larger painting brush and add a thin mix of Payne's Grey. As it becomes sticky in the drying process, lightly brush the pigment into the recesses leaving a light, even coat on the highlights.

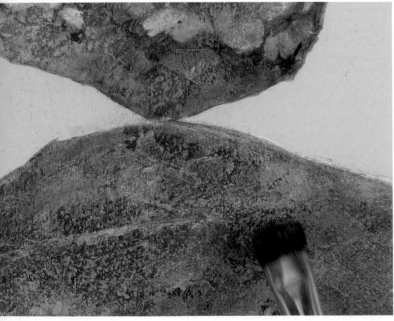

Fig. 8.31.

Extra Contrast

(Fig. 8.32) Sometimes you may want to bring out the highlights more and the brush is proving to be too gentle. Using kitchen towel or a cloth in one light source direction will help bring more contrast. A step further would be to use wet and dry paper, which will dramatically bring back the white gesso.

Adding more detail in the bottom rock: (Fig. 8.33) With the detail brush continue to add shadow cracks and marks.

Tinting the rock brown:
(Fig. 8.34) Water the Raw Umber to a cream consistency and brush over with the main brush (Fig. 8.35). This is the same as tinting the rock earlier (Fig. 8.31), leaving an even layer of transparent brown. Just as it is drying, 'soak off' the top parts where the light is falling from above.

(Fig. 8.36) The rock should start to look browner, and the next layer is to add opaque brown with the palette knife.

(Fig. 8.37) Just like the grey gesso before, add various shades of brown, from light to mid-brown around the rock.

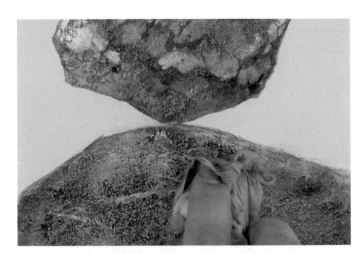

Fig. 8.32.

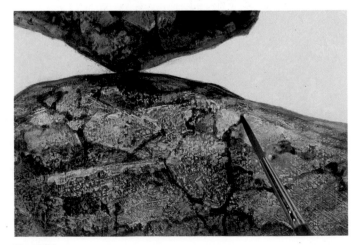

Fig. 8.33.

Final Rock Details

(Figs 8.38 and 8.39) With the detail brush, add little highlights and shadows. Also add some understated little white highlights with the knife, for an extra 'gritty' appearance.

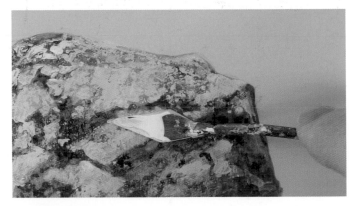

Fig. 8.37.

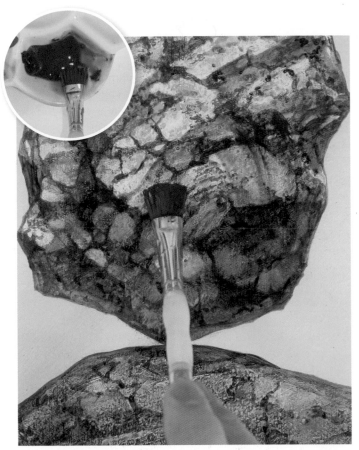

Fig. 8.34 (inset).

Fig. 8.35.

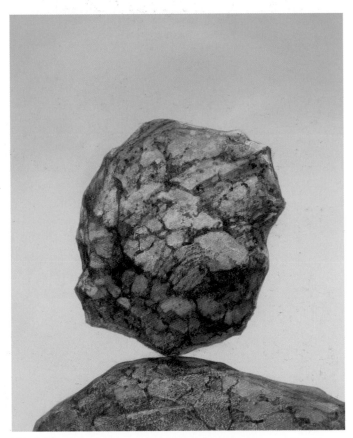

Fig. 8.36.

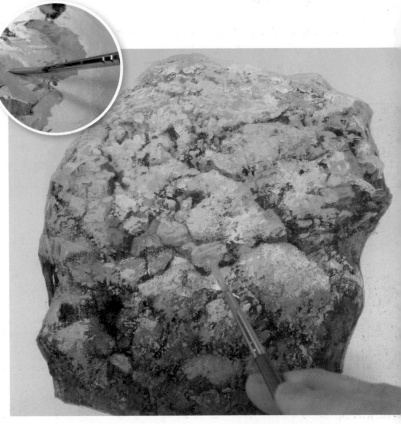

Fig. 8.38 (inset).

Fig. 8.39.

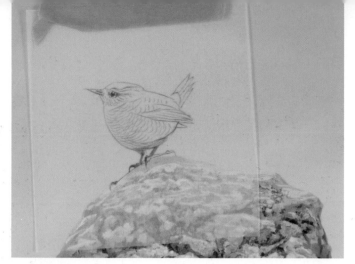

Fig. 8.40.

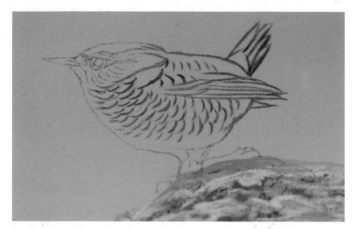

Fig. 8.41.

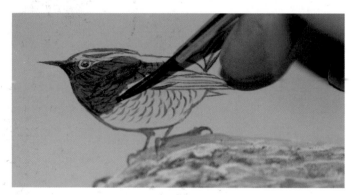

Fig. 8.42.

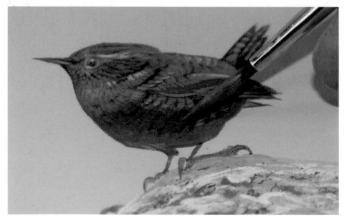

Fig. 8.43.

Adding the Wren

(Fig. 8.40) The pencil drawing at the beginning of this chapter is at the same size. Photocopy it on to tracing paper and trace it down using Imagetrace®, or do it the traditional way using soft lead smudged on the reverse side. The painting sequence here is a typical one for rendering objects.

(Fig. 8.41) Brush in the wren lines. Using the detail brush, it's good practice to paint in the wren as if it were a brushed black and white line drawing. These lines serve as dark details and shadows to make it easier to then apply lighter coats on top, and not lose your way.

(Fig. 8.42) Now block in the mid-brown. Paint an all-over transparent mid-brown, still allowing the dark brush lines to show through.

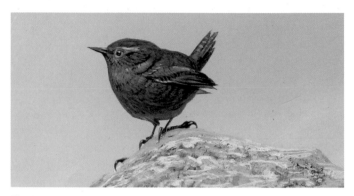

Fig. 8.44.

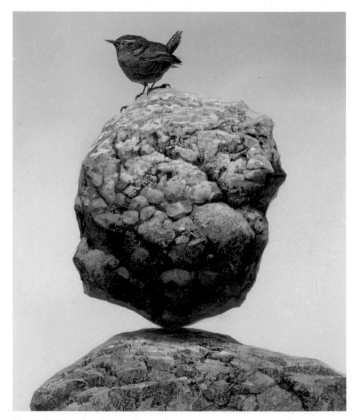

Fig. 8.45 The final painting.

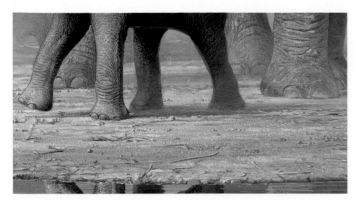

Fig. 8.46.

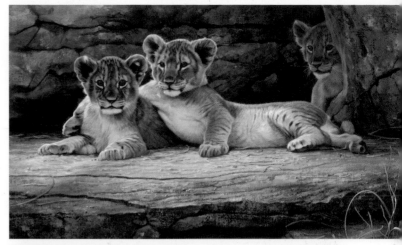

Fig. 8.47.

(Fig. 8.43) Opaque details: Add opaque light brown feathers based on the brush lines underneath. Many of those marks may disappear but they can be ticked back in.

(Fig. 8.44) Final dark detail marks: The feet and beak, eyes and wing all need a few more detail tweaks on top of the opaque body colour. A sweep of brown shadow tint under the belly finishes it off (Figs 8.44 and 8.45).

Applying gesso in paintings as a means of texture is a technique that works best if used sparingly in representational style paintings. It works particularly well on canvas because the knife blade tends to leave gesso on the top of the weave, which becomes part of the overall effect.

Here are some examples of rock and grit which have been applied in paintings. The baby elephant painting (Fig. 8.46) shows a small amount of gesso 'rock' by applying it in a horizontal manner with a palette knife. By contrast, the lion cubs' rock (Figs 8.47 and 8.48) was applied far more generously and in a few layers with tinting back and forth.

(Fig. 8.49) Below, the sand martins' sand bank was painted purely with coloured gesso using a palette knife.

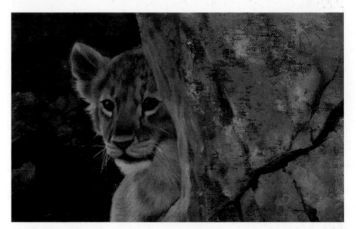

Fig. 8.48.

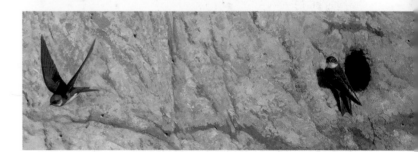

Fig. 8.49.

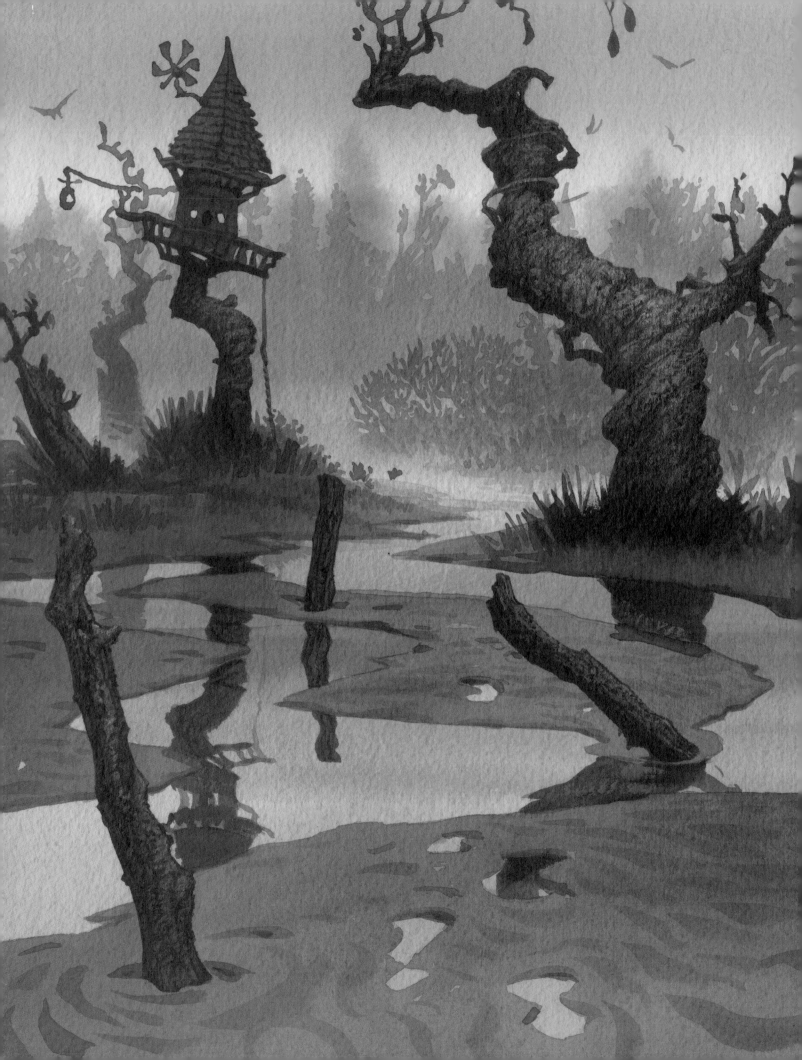

CHAPTER 9

WASHES

The Drawing Guide

The pencil guide drawing (Fig. 9.1) is a rough guide in terms of details and the placement of objects, but it's a good procedure to have one on tracing paper rather than draw directly on to the painting paper. Drawing directly may leave unwanted lines when the paint has dried, and only if the paint is very thin may it be possible to remove them with a putty rubber.

Tape the drawing at the top only, and the only marks you need to make are on each side outside the picture area: these

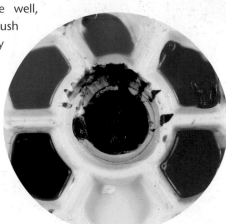

Fig. 9.2 This example is based on the 'Washes' ball exercise in Chapter 1.

denote where the horizontal bands of colour wash will go. This will stay taped until the very end of the painting.

Once the colour is applied and dried, the bands of colour will help give an approximate point for the distant tree line and the following middle-ground trees, all graduating at the bottom edge into the blue mist.

Mixing the Colour Washes

(Fig. 9.3) In a palette well, mix with a mixing brush enough of each watery colour to do full one-load sweeps. Don't worry about having the right colours – after all, it's a fantasy scene, and anything goes. The thickness should be like semi-skimmed milk.

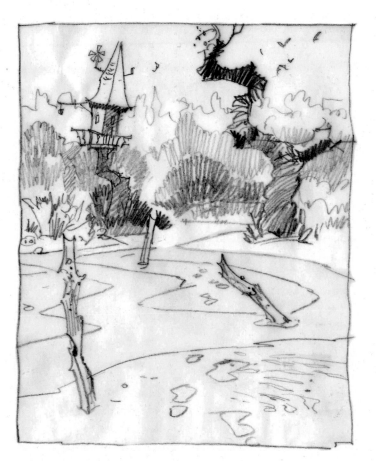

Fig. 9.1 Pencil drawing guide. Scan and print at 275 per cent on to tracing paper.

Fig. 9.3 Pools of watery colour well mixed and ready to be used.

WASHES

MATERIALS NEEDED

- 1.5in soft flat wash brush

- Large round watercolour brush Winsor & Newton Cotman 111, No. 14

- Detail Brush Winsor & Newton 222, No. 6

- Watercolour paper: Arches Rough 640G/M2; or watercolour board

- A board to tape the paper to

- Tubed acrylics: Ultramarine Blue, Cadmium Yellow Medium, Cadmium Red Medium, Quinacridone Violet, Dioxazine Purple, Burnt umber, Payne's Grey

- Tracing paper, Imagetrace® paper and 6H pencil or tracing pencil

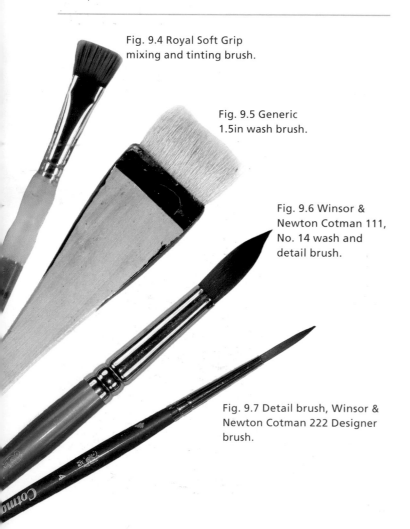

Fig. 9.4 Royal Soft Grip mixing and tinting brush.

Fig. 9.5 Generic 1.5in wash brush.

Fig. 9.6 Winsor & Newton Cotman 111, No. 14 wash and detail brush.

Fig. 9.7 Detail brush, Winsor & Newton Cotman 222 Designer brush.

PREPARING THE PAPER

To minimize or to avoid warping the paper there are three basic approaches. This example uses the first one.

HEAVYWEIGHT LOOSE PAPER

In this example I've used Arches Rough 640G/M2, a heavyweight thick watercolour paper with an inherently rough surface, liked for its aesthetic element and its resistance to warping. It is unstretched by soaking and taping, so a subtle but acceptable buckling of the paper might result. Even the heaviest papers will warp if enough water is applied many times, so if in doubt, always stretch the paper.

MID- TO HEAVYWEIGHT STRETCHED PAPER

Soak and gum tape the paper into position on a piece of MDF or hardboard. This will dry flat, but depending on the amount of water, it may buckle during the painting process and affect the image. (See Chapter 6 regarding stretching paper successfully.)

WATERCOLOUR BOARD

Watercolour or wash board is the best for not buckling, but may be smoother than the heavyweight loose papers.

Wetting the Paper

Place and tape the paper top and bottom with masking tape on a board which you can rotate and incline at about 10 per cent.

Now the paper is in position with guide marks for the colour areas on the far sides, wet the whole paper generously with clear water from the top to the bottom methodically with the wide wash brush (Fig. 9.8). Be sure not to go back up or fuss on the way down because that will leave tide marks or marks later on. This pre-wash will make a smoother running of colours compared to putting it on dry.

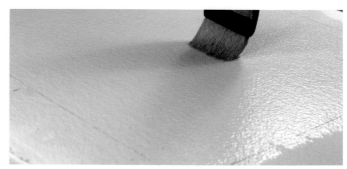

Fig. 9.8.

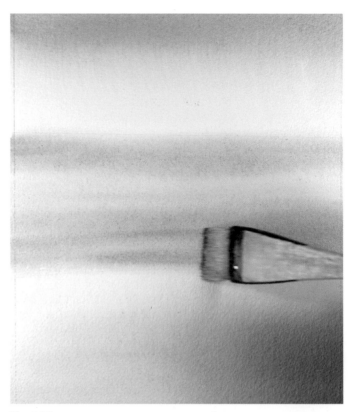

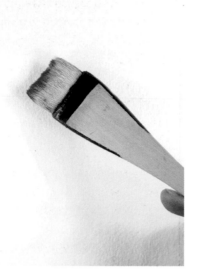

Fig. 9.9.

The Colour Washes

Now comes the fun part. With one eye on the colour reference with all the colours mixed and ready, there is only a short time to apply the colours. As in comedy, timing is everything when it comes to the amount of colour spreading on the surface. If it's too dry it won't run enough, and if it's too wet it'll run out of control.

When the surface looks like satin, dip generously into the Cadmium Yellow and apply to the top and bottom in a few horizontal sweeps (Fig. 9.9).

(Fig. 9.10) Then dip into the red and do the same to the top, bottom and middle areas. Quickly clean your brush, dab dry, and then load up with Ultramarine Blue and sweep it across. Once the blue band is in, dip into the Dioxazine Purple and blend it in with the blue.

The overall aim is for a mid-tone or below. If your mix has been really weak don't worry, let it dry and go over it again. That's hard to do in gouache or watercolours!

Time To Dry

Now leave the paper for 15–30min until it is totally dry in readiness for the distant tree-line.

The Second Clear Wash

(Fig. 9.11) With clean water, methodically wet a horizontal band starting just above the tree line and finishing at the bottom of the blue band. Allow to become satin again.

Fig. 9.10.

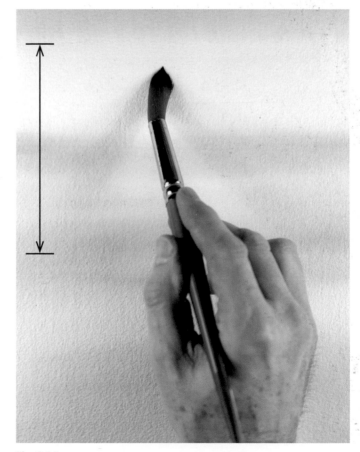

Fig. 9.11.

WASHES TIPS

SLOPING: Have the board on an incline and let gravity do the blending.

A BIG BRUSH: Use a large, round watercolour brush with a great tip for fine lines and fewer dips.

(Fig. 9.12) Load the wash brush moderately to start with (generously will have blobs dispersing quickly), and starting from one side, work your way across, up and down. You may need to re-load the brush a few times. Work your way down and finish the band before you get to the bottom edge of the wetted paper, otherwise if the colour finds the edge it will leave a hard tide line unless you soak it up with a clean brush.

(Fig. 9.13) Optionally, you can go through soaking up some colour with a squeezed damp brush to vary the tones and create a hint of more trees.

The Third Clear Wash and Colour

(Fig. 9.14) When it's dry, run a wide brush of clear water across from the top of the second line of trees to the bottom of the blue band. Don't let the red run too far into the blue.

Wait Until it Turns Dryer than Satin

(Fig. 9.15) This line of trees wants a slightly sharper edge, so let the paper dry slightly more than before. Run the red across in more defined tree shapes. It's a race against time, so speed is of the essence. You may need to soak up the bottom edge with a clean brush as it goes over the purple. Leave it to dry.

(Fig. 9.16) After drying, load up red for the third time and this time apply the paint on dry paper for that sharp edge. Use the very tip to get delicate lines on the top edge; however, every now and then you may need to keep the bottom edge moving so it doesn't reach that drying tipping point.

(Fig. 9.17) Soften the bottom edge with a clean damp brush.

(Fig. 9.18) Load up with a stronger mix of red with a little purple or burnt umber. It must still be fluid, like milk, and detail the mid-ground bushes and tree. Soak up and soften the bottom edge.

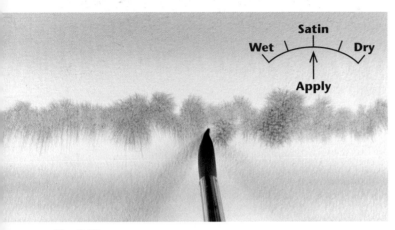

Fig. 9.12.

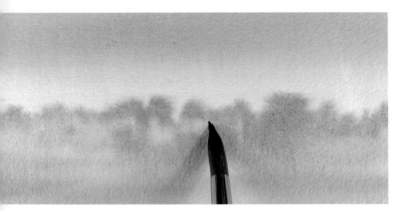

Fig. 9.13.

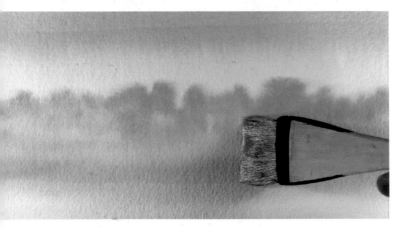

Fig. 9.14.

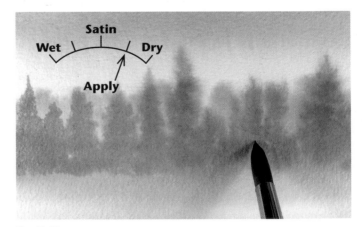

Fig. 9.15.

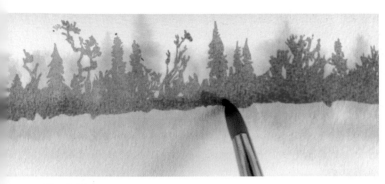

Fig. 9.16.

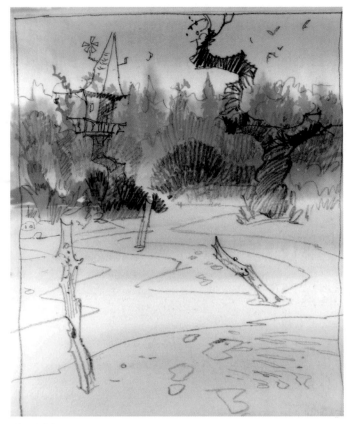

Fig. 9.20.

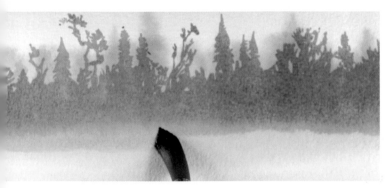

Fig. 9.17.

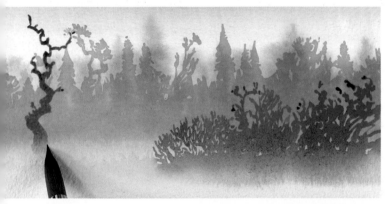

Fig. 9.18.

(Fig. 9.19) Add the foreground foliage with an even darker mix. Each object gets stronger in tone the nearer it gets to the viewer.

(Fig. 9.20) Now is a good time to check on areas of colour and trace through some foreground outlines.

(Fig. 9.21) Place the Imagetrace® paper under the still attached guide, and (Fig. 9.22) gently trace the mud banks, foreground tree, tree house, posts and footprints.

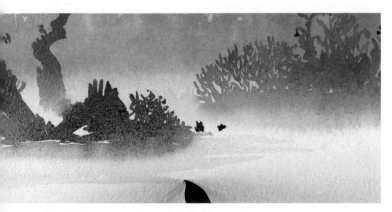

Fig. 9.19.

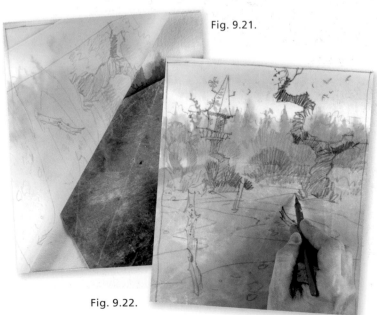

Fig. 9.21.

Fig. 9.22.

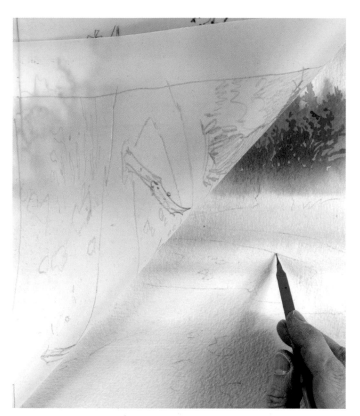

Fig. 9.23.

(Fig. 9.23) The lines should be just visible enough so as not to appear in the final painting. However, because the mud banks are dark, it may be possible to turn any marks into details such as raised mud bank edges.

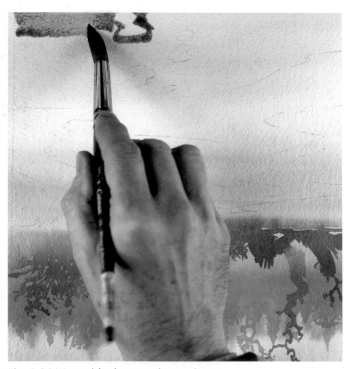

Fig. 9.24 It's upside down and on a slope!

Upside-Down Wash!

The plan here is to let the pigment run from the top, when it is at its strongest, to the bottom, when it becomes most diluted. The nearest mud bank to you is the darkest, and as it recedes into the picture it gets weaker and it can change colour. The paper is dry for sharp edge washes.

(Fig. 9.24) Wet your brush with clear water first, then load it up to dripping point with Burnt Sienna and a violet mix; then fill in from side to side, carefully going round footprints and up to the tracing marks. The clear water will come out last, thereby giving a weaker tone; then load up with the next colour.

(Fig. 9.25) Keep filling down, but introduce a violet mix half way down (Fig. 9.26). Remember to not let areas dry as you fill in the shapes. Let it dry before turning it back round.

(Fig. 9.27) Now it's ready for the details and stronger tones. The board should be sloping towards you again.

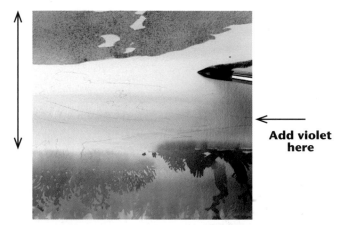

Add violet here

Fig. 9.25.

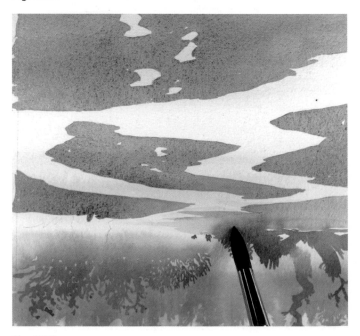

Fig. 9.26.

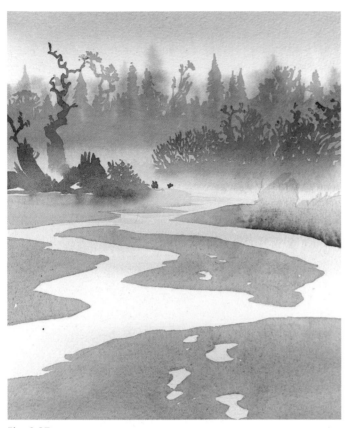

Fig. 9.27.

(Fig. 9.28) Flip the guide over to check and trace through any final guide marks in preparation for painting the trees.

(Fig. 9.29) With a dark wash of Burnt Umber and violet, fill in the tree shapes and the tree house along with the fence posts (Fig. 9.30) with a flat wash. As the brush becomes emptier use the tip to do fiddly little branches and fence posts.

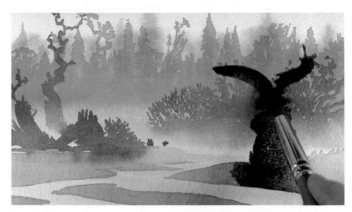

Fig. 9.29.

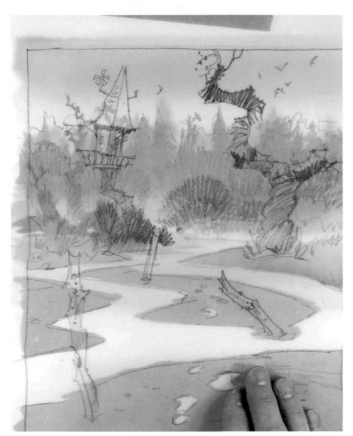

Fig. 9.28 Pencil trace still in position.

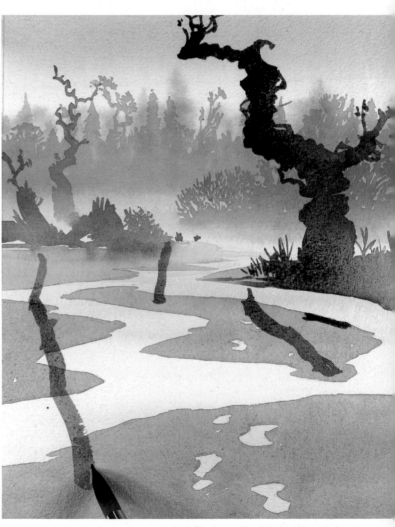

Fig. 9.30.

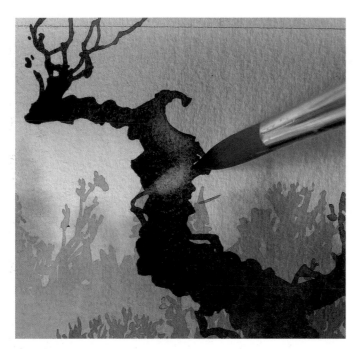

Fig. 9.31.

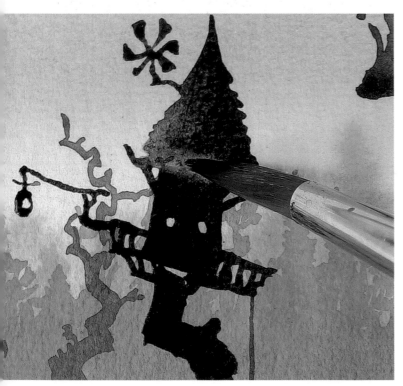

Fig. 9.32.

(Figs 9.31 and 32) With a clean damp brush, soak up colour on the top surface where the light is falling.

(Fig. 9.33) After the first tonal wash, apply an even darker tone on the foreground posts.

(Fig. 9.34) Add a little extra blue on the ground below the tree house with a weak wash: this helps push back and darken this area.

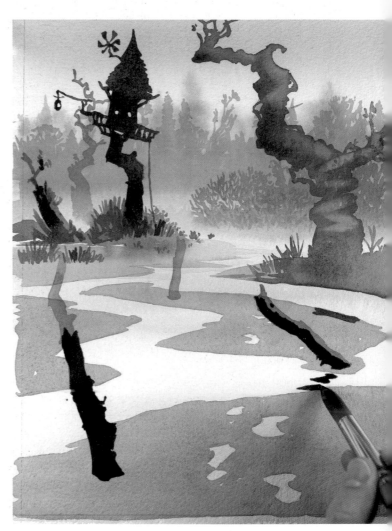

Fig. 9.33.

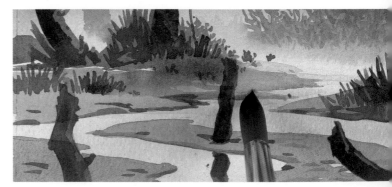

Fig. 9.34.

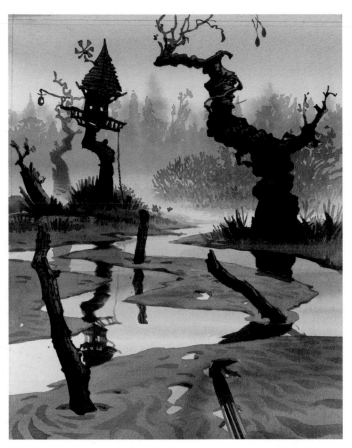

Fig. 9.35.

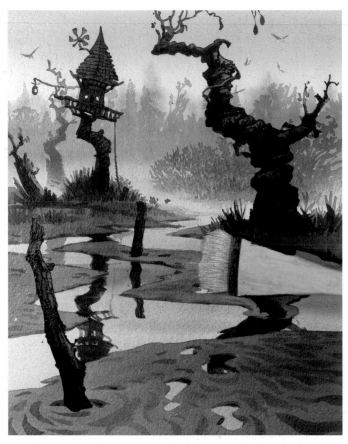

Fig. 9.36.

Line Work And Details

(Fig. 9.35) With a strong mix of Burnt Umber and violet, load the large wash brush and 'draw' with the fine point the shadow areas in the tree bark. Imagine a thick coiled rope as the tree to help imagine those recesses. Add shadow details and edges to the fence posts, and reflections in the water. Add some weird flying creatures, too, with a light orange mix (Fig. 9.36). Don't worry about the next opaque stage, as detail marks will be put in again after.

Washing In More Colour

(Fig. 9.36) If the foreground is too light it's easy to build up the strength of colour. Here I've added another brown wash to the mud banks and then let it dry.

Add another clear wash of water, and as it's turning between satin and matt, brush in more colour, in this case more yellow and red (Fig. 9.36).

This is why acrylics are so good at controlling the strength of tone. It's best to under apply the tonal strength so you have the option to darken it later.

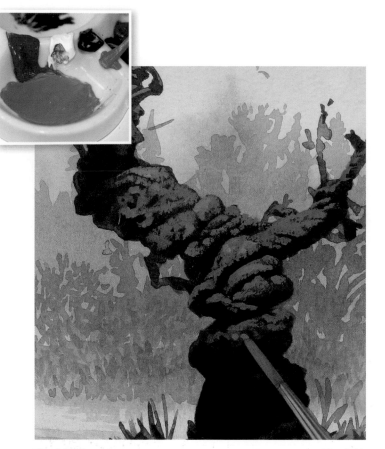

Fig. 9.37 (inset).   Fig. 9.38.

THE OPAQUE DRY BRUSH STAGE

It's time to take this from a pure transparent watercolour style painting into a combination of the opaque and the transparent.

The bit of detailing that's been done on the tree trunk is a guide for the opaque layer. Once done it will need another detailing layer to find the form of the tree trunk again. It's an opportunity to make sense of any twists and turns in the tree structure.

Mixing and Loading the Brush

Using a colour sympathetic with the light in this picture, mix up a terracotta colour using red, Burnt Umber and white (Fig. 9.37).

The thickness of the paint is important as it wants to be thick enough to use as a dry brush technique. Load up the brush and flatten it, so it is flat as it is dragged over at a low angle. Try and get the sort of brush marks shown in Fig 9.38.

(Fig. 9.39) Highlight all the areas except for the shadows, as the undersides can be tinted with shade in the next step of detailing.

(Fig. 9.40) Dragging the brush over the roughness of the paper will help get the right bark effect.

(Fig. 9.41) Build up the marks with successive strokes on all those objects such as the fallen tree and the tree house. In this example I've left the house alone (Fig. 9.42), but it could be done with opaque paint too – perhaps a red-tiled roof and glowing windows in yellow. Maybe add bright green glow-worms in the grass, too?

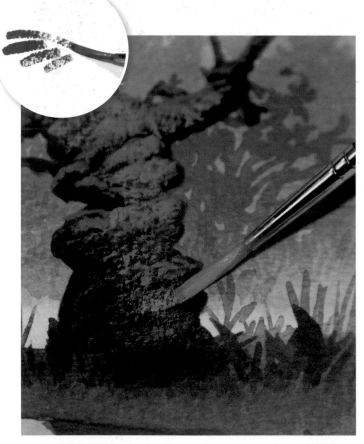

Fig. 9.39 (inset).   Fig. 9.40.

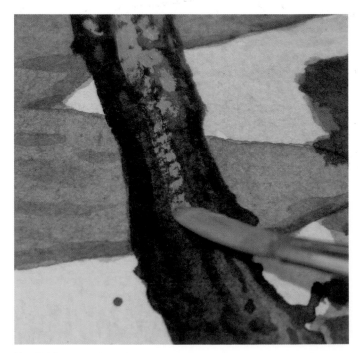

Fig. 9.41.

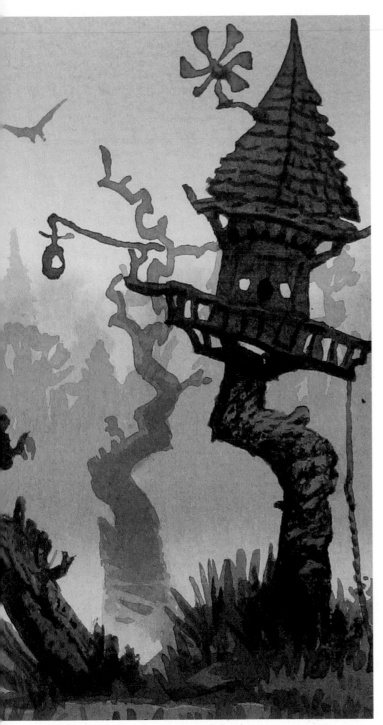

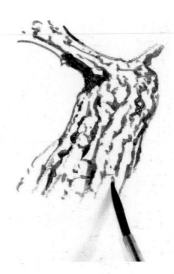

Fig. 9.43.

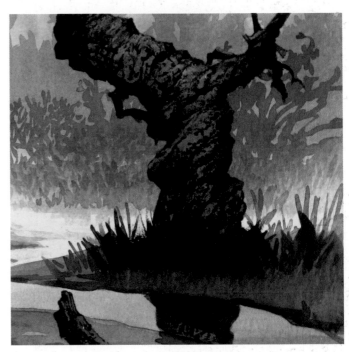

Fig. 9.44.

Fig. 9.42.

Tinting Back in Detail and Shadow

THE DETAILS

(Fig. 9.43) Mix up a deep Burnt Umber with a little violet to get a dark line with the detail brush. Using your opaque marks as a guide, 'draw' in the bark shadows as they twist and turn up the tree. Add a few irregular holes and cracks (Fig. 9.44).

THE TINTING

(Fig. 9.45) With a weak mix of Burnt Umber, wash over the entire tree, which initially will give you a flat colour effect. But then using the soak-up method, remove the paint on the top half where the light will be falling.

(Fig. 9.46) Add tint on the fence posts and in small areas on the water line, to give the mud banks an edge.

(Fig. 9.47) With the final layer of opaque paint the trees stand out in front of the transparent treatments.

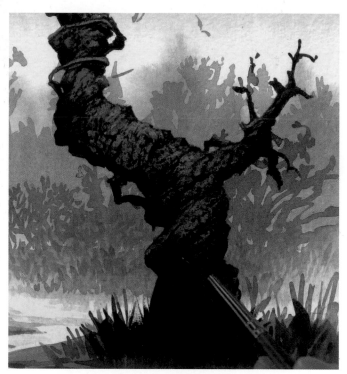

Fig. 9.45.

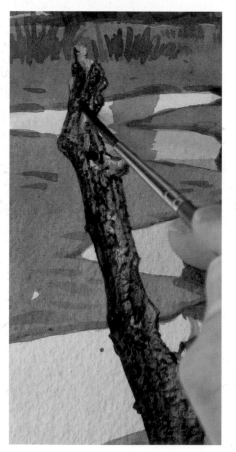

Fig. 9.46.

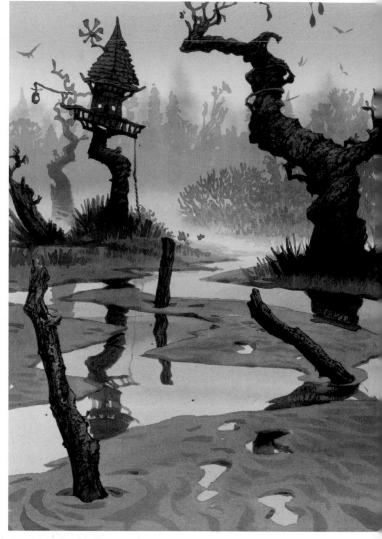

Fig. 9.47 The final painting.

WASHES

Acrylics are particularly good at wash paintings. The fact that you can build up as many layers of wash as you like makes controlling the tone of the painting a joy.

A key lesson in this style of painting is to not be too generous with the pigment and mix it too thickly. It's just like watercolours without the usual constraints.

Initially this example of a fantasy landscape is a wash painting with transparent colours; however, the tree bark and posts introduce an irresistible opportunity to use the dry brush technique followed by a tinting layer. The roughness of the paper lends itself to creating rough textures such as wood and rocks.

Here are a couple of examples of those multi-layered washes. The parrotfish painting (Fig. 9.49) uses both large area washes and small detail washes. It's also a combination of transparent and solid colours, the fish becoming solid colour with tinting layers.

(Fig. 9.50) The light ripples on the fish and the bright plume of the powdered coral are semi-transparent detailed washes of opaque pigments. If opaque areas are to be used in wash paintings it looks better if they are contained within an object.

(Fig. 9.48) The illustration of a loggerhead turtle for a T-shirt design is a typical example of a line and wash approach using the multiple layering qualities of acrylic paint. It's done on watercolour board with latex fluid to create the white outlines and highlight marks. Because acrylics dry so fast it's not long before the latex can be gently removed and either a new wash or more latex marks added. Very difficult to do in either watercolours or gouache!

RIGHT: Fig. 9.49 (inset).
Fig 9.50

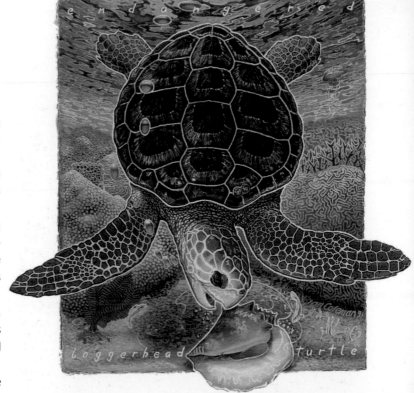

Fig. 9.48.

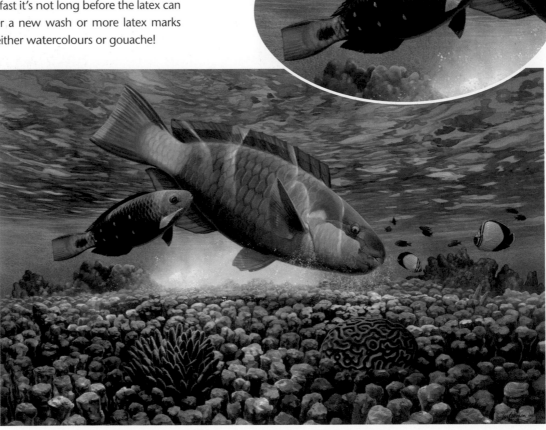

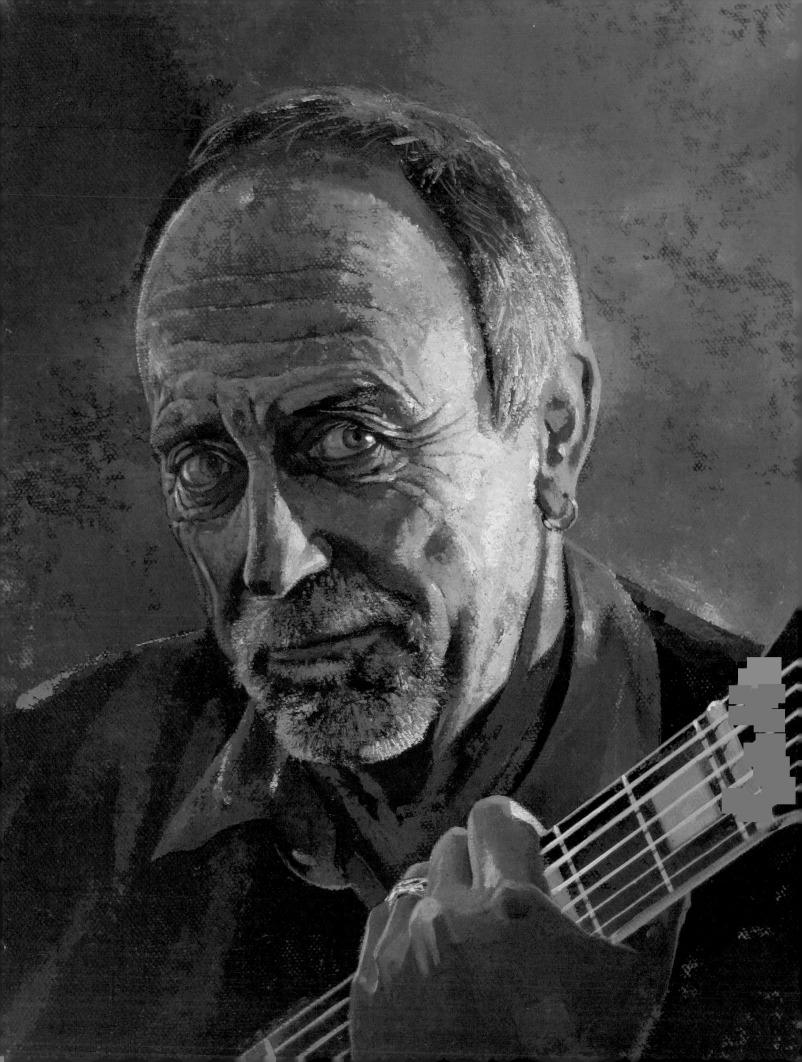

CHAPTER 10

PALETTE KNIFE TECHNIQUE

Palette Knife

Including Detailing and Line Making

In this chapter the following topics are explored:

• **Background blocking in**
• **Palette knife painting**
• **Line making**

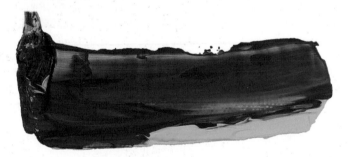

Fig. 10.1.

THE TECHNIQUE

Palette knife paintings are a lot of fun to do, and if you haven't tried one yet I urge you to have a go. You'll soon get lost in its instant and punchy results.

The idea is to use a palette knife for as much of the painting as you can, because in doing so it will create a distinct and stylized look. Brushes will be used for background base colours and details. This painting is done at the same size of this book – 220 × 280mm – which, combined with a subject that is complex in shapes and details, prompts one to use the smallest palette knife, in this case the diamond-shaped 35mm blade palette knife.

Depending on the scale and style of the painting, the right knife is an important consideration. As a general rule larger knives are used for larger paintings. Knives come in a huge variety of shape, size and flexibility, and all give a slightly different result. The bigger the knife, the more paint can be loaded for long, continuous paint marks.

Unusually for acrylic painting, this has a general rule about the sequence of tones: paint the darker tones first, working up to lighter and lighter tones in ever-decreasing areas to create form and shape in representational paintings.

This is a wet-on-wet and dry-on-dry style. Great effects are created blending two wet coats together after the initial blocking in coats. Work in small areas when using wet-on-wet blends.

The Style

The concept and subsequent drawing lay the groundwork for launching the overall style. The paint style is primarily governed by our own mannerism of manipulating the knife. Even though the same knife is used, everyone will dab, scrape and squash the paint differently. Within a short amount of time you will discover your favourite mannerism. My mannerism here is the same as the Gesso Rock chapter, namely small circles, blade and board parallel, with a medium amount of paint.

Preparation

A 10 × 12in canvas board is my preferred choice because it has the canvas tooth and there's no give in the surface tension. However, stretched canvas and gessoed MDF make good alternatives. MDF provides a smoother and therefore a more slippery mark.

Have a spare piece of canvas to make the initial colour mixes before transferring them to the painting and mixing and blending further.

MATERIALS NEEDED

Preparation:

• 10 × 12in canvas board

• White Gesso

• 2in wide bristle brush for background

• Photo reference enlarged to size

• Line drawing supplied enlarged to size

• (Tracing paper if creating your own line drawing)

• Tracing pen or 6H pencil

• Imagetrace® paper

Painting stage:

• 2in Hog flat brush for tinting

• Winsor & Newton Designer 222 No. 6 Detail brush

• Palette knife, 35mm diamond-shaped

• **Background colours:** Cadmium Red and Ultramarine Blue

• **Flesh colours:** Burnt Umber, Burnt Sienna, Cadmium Red Deep, Cadmium Yellow, Titanium White, Payne's Grey, Ultramarine Violet

• **Tints:** Viridian Green, Phthalo Blue Green Shade

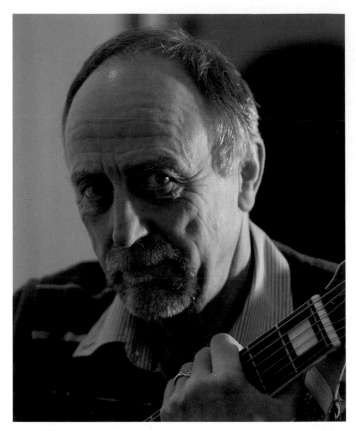

Fig. 10.3.

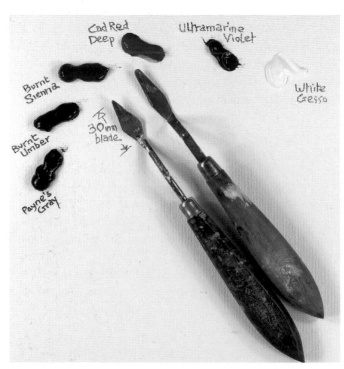

Fig. 10.2.

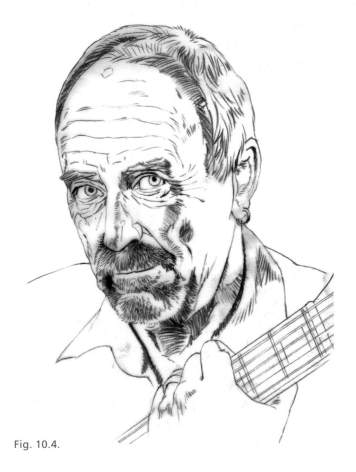

Fig. 10.4.

(Fig. 10. 3) Enlarge the references by 275 per cent on a photocopier on to tracing paper to trace your own drawing, or use the line drawing provided (Fig. 10.4).

The Drawing

Trace down the image on to the canvas board using either the traditional method of soft pencil on the underside (Fig. 10.6) or a carbon paper such as Imagetrace® (Fig. 10.5).

(Fig. 10.7) Apply just enough pressure to get a faint line on the canvas. A 6H pencil or tracing pen is ideal.

(Fig. 10.8) Here we can see how the line looks. It's enough information for the next stage.

Line Painting

(Fig. 10.9) It's very useful to first paint in some exact details as a guide for the less controlled knife paint marks. Many of these marks will be painted over, and some will be put back in towards the end.

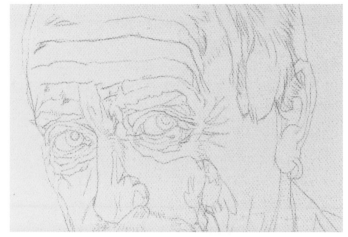

Fig. 10.8.

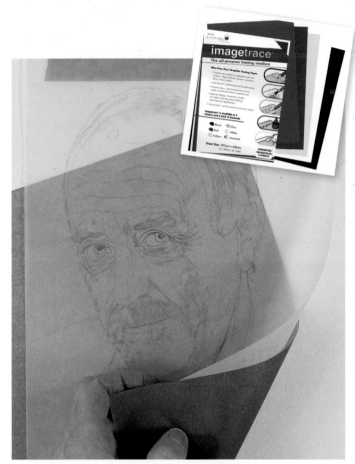

Fig. 10.5 (inset).   Fig. 10.6.

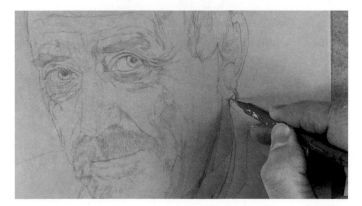

Fig. 10.7.

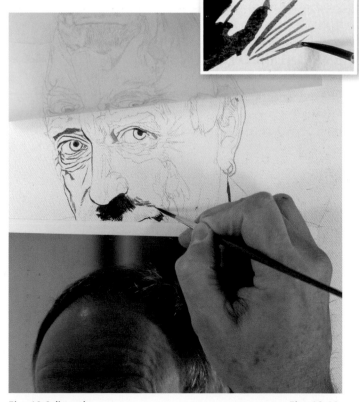

Fig. 10.9 (inset).   Fig. 10.10.

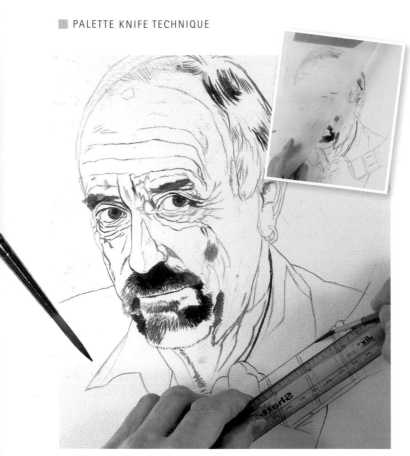

Fig. 10.11 (inset).   Fig. 10.12.

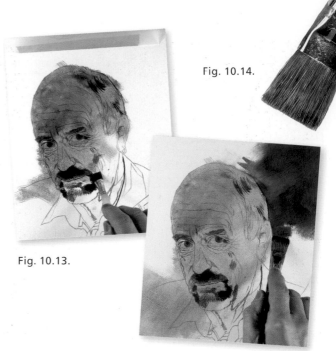

Fig. 10.13.

Fig. 10.14.

Fig. 10.15.

Using the detail brush, Winsor & Newton 222 No. 4 Designer Brush, mix a fluid Burnt Umber. Load your brush by rolling and then dabbing flat. If it's fluid it will give you at least 12in of line (Fig. 10.10).

It's useful to have the photo reference close by, and the trace securely taped, to be reminded of what the lines meant.

(Fig. 10.11) Once all the line painting guides are in, leave to dry for ten minutes. (Fig. 10.12) Use a ruler held at 45 degrees to paint in straight lines by running the metal ferule along the edge.

PALETTE KNIFE TIPS

KEEP THE BLADE PARALLEL: Avoid stabbing with the tip, and keep the blade flat and parallel with the surface.

CLEAN OFTEN: Paint builds up and affects the predictability of the mark.

USE THE EDGE: Using the edge can give little line details and grooves to contrast the flat area paint marks.

GO OVER SEMI-DRY PAINT: As the paint dries, a second squashing can make interesting effects.

Adding the Colour

(Fig. 10.13) With the ½in synthetic soft brush, mix a mid tone of Burnt Umber and cover the face.

Use a bristle brush (Fig. 10.14) with a thicker mix of deep blue to block in the background (Fig. 10.15).

(Fig. 10.16) On the far left side add a thick Payne's Grey and Spectrum Violet in the centre to blend with the still wet blue. It doesn't matter if you go over the head. The aim is to remove all the white board.

(Fig. 10.17) The aim is to be fairly loose and sketchy with your brush work. There's an element of hoping for happy accidents with little areas of light and shade that may end up in the final painting. The contrast with light and dark blues might peek through the palette knife layer which will be all over but open enough. Try not to be too thorough in covering every millimetre.

(Fig. 10.18) With the Designer 222 soft detail brush, tweak in the eyes with a mixture of grey-blue mix, then the pupils and eyelids with black, with yellow ochre for the iris.

Putting the eyes in now will help to connect all the other marks radiating around the eyes, and to preserve them. There's a danger that if you palette knife first around the eyes, you will lose the line guides.

Adding the Skin Tones

(Fig. 10.19) Put in the shadow areas. The darker shadow skin tones are applied first with the palette knife. A variety of basic skin colour tones can be achieved with the colours above on

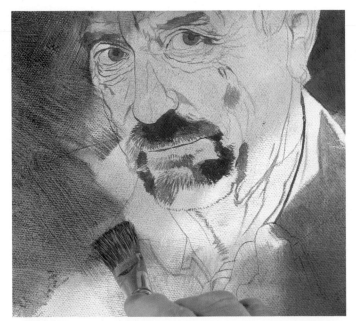

Fig. 10.16.

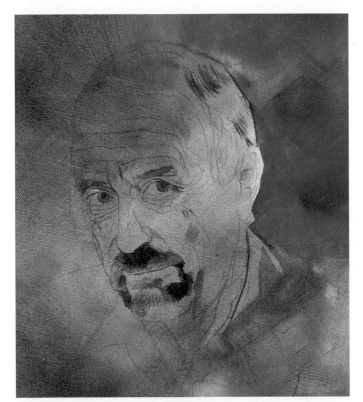

Fig. 10.17.

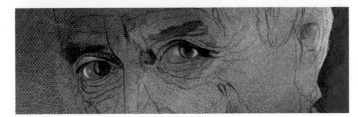

Fig. 10.18.

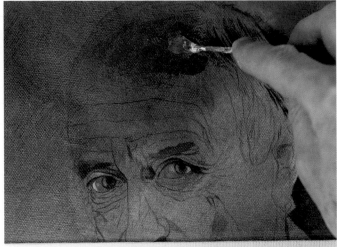

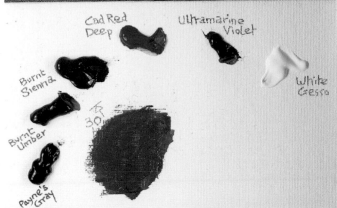

Fig. 10.19.

the palette ready for mixing. Start with Burnt Sienna, a little red and Ultramarine violet with a touch of white to give it opacity.

Alternatively try Burnt Umber instead of Burnt Sienna, or Payne's Grey instead of Violet for a duller shadow tone.

(Fig. 10.20) Start from the top with the darks, and as half the forehead is covered, mix a lighter paint and add it on top of the wet paint where appropriate according to the photo reference,

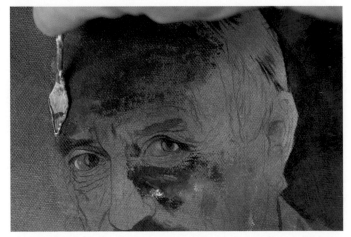

Fig. 10.20.

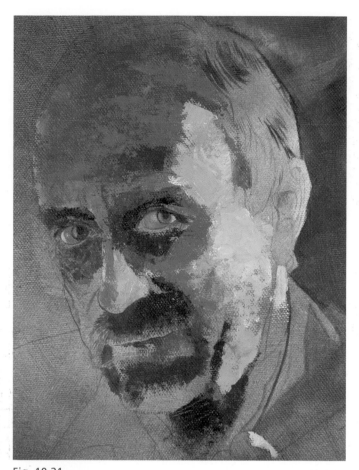

Fig. 10.21.

with small circular blending movements. Some parts will have dried, but that's all right.

(Fig. 10.21) Put in the light areas. A lighter skin colour is mixed for the right side of the face using proportionally higher amounts of Cadmium Yellow and white to the forehead shadow colour.

(Fig. 10.22) When the left shadow edge of the face is blocked in, the dark brown and black background is put in accurately along the face profile. Using that colour, all the other hair areas are put in, too.

(Fig. 10.23) Next paint in the guitar, with Violet and white added to the black and a few cooler skin tones mixed for the hand. Use Payne's Grey highlights on the hair and beard, with a lot of blade edge markings.

(Fig. 10.25) Block in with dark brown – a black and Burnt Umber mix – on the jumper. Then a violet mix for the shirt, returning to a mid-brown highlight for the jumper folds.

Details: (Fig. 10.26) Check where the shirt edges lie, also the frown and the laughter lines, especially around the eyes. Add any guitar details if necessary, and trace the lines through faintly. Alternatively, do it by eye and keep flipping the trace up and down.

(Fig. 10.27) Adding highlights and dark lines with the Designer 222 brush.

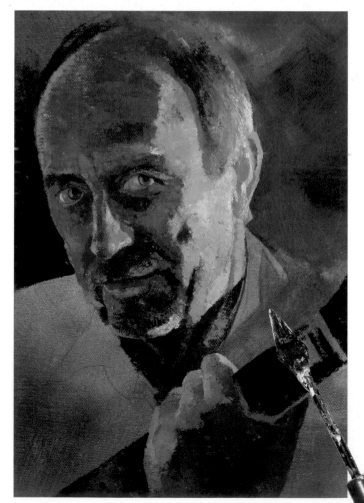

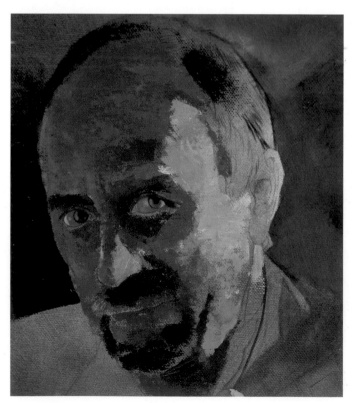

Fig. 10.22.

Fig. 10.23.   Fig. 10.24 35mm diamond-shaped palette knife.

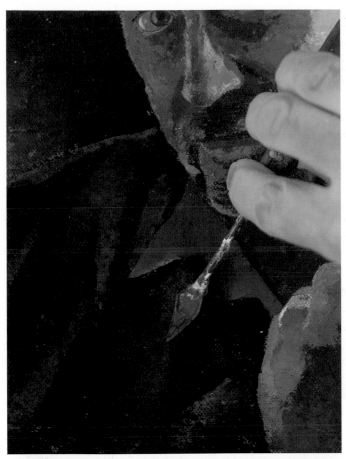

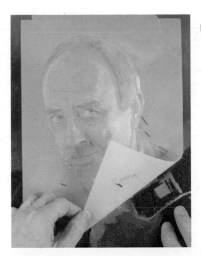

Fig. 10.26.

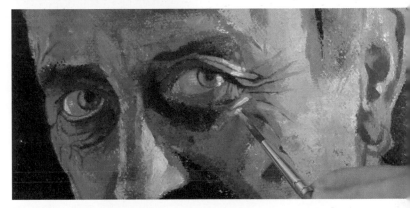

Fig. 10.25.

Fig. 10.27.

(Fig. 10.28) Continue with the shadow details, frown lines, eyelids, and any small areas of colour with a view to using a tiny bit of palette knife colour over it.

(Fig. 10.29) Find the collar edge and use the brush to fill in any colour gaps.

(Fig. 10.30) Finish the background with wet-in-wet blending, dark grey violets into blues.

(Fig. 10.31) The illustration shows the palette so far, with all the various shades of each colour.

(Figs 10.32 and 10.33) Work on the light areas: the side of the face may take two or three layers of increasing brightness to create a high contrast to the shadow side. White and light paint tend to fade a little, and so often need topping up.

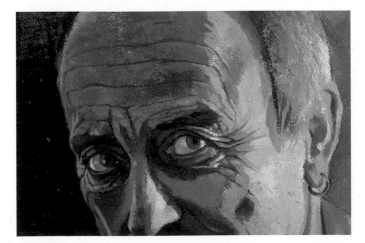

Fig. 10.28.

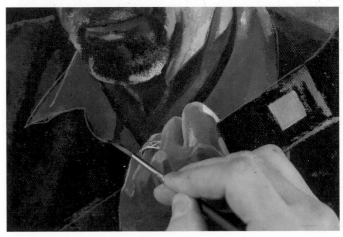

Fig. 10.29.

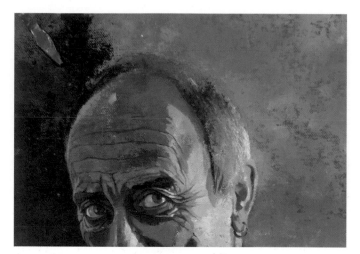

Fig. 10.30.

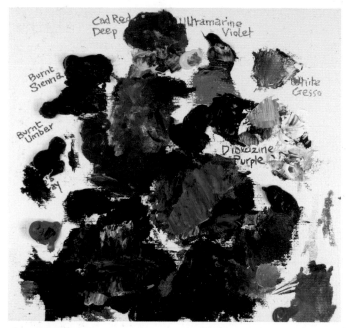

Fig. 10.31.

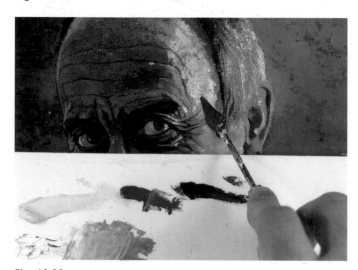

Fig. 10.32.

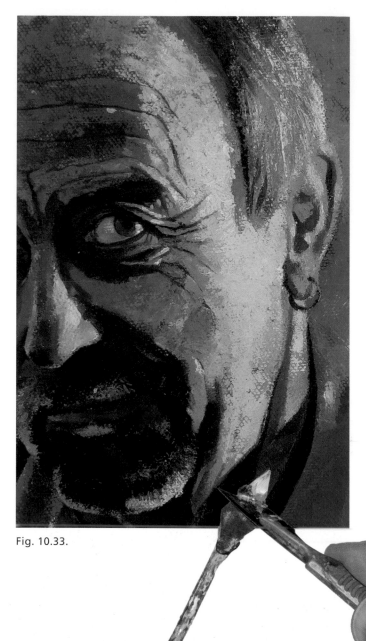

Fig. 10.33.

Fig. 10.34 Clean the blade occasionally.

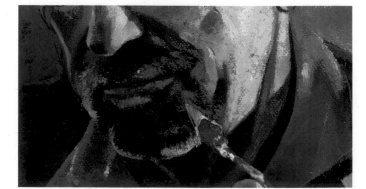

Fig. 10.35.

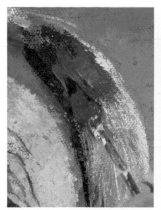

Fig. 10.36.

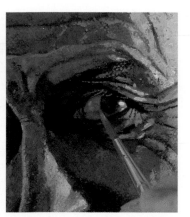

Fig. 10.37.

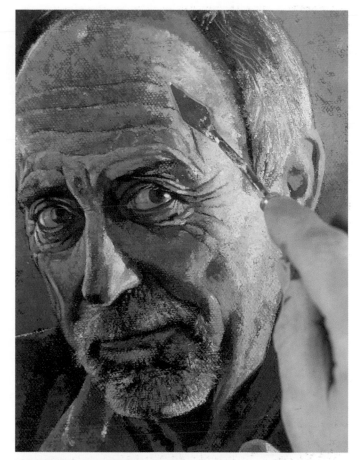

A separate flesh tone mix as shown above consists of a white base with yellow and red added in tiny amounts.

(Figs 10.35 and 10.36) Next concentrate on the beard and hair: use a mid-brown mix with an emphasis on using the edge of the blade to create longer marks, followed by a lighter detailing.

(Fig. 10.37) Put in the final detailing in the eyes, with a little shade tinting and highlighting on the eyelashes and eyebrows.

(Fig. 10.38) Put in the final highlights on the face, using a predominantly white mix with a little yellow and red. Use mauve highlights on the left side of the forehead and nose.

Fig. 10.38.

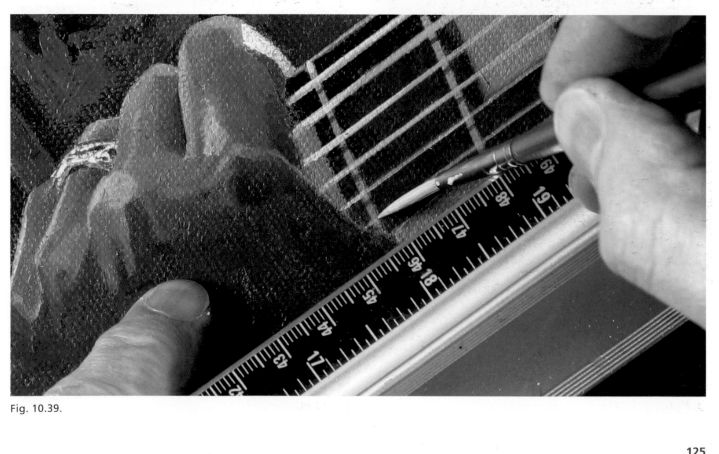

Fig. 10.39.

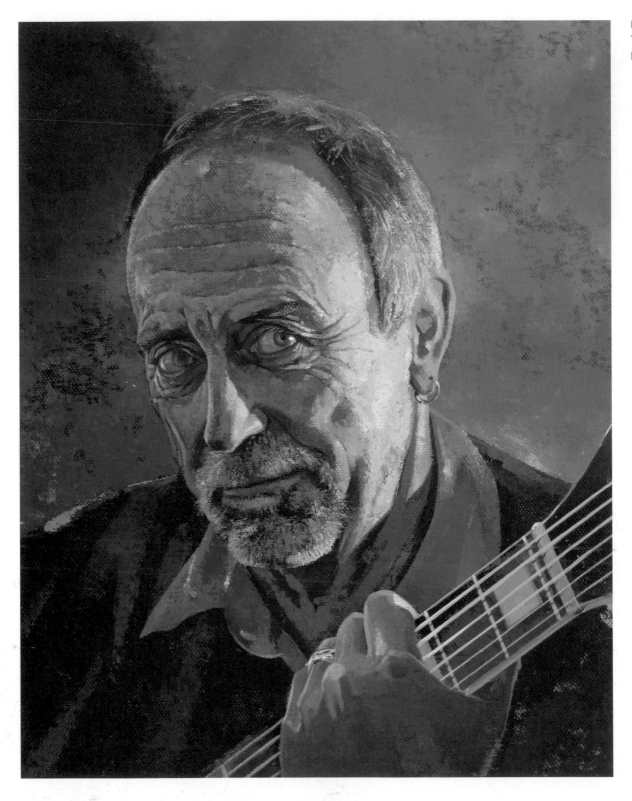

Fig. 10.40
The finished
painting.

(Fig. 10.39) Line making: Load the brush with paint that is fluid enough to be drawn out of the brush. Load it by rolling it and then flattening it to a small blade. It is tempting to make the mix very opaque and thick, but it won't make thin lines. Run the ferrule along the edge of the ruler, which is held at 45 degrees, and make two or three strokes.

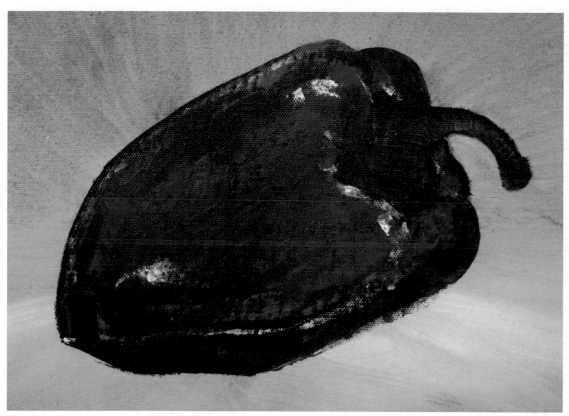

Fig. 10.41.

Palette knife paintings can create really solid colour paintings with sharp edges and wonderful blends, with popping out colour accents here and there.

Good subjects can be still-life objects such as flowers and fruit: here are some 'in progress' pieces showing washed-in backgrounds before the palette knife layers – and no other backgrounds work quite as well (Figs 10.41 and 10.42).

Have a go with some fruit and let your colour schemes go wild!

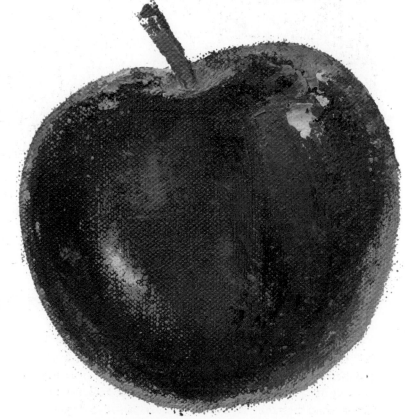

Fig. 10.42.

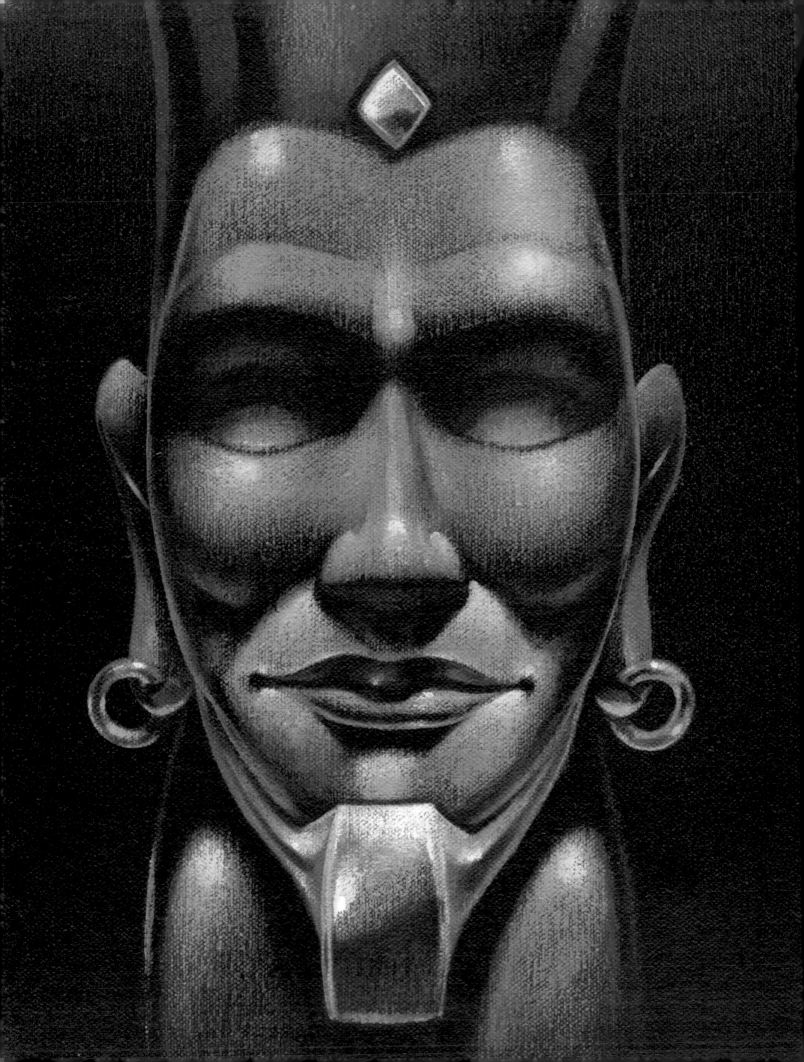

CHAPTER 11

DRY BRUSH TECHNIQUE
Shading Using Canvas Texture

Fig. 11.1.

It is called 'Dry Brush' because you rarely add any water to the paint and then you remove most of the paint from the brush before applying it.

This technique is one that needs a little practice, so don't give up too soon because when you get the idea, the brush work creates a great effect for small to medium areas. The scale of the canvas weave is important in relation to the overall picture size. This work is best for paintings A4 size or larger.

I use this technique mainly for shading lighter tones on top of darker tones. Dark on top of light tends to look too harsh, whereas light on top of dark looks subconsciously like highlights of detail.

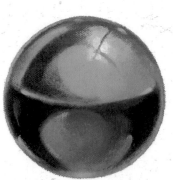

Fig. 11.3 The Dry Brush exercise in an early chapter.

Preparation

The first thing to do is make sure you have an even and close weave on your canvas; this will provide the best illusion of graduating colours (Fig. 11.5). Make sure if you are using stretched canvas that it is nice and taut so the frame edges underneath don't interfere, because in later layers we need to apply more pressure.

The dry brush shading starts after we have blocked in the background in the more conventional way using a small amount of water.

For the background use a 1.5in wide hog hair brush for applying the colours, and a 3in softer one for blending the colours without leaving streaks. (Fig. 11.7). Have a large pot of water to dampen your brush – though don't take up too much water in the brush otherwise the paint will get thin. Dampen the brush to allow the pigment to be taken up fully within the brush and so

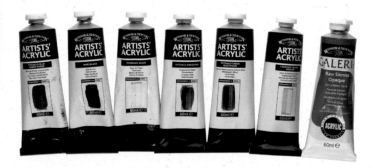

Fig. 11.2
Colours Used:
Phthalo Blue Green Shade
Mars Black
Titanium White
Phthalo Turquoise

Phthalo Green Blue Shade
Cadmium Yellow Medium
Raw Sienna Opaque

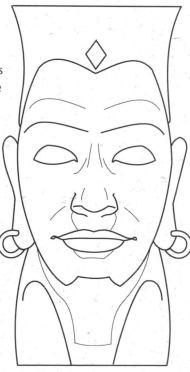

(Fig. 11.4) Photocopy line drawing guide to 318 per cent.

129

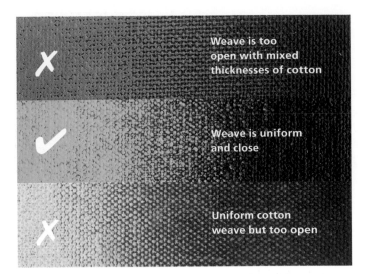

Fig. 11.5.

Fig. 11.7.

minimize streaks (Fig.11.8). Use a transparent dark paint, Phthalo Blue Green Shade, or try any other transparent dark colour. Use it throughout in the subsequent layers in combination with white. Note that some reds, such as Cadmium Red, have white in them to make them opaque; here we are keeping it transparent so the foreground opaque colours stand out.

(Fig 11.6) For the foreground use a couple of flat brushes for the small areas of shading, one Winsor & Newton Short Flat/ Bright Fine Hog hair, and a small soft Royal No. 4 SG155 synthetic for the really detailed areas. Practise a little with them so you can see how the paint 'drags out' of the brush at a low angle across the canvas weave.

MATERIALS NEEDED

Preparation:
- Rosemary & Co, Series 2015, No.16 1.5in Hog
- Generic 3in Hog brush
- Winsor & Newton No8 Short Flat/Bright Fine Hog
- Synthetic Royal No. 4, Sg155
- 12 x 8in canvas board or stretched canvas
- Line drawing photocopied to size
- Imagetrace® paper

Technique

Blocking in the Background

If you are using a piece of loose canvas, tape it to a board with masking tape top and bottom and lay it flat. Make sure your image lies within the edges by about 6cm, so the sweeping brush strokes don't catch the canvas edges and pick up blobs of paint and dust.

Take your tube of Phthalo Blue Green Shade and squirt a 3cm line directly near the top of the canvas (Fig. 11.9). Dampen your smaller bristle brush, and wipe off the excess. You only need a tiny

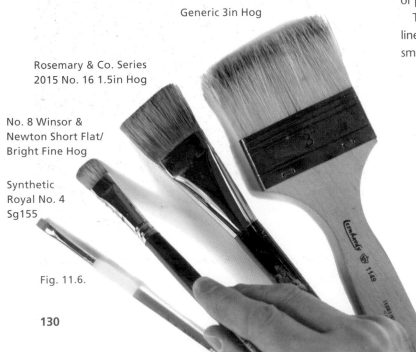

Generic 3in Hog

Rosemary & Co. Series 2015 No. 16 1.5in Hog

No. 8 Winsor & Newton Short Flat/ Bright Fine Hog

Synthetic Royal No. 4 Sg155

Fig. 11.6.

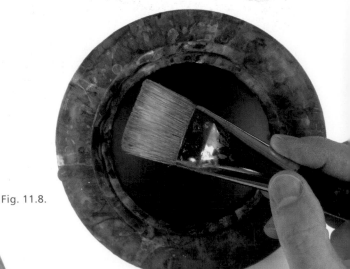

Fig. 11.8.

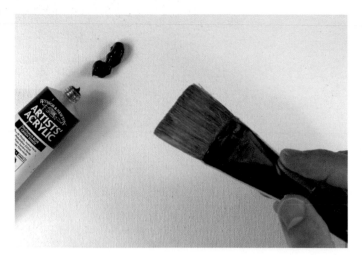

Fig. 11.9. 1.5in Hog.

Fig. 11.10 Keep the paint on the move until you are happy with it or it will start drying.

amount of water, but add a little more if the paint is too dry or too thick and won't dilute enough. However, it is very easy to use too much water and get a weak colour tone with lots of streaks, so as a general rule go easy with water.

Sweep the paint from side to side across the canvas (Fig. 11.10), often varying the angle so you smooth down the thickness of the paint and get a uniform look. Keep working your way to about three-quarters of the way down the canvas, spreading the paint so that it is an even mid tone (Figs 11.11 and 11.12). Keep an eye out to avoid the 'parallel' effect of repeated horizontal strokes. Vary the directions vertically to horizontally, but always long sweeps. As the paint starts to get tacky, make the final sweeps.

Sweeping up at a slight angle tends to look better even if you end up with some brush lines. The aim is not to make brush marks invisible but to make them subtle. Working quickly, mix in the black before it gets too dry, otherwise the brush will lift the paint and you will be left with the white of the canvas again, and it's almost impossible to blend it back without forming ridges.

Squeeze the same amount of black paint near the bottom, and, using your uncleaned brush, sweep the paint back and forth until it is thin and uniform; then take it up into the colour. Each time you sweep up from the bottom the paint begins to smooth out. (Fig. 11.18) Avoid forming ridges and parallel sweeps.

Leave to dry for about 30 minutes.

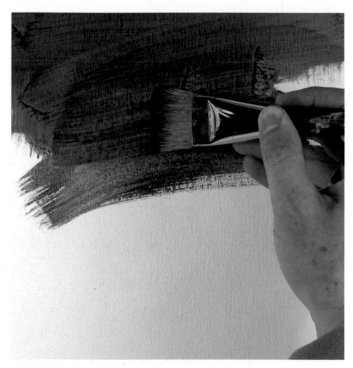

Fig. 11.11.

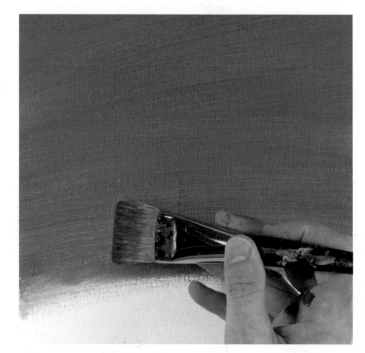

Fig. 11.12 When the paint begins to get tacky it's easier to blend smoothly.

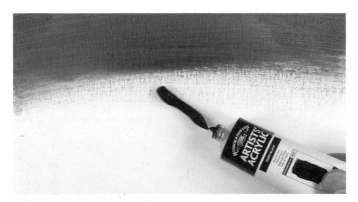

Fig. 11.13: Apply Mars Black straight from the tube. Add a tiny amount of water to help blend into the wet blue colour.

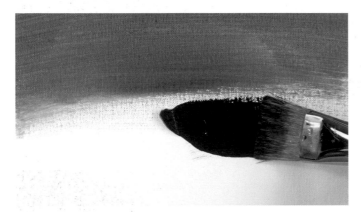

Fig. 11.14 *Important: the whole background blend is done quickly so the first colour does not have time to dry.

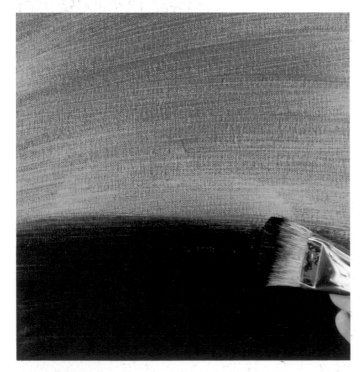

Fig. 11.15 Once you have it roughed in, switch to the wide, dry bristle brush and gently blend over the whole area using long, gentle sweeps.

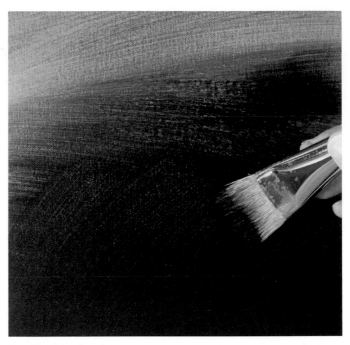

Fig. 11.16.

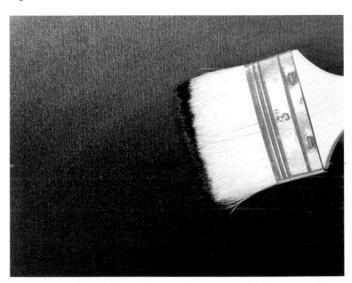

Fig. 11.17 Once you've blocked in the bottom part, sweep right across back and forth working your way up into the blue. You may need to do this several times.

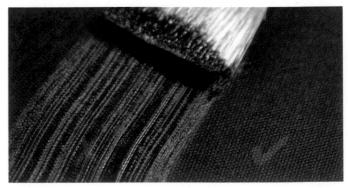

Fig. 11.18.

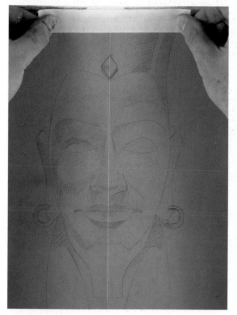

Fig. 11.19.

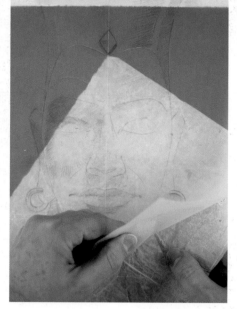

Fig. 11.20.

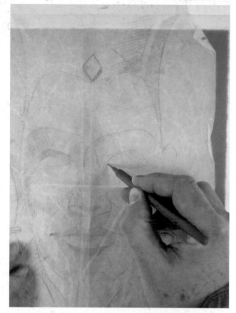

Fig. 11.21.

DRAWING THE HEAD

(Fig. 11.19) Using the line drawing guide provided at the beginning, centre the drawing and tape it securely all along the top with masking tape.

(Figs 11.20 and 11.21) Using Imagetrace® paper (see Chapter 1, Tools and Materials) or the conventional way of soft pencilling the back of the lines, trace the design on to the painted canvas. I've used a white Imagetrace® paper to make this easier to see. Apply just enough pressure to see the line. Use a 6H pencil, or a tracing pen with a ballpoint-shaped nib.

Here I have used the original drawing on tracing paper, however you can use the line drawing provided enlarged on a photocopier at 318 per cent on regular white A4 paper, or feed through a sheet of tracing paper.

Slide the Imagetrace® paper wax side down under the guide.

TOP TIP

Always keep your line drawings taped on all the time until you have nearly finished the painting. It's surprising how easily you can lose your way, and having this as a back-up is a lifesaver.

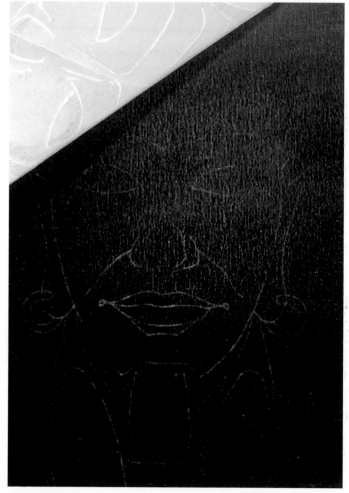

Fig. 11.22

THE FOREGROUND LAYERS

The Black Areas

Use a hog bristle brush because you need to vary the pressure to 'get into' the weave. Soft brushes don't work as well. Load the Short Flat Winsor & Newton Hog No. 8 bristle brush with black paint neat from the tube. Do not use water. Pat it flat so the paint is loaded through the bristles, and remove any excess blobs of paint. For flat black areas be more generous with the amount of paint in the brush, but for the 'feathering' areas where it shades from dark to light, remove most of the paint from your brush. Use a residual amount of paint to create the illusion of shading. Block in areas of black by gently doing the drag technique (Figs 11.24, 11.25): for this, hold the brush close to you to start, and

sweep away to decrease the pressure and get the desired feather effect (Fig. 11.26).

The first layer looks a little rough, but as you go over the previous dry layer it starts to fill in and become smoother (Fig. 11.27). Block in those solid black areas first and come back to softening the edges. Be careful not to fill too much: it is very easy to put on too much paint.

Once all the blacks are roughly done, put on the first layer of opaque mid-tone turquoise.

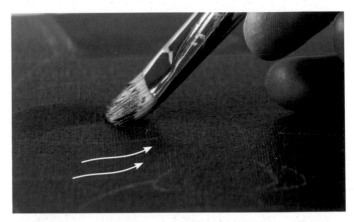

Fig. 11.24.

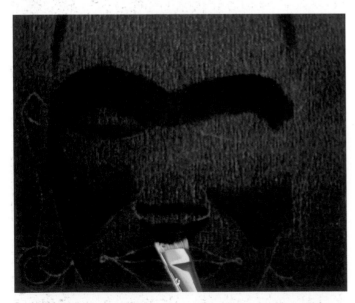

(Inset) Fig. 11.23 Short flat Winsor & Newton Hog No. 8 bristle brush. ABOVE: Fig. 11.24.

Fig. 11.25 Don't try to get to the end result in one layer. This may take a few coats.

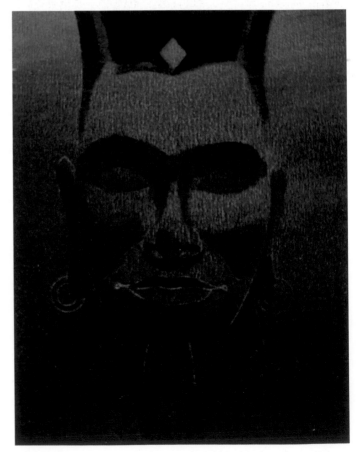

Fig. 11.27.

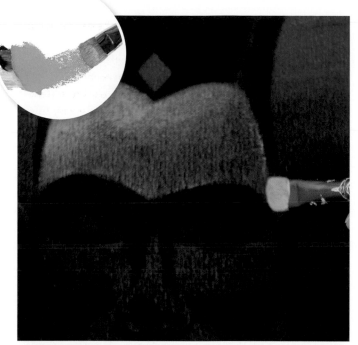

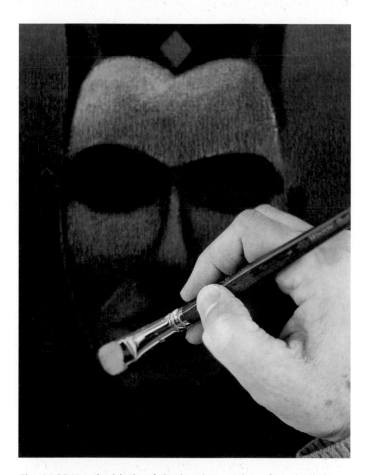

THE MID-TONE COLOUR

The First Opaque Layer

In this layer we add white to our colour. Using a clean, dry brush, take Phthalo Blue and Titanium White and mix thoroughly in equal amounts on your mixing palette with your painting brush. No water. Make sure the paint is dispersed through the bristles, and drag off any excess paint so no blobs are visible. As you start painting, try to get a 'light dusting' effect as you drag the brush at 45 degrees or less (Fig. 11.28).

Starting at the top with the forehead and imagining you are replicating the light coming from above, gently apply the paint (Fig. 11.29).

You may feel there's not enough paint in the brush, however it will build up bit by bit. Move to adjacent areas to let the previous area dry before going over it, and only re-charge your brush when hardly any marks are being left (Fig. 11.30). You may want to turn the painting at a different angle to suit your brush-stroke direction.

Fig. 11.28 (inset) Mid blue mix.   Fig. 11.29.

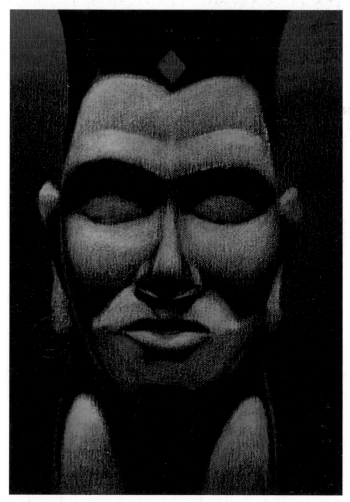

Fig. 11.30 Use the blade of the brush to make soft and subtle marks: like the cheek profile above, this is best done when your brush is near empty. Also you may have to apply more pressure as the paint begins to run out.

Fig. 11.31.

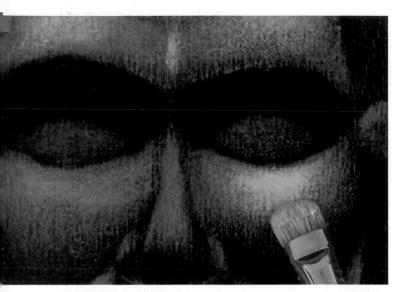

Fig. 11.32.

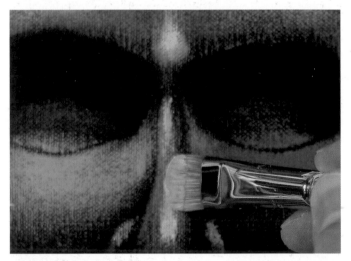

Fig. 11.33.

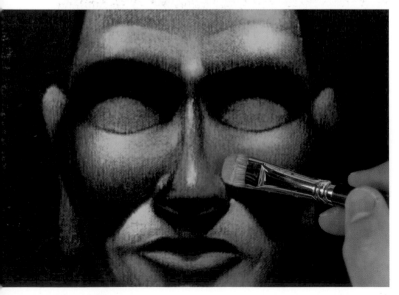

Fig. 11.34.

The Second, Third and Fourth Layers

For the second layer, mix a lighter tone and apply this to mark out highlights, the top of the forehead, the brow, the cheekbones, the nose bridge (Figs 11.32 and 11.33). As you get used to dragging the residual paint out of the brush you can be more generous with the paint, and vary the direction to get a more solid, flat and uniform highlight.

When the second layer is dry, work your way round again with the same colour for the third layer (Fig. 11.34). This time focus on the centre of the highlights and do not fade out quite as far.

Finally for the fourth layer mix an even lighter blue and do the same over again, but not as far out as the previous layer (Fig.11.35).

Adding the gold beard: With a clean, dry brush using a yellow ochre made from Cadmium Yellow Medium and Raw Sienna Opaque, fill the brush as before. Use the blade and the flat side for a first coat on the head gem and beard (Fig. 11.38). This again will seem weak and faint, but don't worry – let it dry and repeat the process (Figs 11.39. and 11.40).

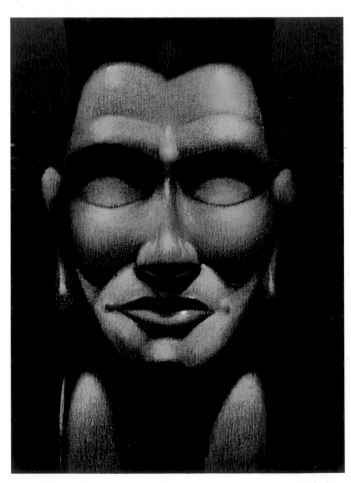

Fig. 11.35 Remember to let each area dry before going back and building it up again. The centre of the brightest areas may need four or five applications.

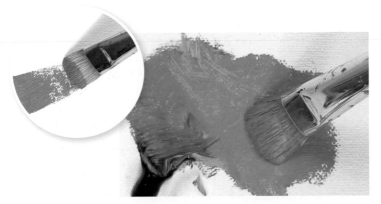

Fig. 11.36 (inset)

Fig. 11.37.

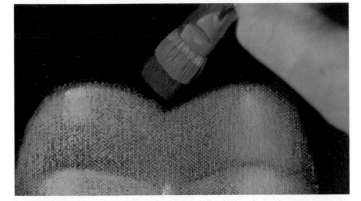

Fig. 11.38.

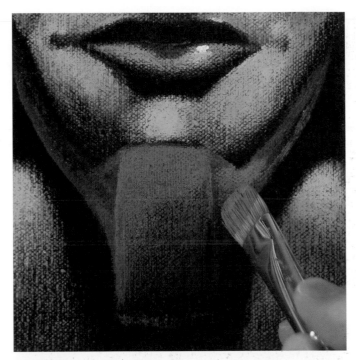

Fig. 11.40.

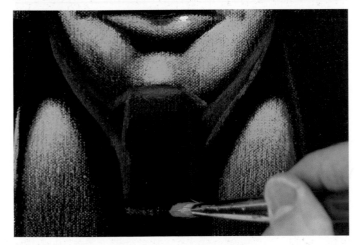

Fig. 11.39.

Adding the Light Green Reflected Light

Repeat the process, using a Phthalo Green and Titanium White (Figs 11.41, 11.42 and 11.43); this detailing will test your brush skills using the corner of the brush! Don't worry if you feel your brush is hard to work with in small areas: there is a chance to tidy up later using a smaller brush around the mouth, nose and jaw line.

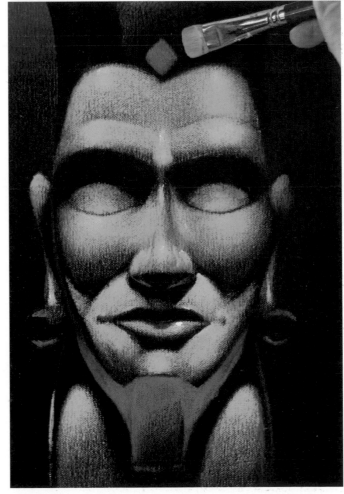

Fig. 11.41.

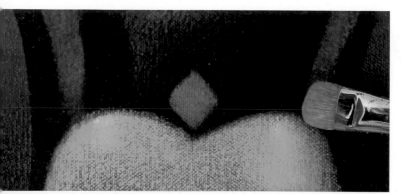

Fig. 11.42.

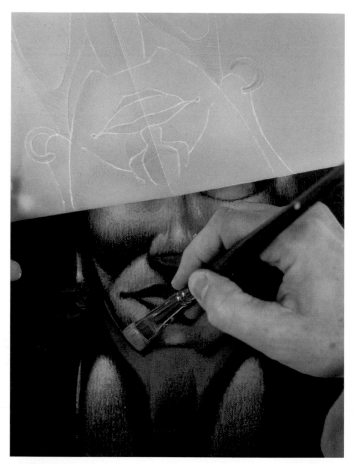

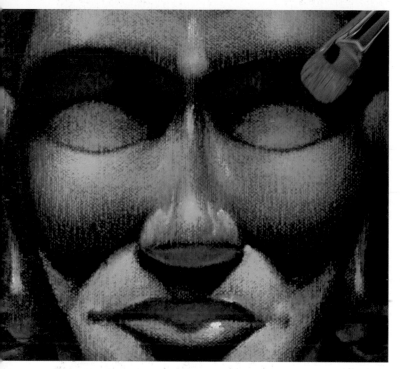

Fig. 11.43.

Fig. 11.44.

Adding the Reflections

The final layer before using the small detail brush is to add the reflections. This may be a good time to use the line guide (Fig. 11.44) to see how near you are to the drawing. Flicking it up and down quickly gives you an idea, but if it needs major adjusting it's best to re-trace the lines on to the canvas.

Finish off the jaw line, ear lobes and the bottom of the beard with a lighter mix of green, Phthalo Green and White. Continue with the headdress, below the eyebrows and top lip, and finally the nose (Fig. 11.45).

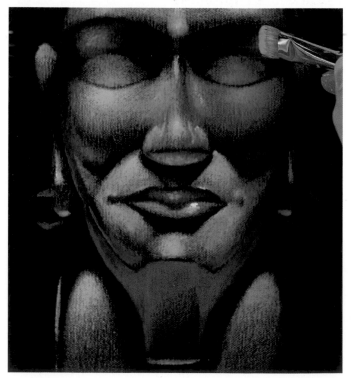

Fig. 11.45.

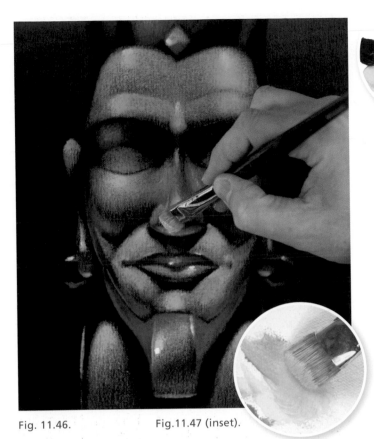

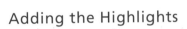

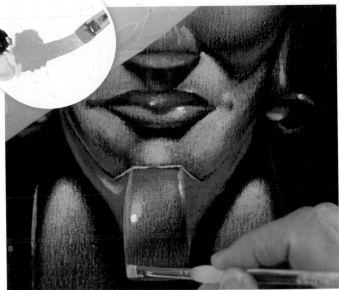

Fig.11.48 (inset). Fig. 11.49.

Fig. 11.46. Fig.11.47 (inset).

Adding the Highlights

Mix a bright yellow of Titanium White and Cadmium Yellow (Fig. 11.47), again using no water, with the corner of your brush, and drag it across the middle of the beard a few times. Do the same over the gem stone and the earrings.

Now is the time to add a nice generous blob on the edge of that beard, the earrings and the gem stone – and hopefully it looks really shiny!

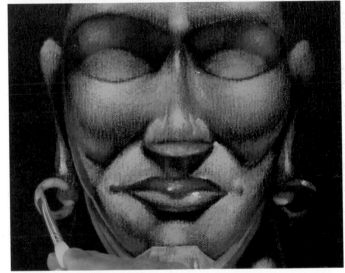

Fig. 11.50.

Adding the Details, Sharpening the Edges

The marks now need to be more exact, so switch to a smaller brush; in this project it is the synthetic Royal flat brush. It is soft, unlike the hog bristle, and gives the paint a more solid line as well as going into the weave without too much pressure.

Using bright yellow, define the edges of the beard (Fig. 11.49). Yellow is particularly weak in terms of opacity, so again a few layers may be required. Load the brush the same way, patting it flat so you get a nice line.

Do the same with the bright green over the earrings (Fig. 11.50) and under the beard, and sharpen the outline of the head (Figs 11.51 and 11.52) and ears with a mix of mid-tone blue.

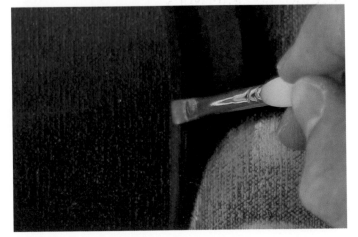

Fig. 11.51.

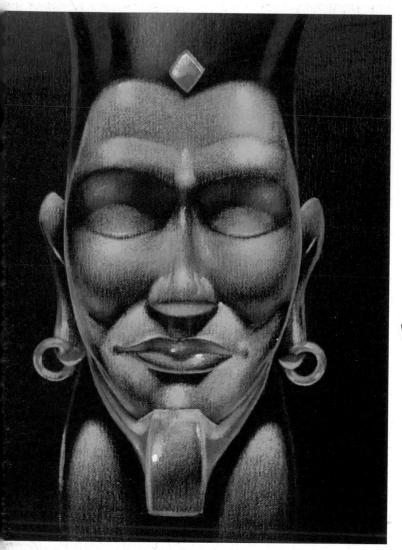

Fig. 11.52.

The Dark Details and Tidying Up Shadow Areas

(Fig. 11.54) Using the same small detail brush, mix a dense black using 75 per cent Mars Black and 25 per cent Phthalo Blue. A tiny drop of water may be necessary to make the paint flow from your brush. Load the brush and then flatten both sides. Using the 'blade' corner, put in the mouth corners, and with the flat blade, define the join between the top and bottom lip. The eye sockets, nose and ears may also need a little attention.

Depending how light your main background is, there may be other key areas that need the shadow strengthening such as on the neck and the headdress.

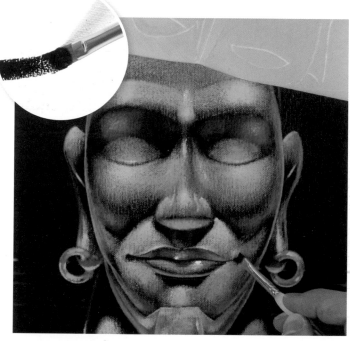

Fig.11.53 (Inset).   Fig. 11.54.

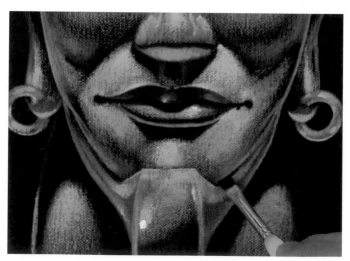

Fig. 11.55.

DRY BRUSH TIPS

TURN THE CANVAS: Make sure you can turn your canvas at any angle for easier brush strokes.

DARK TO LIGHT: Shading in this technique tends to look best when finishing with lighter colours.

LOW ANGLE STROKES: Hold the brush at an acute angle, 45 degrees or less. Repeat strokes in approximately the same direction.

LAYERS: Make sure each layer is dry (a couple of minutes) before going over it again and building up the strength of colour.

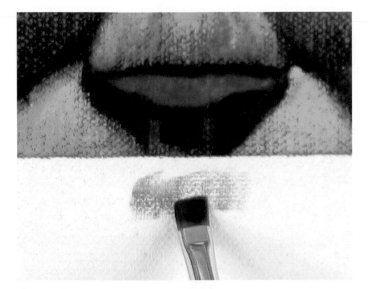

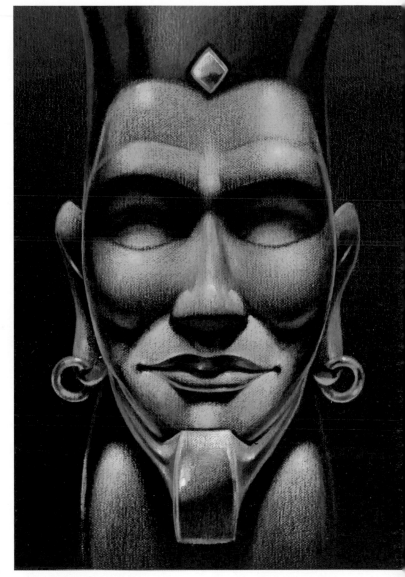

Fig. 11.56.

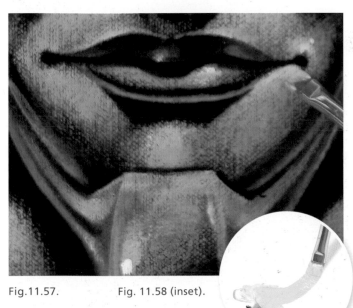

Fig.11.57.   Fig. 11.58 (inset).

Fig. 11.59 The finished picture.

If some areas are too strong it is possible to 'tint' them back to a more muted colour. Taking the same brush, use more water in your black and remove most of the moisture until you get a damp mark (Fig. 11.56). Using this mix, tint some shadow under the nose and in the eye sockets so only part of the eyelid is lit. See the comparison between Figs 11.55 and 11.56.

Light Highlights

Finally the best bit – putting on sparkly highlights, the white shines at the corner of the mouth (Fig. 11.57), and those on top of the earrings. Finished! (Fig. 11.59)

I hope you've had fun trying this form of graduating tones using the canvas weave. If you try different brushes in combination with different canvases you are bound to discover which is your favourite. Good luck!

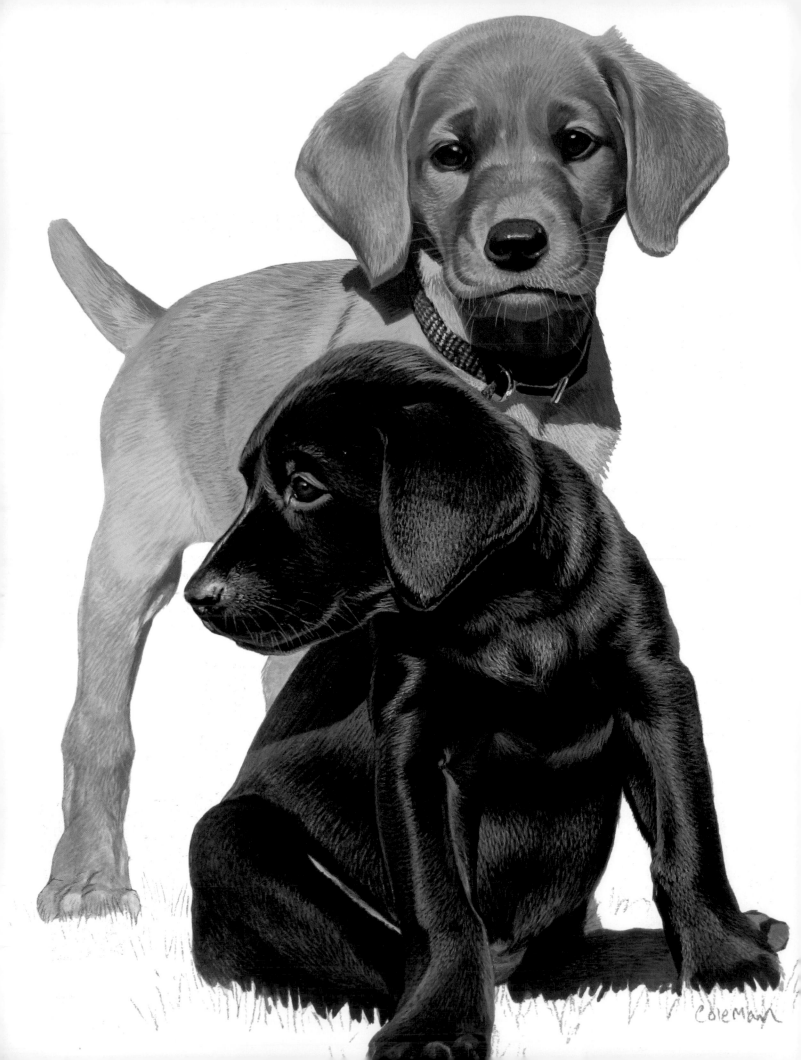

CHAPTER 12

ILLUSTRATION
Including Fur Technique

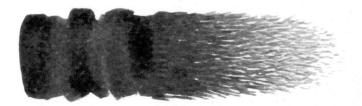

Fig. 12.1

In this chapter the following topics are explored:

- **Illustration style fur technique**
- **Semi-opaque layers**
- **Tonal washes**

Introduction

The illustration in this chapter is based on the stippling shading exercise in Chapter 1.

This technique takes line and wash a stage further by moving from a transparent wash to a semi-opaque painting. Here the whole area is given a medium tone wash after the line work, and then the highlights are put back in with semi to opaque brush strokes. This achieves a beautiful 'solid' look to the subject, and once again uses the core quality of acrylics: the multiple layers.

This wash and semi-opaque technique is a universal way of creating illustrations especially for publication. It is quick and effective, and has plenty of scope for adaptation should the painting need more work than expected by becoming a completely opaque painting.

Fig. 12.2

In this example the surface is a watercolour board because it takes line washes and thicker opaque paints smoothly, and most importantly of all it doesn't bow or buckle. These boards are available in different surface papers, but this style lends itself to a smooth surface.

Normal smooth watercolour paper would work well with the line work, and will resist warping with a light wash. MDF (medium density fibreboard) will also work extremely well if gessoed and sanded to a uniformly smooth surface. Tints on that surface require less water as the surface is less absorbent.

Preparation

A 10 × 12in watercolour board is my preferred choice. A 'stay wet' palette is useful if returning to the painting later, but very small washes and paint are used in this example. A spare piece of watercolour board would be useful to mix and to prime your brush, shape the tip and make a test mark.

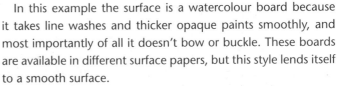

Fig. 12.3

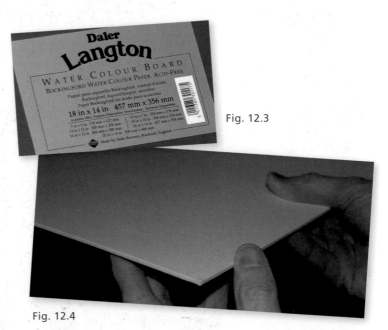

Fig. 12.4

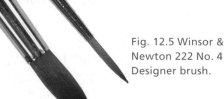

Fig. 12.5 Winsor & Newton 222 No. 4 Designer brush.

Fig. 12.6 Winsor & Newton Cotman 111 No. 14 Watercolour brush.

MATERIALS NEEDED

- 10 × 12in watercolour board

- Photo reference enlarged to size

- Line drawing supplied enlarged to size

- (Tracing paper if creating your own line drawing and 2B propelling pencil)

- Tracing pen or 6H pencil for tracing down

- Imagetrace®

- 'Stay wet' palette or spare piece of board

- Water jar

Painting stage:

- Winsor & Newton Designer 222 No. 6 Detail brush

- Winsor & Newton Wash brush No. 14

- Dogs: Raw Sienna, Burnt Sienna, Payne's Grey, Mars Black, Titanium White, Ultramarine Blue, Ultramarine Violet

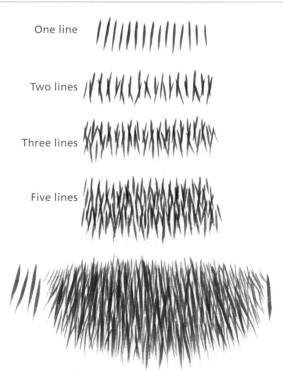

One line

Two lines

Three lines

Five lines

Fig. 12.8 Longer lines.

TECHNIQUE

Painting Fur

Here is a technique to create a realistic result with fur and hair. The principle is to vary the direction of each line so there is a build-up of cross-hatching. There has to be an element of frequent irregularity even though it is based on a pattern.

The black line drawings give a sequence to the build-up.

(Figs 12.7 and 12.8) This is an effective system of creating fur in all colours and lengths. This black and white version illustrates the cross-hatching style and the tapering brush strokes.

The secret to making many marks before you have to re-load your brush is to have the right viscosity: too weak and the marks are insipid, too thick and the paint won't flow out. Once you have the mix like single cream, make a row of hairs.

The second row starts a little further along and this time subtly cross-hatch over the previous lines. Vary the direction occasionally. Once it has reached a convincing state in one tone, it can be made more 3D by adding lighter and opaque hairs, this time less densely spaced. After that make a third layer of occasional darker hairs. Finally areas can be tinted a colour, either to change the hair colour or create a shaded area.

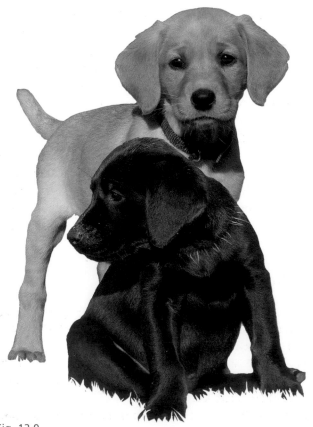

Fig. 12.9.

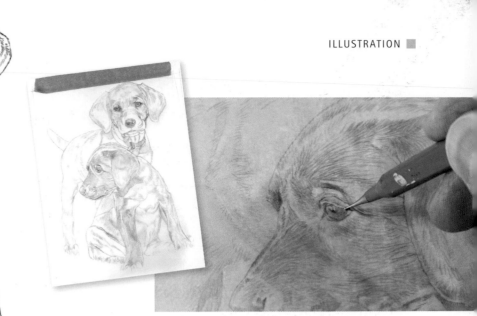

Fig. 12.10.

Fig. 12.11.   Fig.12.12.

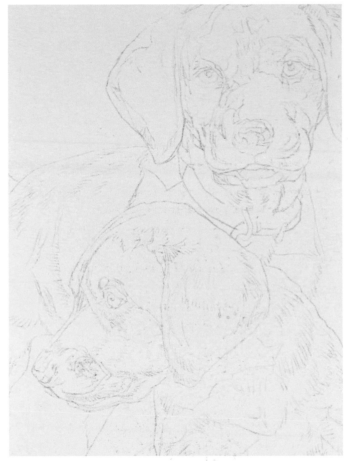

The Drawing

(Fig. 12.9) Enlarge the references by 240 per cent on a photo-copier on to tracing paper to trace your own drawing, or use the line drawing provided below (Fig. 12.10).

(Fig. 12.11) Tape the line drawing securely to the watercolour board ready for tracing down. The trace will stay there until the end. Insert the carbon paper, such as Imagetrace®, underneath shiny side down.

(Fig. 12.12) The trace will leave a heavy line if too much pressure is applied, so aim for a line that's just visible. Because the line drawing is taped in place, only trace through enough lines to guide you along. The line drawing can be flipped down as you paint, or you can make more guide lines.

(Fig. 12.13) The final line on the watercolour board is just visible.

The Illustration

(Fig. 12.14) Using Burnt Sienna, create a watery pool: load up the brush, then remove some of it until you get a nice line. Now it's ready to 'draw' like a pencil.

(Fig. 12.15) This colour will form the darker areas, especially when a second and third coat is added. Brush in the darker areas from the photo reference.

(Fig. 12.16) The darkest areas for the golden puppy are now complete: now we can start the black puppy.

Fig. 12.13.

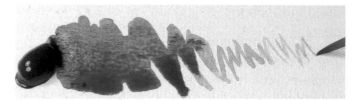

Fig. 12.14.

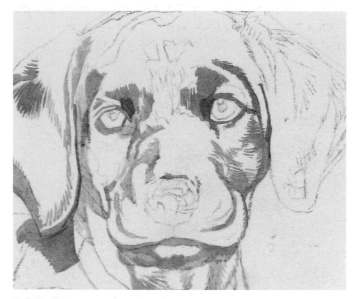

Fig. 12.15.

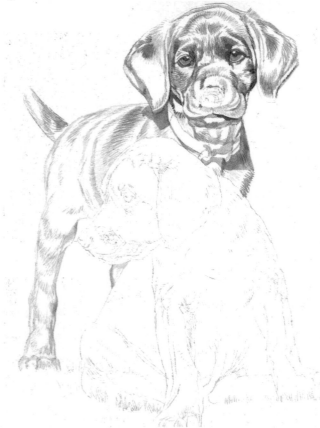

Fig. 12.16.

SEMI-OPAQUE TIPS

WATERY VISCOSITY: If it's too thick it will be too opaque.

BUILD UP IN LAYERS: To achieve the exact tone it's quicker to build up than to lighten back down.

USE TINTS TO SHADE: Tint on top of opaque paints or transparent paints.

PAINT WITH THE BRUSH BLADE: Hair and fur can be best painted using the brush dabbed into a blade rather than a round point.

KEEP OPAQUE LAYERS TO THE FINAL HIGHLIGHTS: The brightest areas are the opaque areas.

(Fig. 12.17) With Payne's Grey, make a watery mix and flatten the brush to get a broader wash-in tip.

(Fig. 12.18) Wash in the golden lab's nose as a first coat.

(Fig. 12.19) The same flat blade can be used to make the fur marks.

(Fig. 12.20) Start brushing in all the darker areas with a mixture of hair marks and flat shaded areas, for example under the neck. Use the line drawing trace if needed to find areas.

(Fig. 12.21) Work methodically around the subject; after the fur marks have dried, add tints over areas as you go – for example, the shadow on the back and around the face.

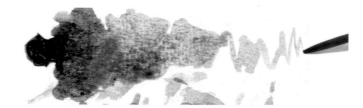

Fig. 12.17.

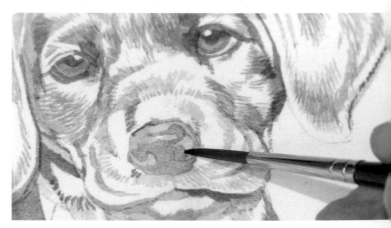

Fig. 12.18.

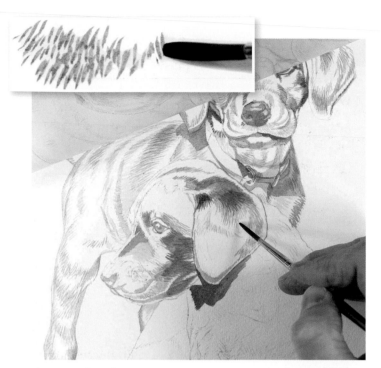

Fig. 12.19 (inset).   Fig. 12.20.

(Fig. 12.22) Once the Payne's Grey marks have covered a majority of the dog, it's time to add the next layer of washes and marks with Mars Black.

(Fig. 12.23) Mix another wash of black tint. It's better to be too weak at first and re-mix the strength for another coat.

(Fig. 12.24) Add a small pink wash of Cadmium Red on the tummy before the over-all blue and violet wash.

(Fig. 12.26) Mix Ultramarine Blue and Ultramarine Violet with the large wash brush and brush it over evenly ready for the opaque layers (Figs 12.27 and 12.28). It will look alarmingly violet.

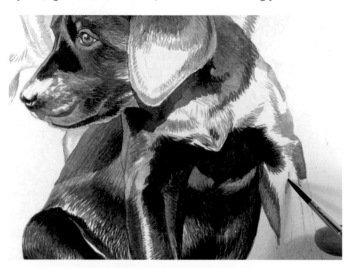

Fig. 12.22.

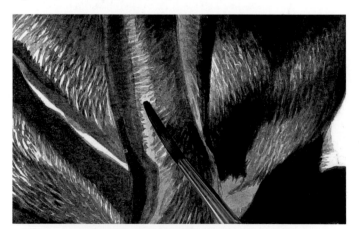

Fig. 12.23.

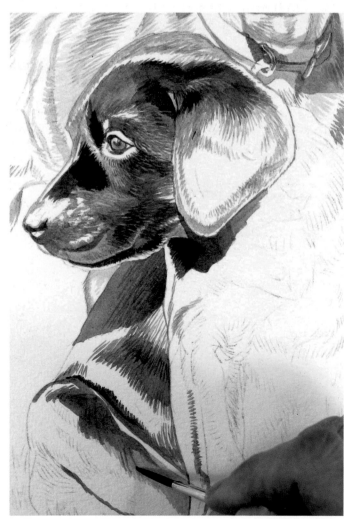

Fig. 12.21.

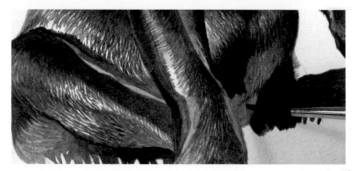

Fig. 12.24.

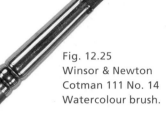

Fig. 12.25
Winsor & Newton
Cotman 111 No. 14
Watercolour brush.

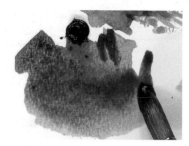

Fig. 12.26.

Contrast

Go back to the designer detail brush and continue to make hair marks in black; lightly tint over those marks when dry to build up the darkest tones (Fig. 12.29). It will begin to look a little less violet!

But first the golden lab needs to be at that stage too.

(Fig. 12.31) Add a little Payne's Grey to your Burnt Sienna, and wash in the shadow area under the chin.

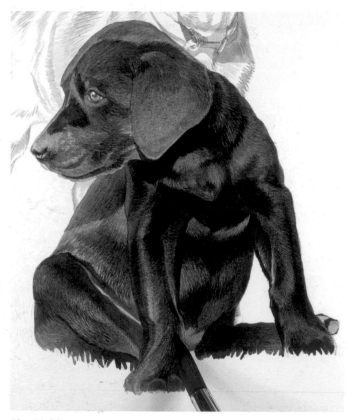

Fig. 12.27.

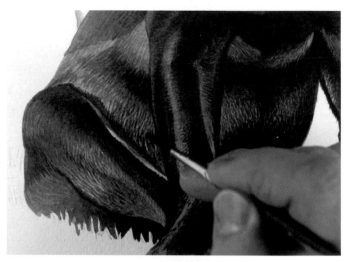

Fig. 12.29.

Fig. 12.28.

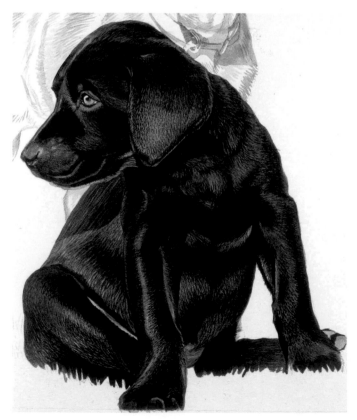

Fig. 12.30.

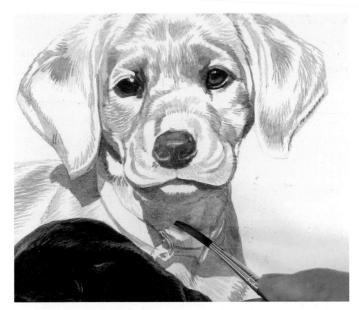

Fig. 12.31.

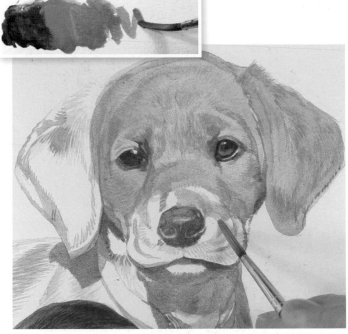

Fig. 12.32 (Inset).   Fig. 12.33.

(Figs 12.32 and 12.33) Semi-opaque wash: Add a little water and white to the Burnt Sienna until you have a teaspoon of liquid to wash in a uniform layer over the dog's head and body. Note it is not thick enough to cover the fur lines.

(Fig. 12.34) After the body wash, add in a mid-blue wash for the collar; then add the darker grey-blue shadow details in the material.

Detailing: Add highlights to the weave on the collar (Fig. 12.35).

(Fig. 12.36) Add a pre-final layer of dark fur lines to continue the marks from underneath and to finish off the nose.

(Fig. 12.37) As the tones and details build up, move to thicker mixes of almost opaque paint for the lightest areas – the top of the head, cheeks and nose and thighs – using white and a small amount of Burnt Sienna.

(Fig. 12.38) Now the head will have a whiter and lighter appearance ready for the final darker tints and lines.

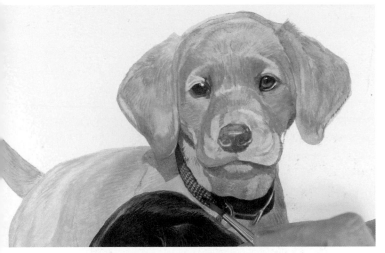

Fig. 12.34.

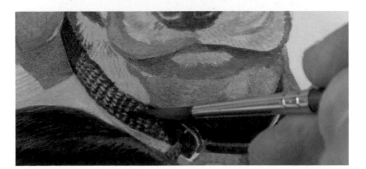

Fig. 12.35.

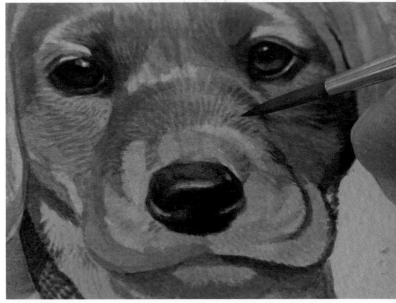

Fig. 12.36.

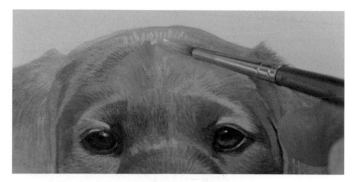

Fig. 12.37.

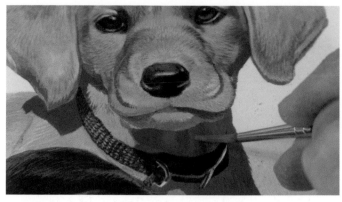

Fig. 12.40.

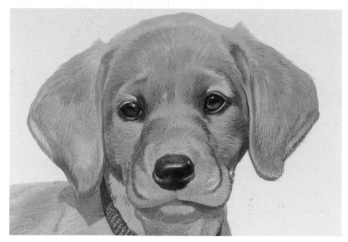

Fig. 12.38.

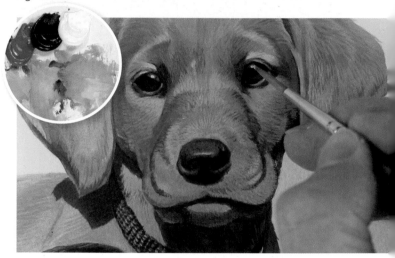

Fig. 12.41 (Inset).   Fig. 12.42.

Chin shadow: Mixing in order of amount, a solid semi-opaque layer of Burnt Sienna, Payne's Grey, Ultramarine Violet and white (Fig. 12.39).

(Fig. 12.40) Add a few layers of the chin shadow colour with lighter highlights painted in whilst it's wet.

(Fig. 12.41) Use different dilutions of Burnt Sienna, Raw Sienna and white.

(Fig. 12.42) The eyes are a mix of Raw Sienna and Burnt Umber with white: Raw Sienna at the bottom of the iris, and a white dot highlight can be added.

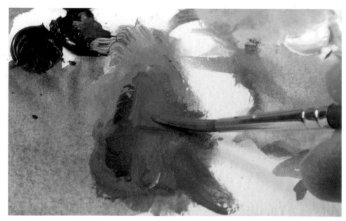

Fig. 12.39.

Semi-opaque blue-greys: With the same semi-opaque viscosity, use Payne's Grey, blue and violet with white to get a mid-tone colour for the highlights on the fur (Fig. 12.43). Apply these to match with your dark fur marks.

(Fig. 12.44) Use an even whiter mix on the brightest areas according to your reference.

(Fig. 12.45) Continue adding the final highlights to the fur on the leg.

(Fig. 12.46) All the black puppy's highlights are now in.

(Fig. 12.47) A final eye detail and whiskers will be put in at the end.

(Fig. 12.48) Add a dark wash of Burnt Sienna over the back to match the tones of the reference. Whilst it's drying, put in the whiskers.

Whiskers: With a single cream-like viscosity, load up and tap the tip into a blade, and practise a few lines (Fig. 12.49). To get an even line, use your little finger as a prop to maintain a constant height.

(Fig. 12.50) If a sweeping action doesn't feel comfortable, try bringing the brush into your palm, still using the little finger as support. This only works for short marks.

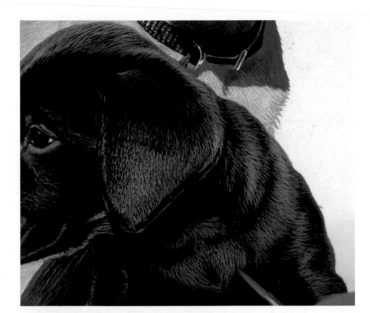

Fig. 12.43.

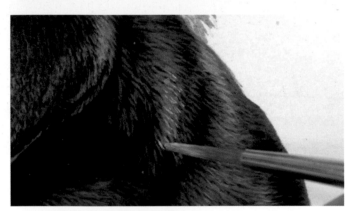

Fig. 12.44.

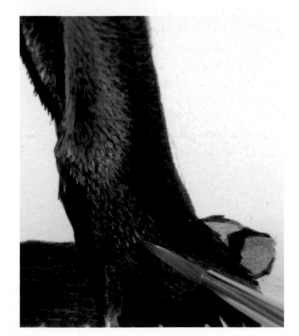

Fig. 12.45.

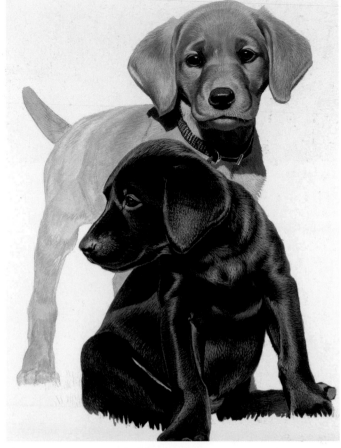

Fig. 12.46.

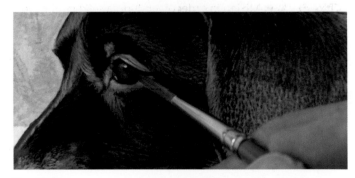

Fig. 12.47.

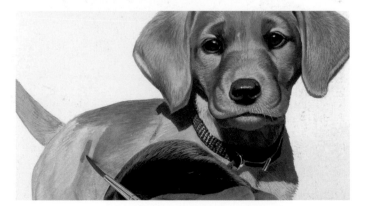

Fig. 12.48.

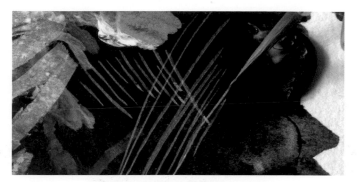

Fig. 12.49.

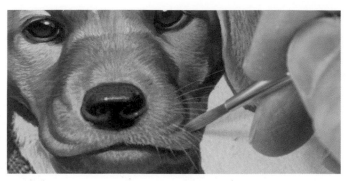

Fig. 12.50.

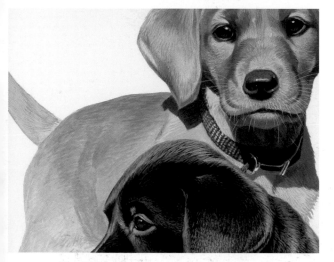

Fig. 12.51.

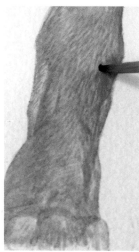

Fig. 12.52.

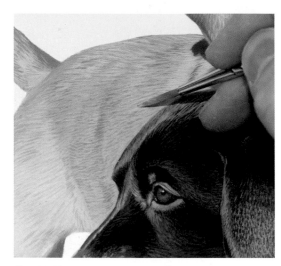

Fig. 12.53.

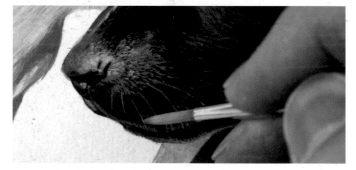

Fig. 12.54.

(Fig. 12.51) The wash on the back is finished. This should look darker than the reference, ready for the opaque lighter fur marks.

(Fig. 12.52) Finish off the darker fur marks down the leg in transparent Burnt Sienna.

(Fig. 12.53) Mix a tiny amount of Burnt Sienna and Yellow Ochre into white. You can use White Gesso, too, for really opaque lines. Use the same brush mark technique of cross-hatching, and double up layers where it needs to be lighter.

(Fig. 12.54) Last but not least, put in the whiskers. Remember to try one or two strokes first. Then take a deep breath…

(Fig. 12.55) The final painting.

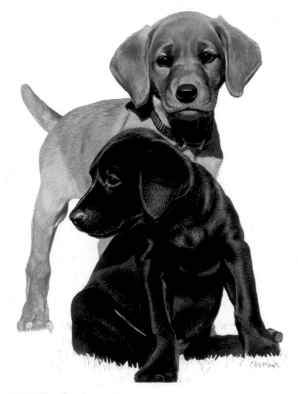

Fig. 12.55 The final painting.

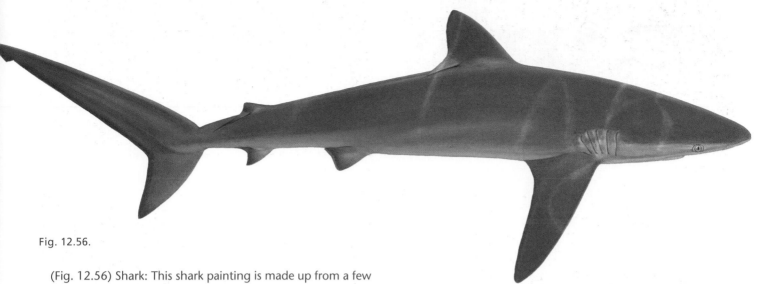

Fig. 12.56.

(Fig. 12.56) Shark: This shark painting is made up from a few layers of washes. Mid body shadows are a single stroke placed on when the board is damp. Again, subtle semi-opaque washes are placed from the top on damp board to give a slightly solid paint feel. Watercolour board, 3 × 9in.

Panda bear: The bear is a bit heavier, with the fur opaque compared to the black puppy, but the whole illustration started out with a wash covering (Fig. 12.57). Watercolour board, 7 × 5in.

(Fig. 12.58) Octopus: A wash painting with lots of little details in opaque acrylics. Watercolour board, 14 × 10in.

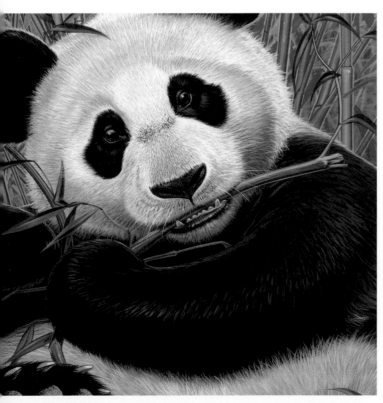

Fig. 12.57.

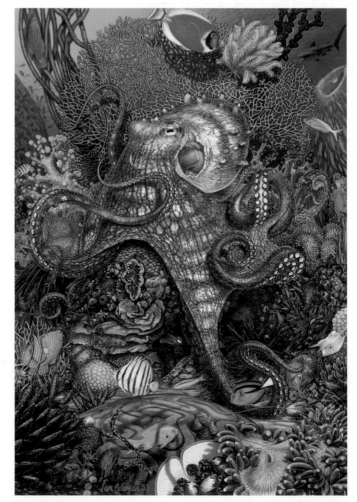

Fig. 12.58.

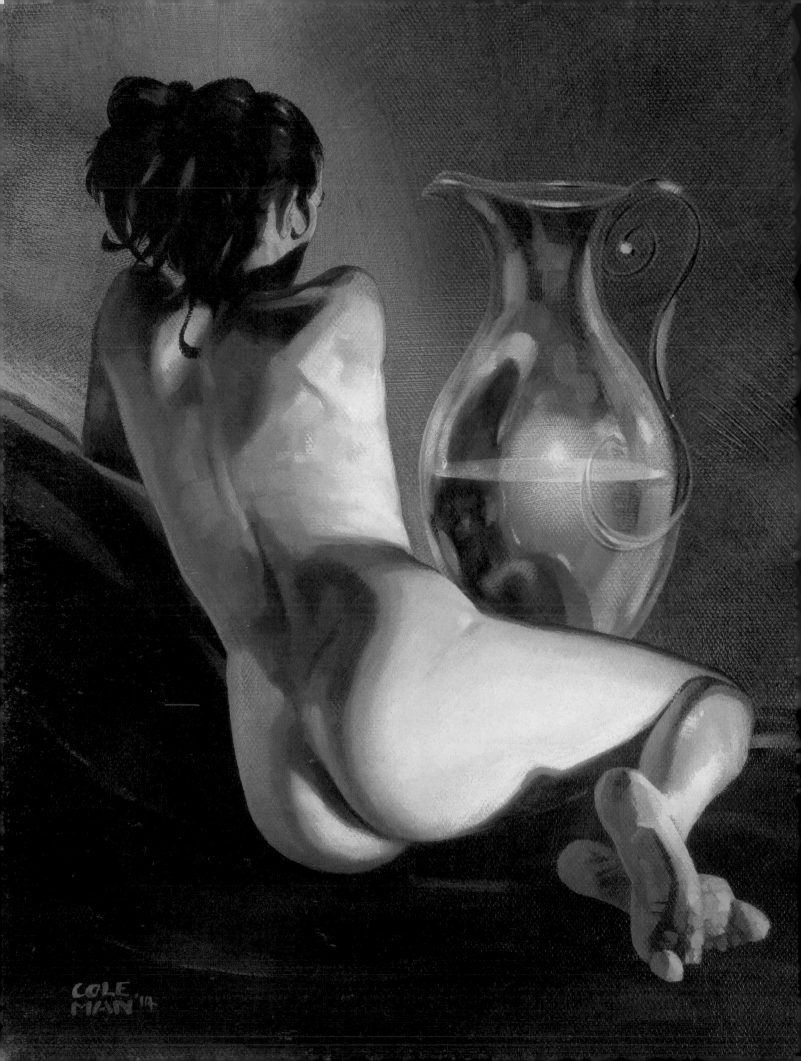

CHAPTER 13

THICK AND THIN

Including dry brush, large area tinting and highlighting

In this chapter the following topics are explored:

• **Thick and thin painting**
• **Multiple layers**
• **Tinting large areas**
• **Removing paint as a method of creating a vignette**

THE TECHNIQUE

This technique is probably the most popular way of using acrylic paint. It has areas of thin washes and heavy dabs, and it uses the best feature of acrylics, which is multi-layering back and forth. By that I mean there is no rule of thin on top of thick, or vice versa: you can apply the paint in any viscosity, in any order.

This is particularly noticeable on the vase, as I happened to go the 'long way round' to get a satisfactory result. This can often happen, and is why I love acrylics so much: they are great at repairing mistakes. You'll notice quite often that colours used for blocking in don't end up in the final picture, but they may be there peeking through. I show you this painting as it evolved with all its twists and turns, but if you digest it all first you may note there are some small shortcuts to be had.

THE STYLE

I wanted to show a few effects in this life drawing example, so I've been less strict about keeping to one technique within the painting. The vase is a little less 'impressionistic' than the figure, for example, and I've used both dry shading and wet shading. Normally I'd try to keep it within a style and leave the middle ground by either making the style looser or tighter throughout.

The choice of brush type is important, and I've chosen a few flat short brushes to get that 'angular' mark making.

This example is painted at this book size of 220 × 280mm.

PREPARATION

This piece is on canvas board, though it could have been done on stretched canvas. Neither normally has an advantage in this context, except it was easier to show it for the camera. I work flat for the tinting, and can rotate the painting easily for the details.

I've added another layer of white gesso on the pre-gessoed canvas board. It sometimes adds another texture feature if there's more than the uniformity of the canvas weave. You can see sweeping horizontal gesso marks left and right of the water vase.

Have a 'stay-wet' palette ready for keeping your paint mixes usable for longer, or a palette board and have water, brushes and kitchen towel. A spare or end piece of canvas can be useful to preview the strength of your tint.

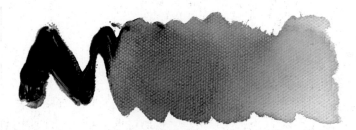

Fig. 13.1 Thick and thin.

MATERIALS NEEDED

Preparation:

• 10 × 12in canvas board

• White gesso

• 2in wide bristle brush for gesso

• Photo reference enlarged to size

• Line drawing supplied enlarged to size

• (Tracing paper if creating your own line drawing)

• Tracing pen or 6H pencil

• Imagetrace® paper

Painting stage:

• ½in flat synthetic for main work

• 2in Hog flat brush for tinting

• ½in short flat bristle No. 8

• ¼in Royal No.8 Soft Grip Synthetic flat brush

• Winsor & Newton Designer 222 No. 6 Detail Brush

• Kitchen towel

• Background colours: Cadmium Red and Phthalo Blue Green shade and Payne's Grey

• Flesh colours: Burnt Umber, Cadmium Red, Cadmium Yellow, Cadmium Deep Red, Titanium White, Dioxazine Purple

• Background tints: Viridian Green, Phthalo Blue-Green Shade

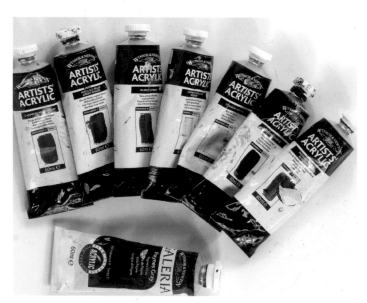

Fig. 13.2.

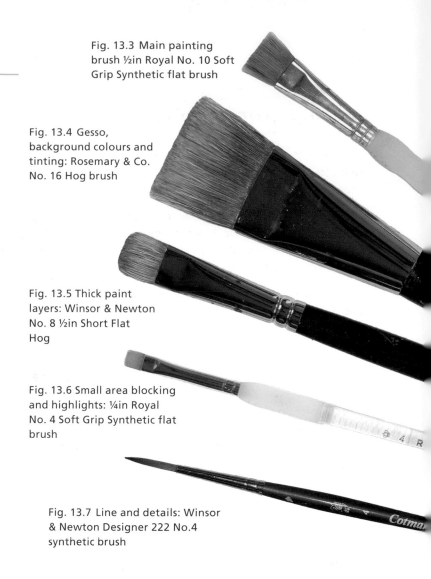

Fig. 13.3 Main painting brush ½in Royal No. 10 Soft Grip Synthetic flat brush

Fig. 13.4 Gesso, background colours and tinting: Rosemary & Co. No. 16 Hog brush

Fig. 13.5 Thick paint layers: Winsor & Newton No. 8 ½in Short Flat Hog

Fig. 13.6 Small area blocking and highlights: ¼in Royal No. 4 Soft Grip Synthetic flat brush

Fig. 13.7 Line and details: Winsor & Newton Designer 222 No.4 synthetic brush

THE BRUSHES

There's not a hard and fast rule with this technique as the five brushes below offer all the mark-making varieties needed. The two ½in brushes could be the more rounded filbert brush types, and the 222 Designer brush could be a rigger brush. Each brush shape will influence the style.

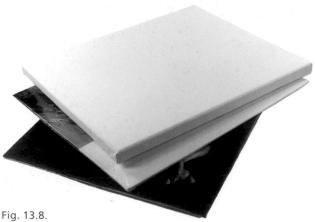

Fig. 13.8.

THICK AND THIN TIPS

START THIN: As a general rule, block in areas with a transparent wash, each subsequent coat becoming thicker.

KEEP THE PAINT MOVING: Don't stop moving the paint until you're happy with it. A wet bristle brush will move thin paint even if it feels touch dry, and thicker paint if it's still tacky.

LAYERS: Often three thin layers can be better than one thick layer.

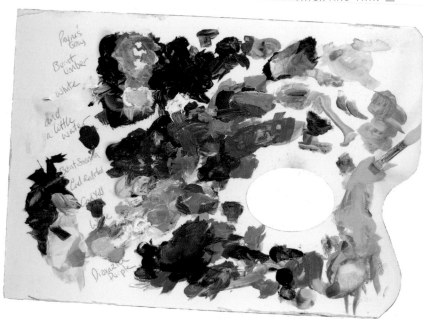

Fig. 13.9 The palette at the end of the painting.

(Fig. 13.8) Canvas board or stretched canvas will work on this example. Both will need cleaning with a little soapy water and a sponge if previously wrapped in cling film, to avoid the paint being repelled.

(Fig. 13.10) Enlarge the reference by 275 per cent on a photocopier to trace a line drawing, or use the line drawing provided below (Fig. 13.11).

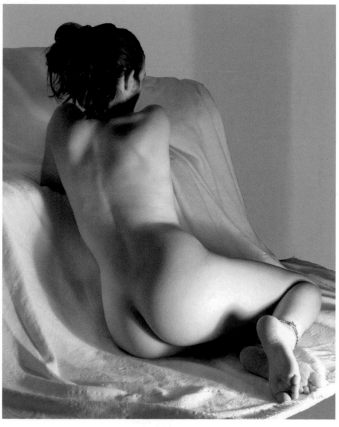

Fig. 13.10.

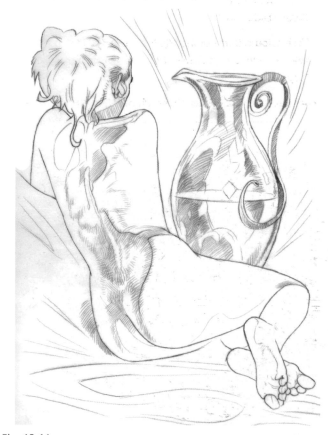

Fig. 13.11.

THE DRAWING

Quite often with a life drawing the form is observed and sketched with a degree of interpretation, so the proportions and placements are not picture perfect. To that end, this first step of using the photo as a tracing guide could be left out, and instead you could draw straight on to the canvas board by sight using the photo reference opposite.

However, I wanted to give you the option of using this drawing as a first try, to follow the same process and leave less room for going off course.

AN EXTRA GESSO LAYER

Before drawing on to the board there's an opportunity to add another layer of texture. Roughly sketch with charcoal or very lightly with pencil where the figure is to go (Fig. 13.12). Using neat white gesso, brush a thin layer with a wide brush in sympathetic directions over the body. You can just see the drawing under the gesso (Fig. 13.13). Normally this would be in a cross-section direction or diagonally, but not in parallel with the form. Let that dry thoroughly before using the accurate outline trace.

(Fig. 13.12) The rough trace taped in position and traced through.

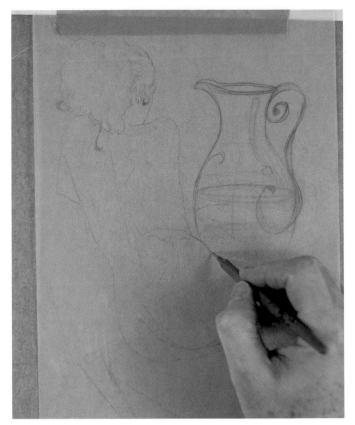

Fig. 13.15.

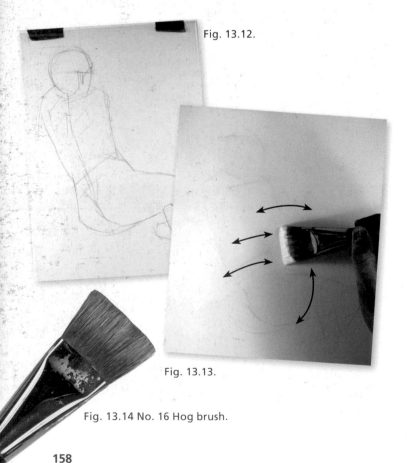

Fig. 13.12.

Fig. 13.13.

Fig. 13.14 No. 16 Hog brush.

(Fig. 13.15) With the Imagetrace® paper in position, trace through your pencil tracing or the one provided with just enough pressure to make a mark. This will still be visible after the background washes of colour.

BACKGROUND COLOUR

(Fig. 13.16) Apply a blob of paint straight on to the canvas board. I've chosen Cadmium Red, but any warm colour could work – browns, yellow-greens, purple for example.

Have clean water ready and a flat wide brush. I've chosen an old, stiff, synthetic ½n-wide brush, but a bristle brush would also work.

(Fig. 13.17) Dip the brush in water, and blend the colour back and forth across the board. Remember that as long as the paint is kept on the move you can spread it around and thin it.

(Figs 13.19 and 13.20) Don't wait for the red to dry, but add a blob of Phthalo Blue-Green Shade and blend in the same way, and purple colours may form. It may dry quickly but it's all right to have dry shading over the red areas.

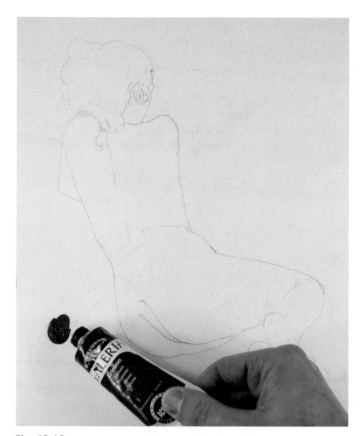

Fig. 13.16.

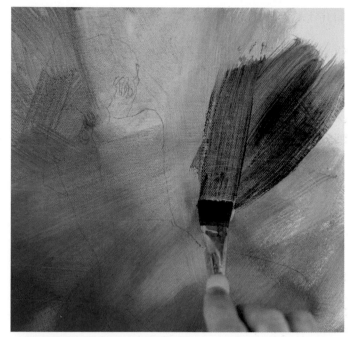

Fig. 13.19.

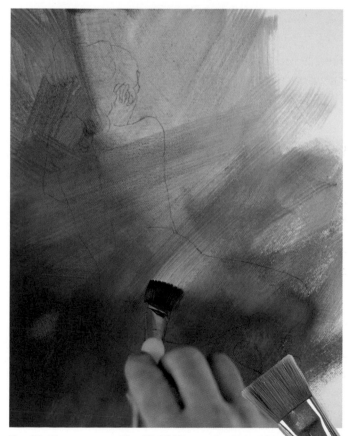

Fig. 13.17.   Fig. 13.18 ½in synthetic brush.

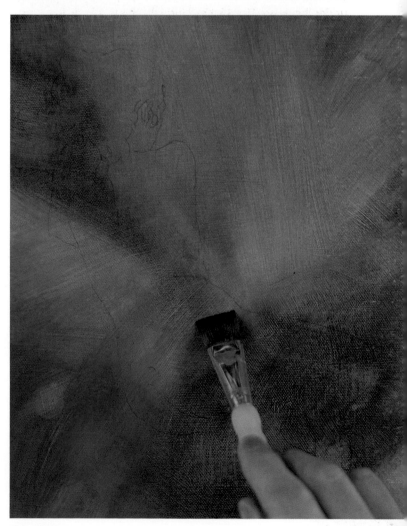

Fig. 13.20.

SHADOW AREAS

(Fig. 13.21) There's not a huge amount of paint on this painting so mixing on a palette is convenient. A mixture of Payne's Grey, Burnt Umber and a tiny amount of white will give it opacity to roughly block in the shaded areas.

The background acrylic paints are transparent so the outlines are still visible; but if, for some reason, they have disappeared, they can be traced on again. It's always a good habit to leave any tracings securely taped until the very end.

(Figs 13.22 and 13.23) Use the same background brush. This grey-brown mix is fairly thick, but as it is pushed around it becomes thinner, so you can influence where you want darker areas to be.

Fig. 13.24: ½in Hog flat brush.

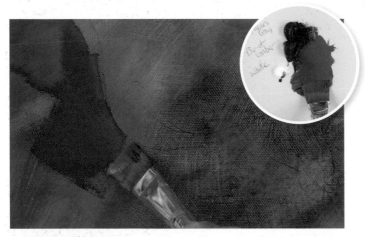

Fig. 13.21 (inset).   Fig. 13.22.

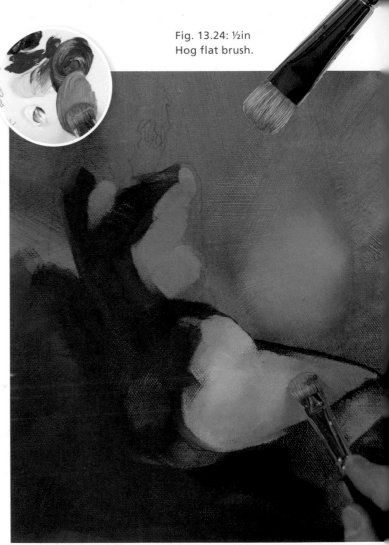

Fig. 13.25 iInset).   Fig. 13.26.

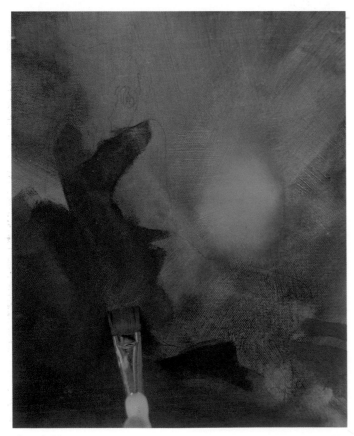

Fig. 13.23.

PAINTING THE FIGURE

FLESH TONES

(Fig. 13.24) I've changed to a Bristle Hog brush so there is more scope to pull and drag semi-drying paint about. Also the paint can be dragged for longer, creating elements of dry shading.

(Fig. 13.25) Flesh tones can be made up from numerous colours, and here I've used a basic blocking-in dark to mid tone, made from equal parts Burnt Sienna, Cadmium Red, Cadmium

Yellow with a little white. The lighter the flesh tone the more white will be needed.

(Fig. 13.26) Having started with the darkest flesh tone, dip in and out of your flesh mix frequently re-mixing either the same tone or lighter or darker as and when you feel you need to, but with a general progression of getting lighter and lighter in the appropriate areas.

FEET, FACE and SHADOWS

(Fig. 13.28) Switching to the flat detail brush, apply the light highlights in the tricky areas such as the feet and face. Build up the tones in the same way, darker to lighter, using every angle of the brush tip. It's very useful to rotate the artwork to make it easier to make fine precise marks.

A deep purple has been added on the hamstrings, and a red cast to the bottom.

RED LIGHT AND HAIR

(Fig. 13.29) Continue with the red cast all the way up to the shoulder. This should still shine through, with subsequent semi-opaque layers of more muted tones on top.

Add the black hair: it may take a few thin layers to get a solid black, and you may need to rotate the canvas again.

(Fig. 13.30) Dull down the red on the left body side with a transparent wash, and (Fig. 13.31) sharpen up the right body side profile with a lighter flesh mix.

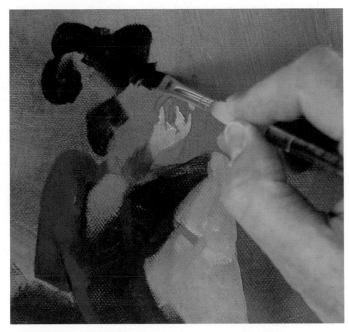

Fig. 13.29.

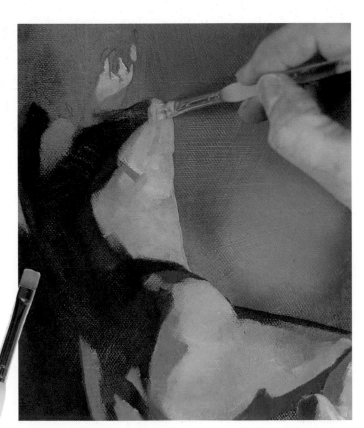

Fig. 13.27 ¼in No. 4 Detail brush.   Fig. 13.28.

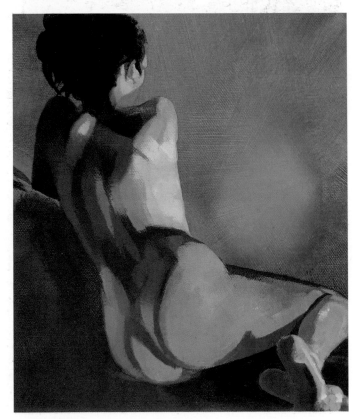

Fig. 13.30.

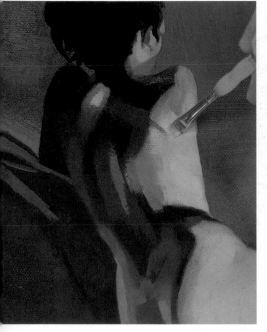

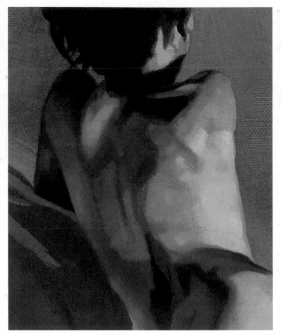

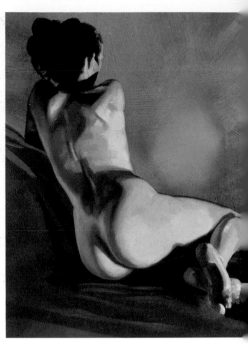

Fig. 13.31.

Fig. 13.32.

Fig. 13.33.

(Fig. 13.32) Soften the contrast on the back by adding smaller areas of colour which are closer in tonal values. Add the collarbone detailing. This is where changing tonal strengths may require multiple layers of trial and error.

VASE

The vase is an opportunity to use tinting layers, using thin coats in either opaque or transparent mixes. In this example I went back and forth with light and dark versions showing how you can discover the right colours by continuing to work over the previous tones.

(Fig. 13.34) Flip back the outline trace, or re-align it if it has become detached; use white Imagetrace® paper or regular grey carbon paper to trace the vase on to the board (Fig. 13.35).

(Fig. 13.36) Using the synthetic flat detail brush, mix a little white to a skimmed milk-like consistency. Remove the excess

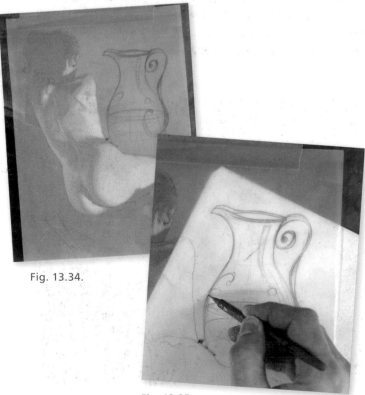

Fig. 13.34.

Fig. 13.35.

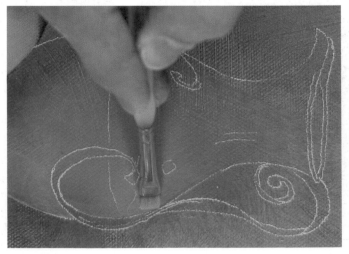

Fig. 13.36.

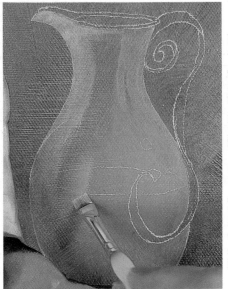

Fig. 13.37.

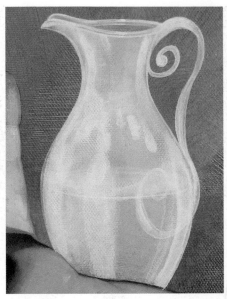

Fig. 13.38.

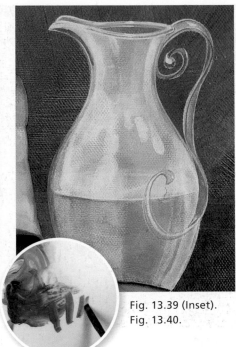

Fig. 13.39 (Inset).
Fig. 13.40.

paint from the brush, and with the residual amount apply thin coats. The white carbon lines will dissolve as you go over them.

(Fig. 13.37) As each layer builds and ideas of reflections take shape, it's possible to increase the opacity so the end result is a frosted white vase (Fig. 13.38) ready for darker shading with more tints.

DARKER DETAILS

(Figs 13.39 and 13.40) With a thin mix of semi-transparent mid-blue – using blue, Payne's Grey and a tiny amount of white – paint the details of the scrolling handle, vase spout and water line.

(Figs 13.41 and 13.42) With a thin blue wash, tint the neck, water and handle. Some of the whiter highlights will almost disappear, but will still show subtly in the final result.

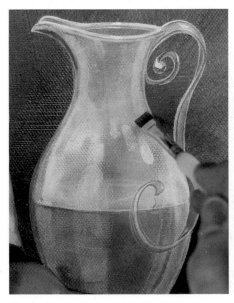

Fig. 13.41.

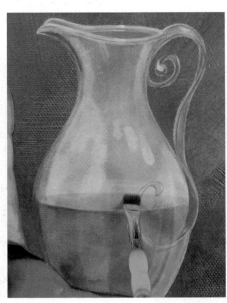

Fig. 13.42.

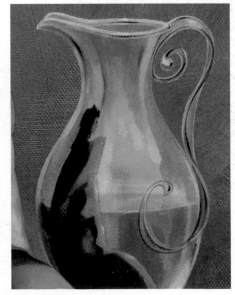

Fig. 143.

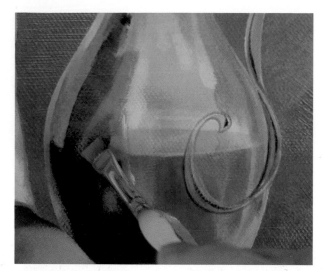

Fig. 13.44.

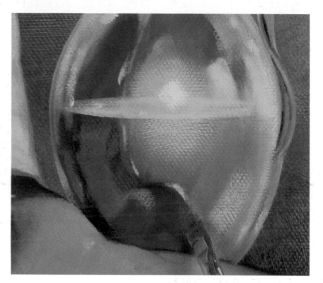

Fig. 13.45.

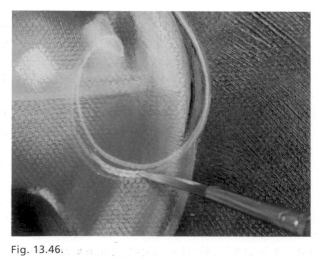

Fig. 13.46.

(Fig. 13.43) Quite often a reflection's colour is influenced by other factors, such as the texture, the colour of the object and the atmosphere. A transparent glass vase will reflect a small proportion compared to a mirror, and one way of approaching this is to treat the object as if it were a mirror, and then dilute those tones with a tint.

(Fig. 13.44) A diluted mix of opaque blue is applied a few times until it is just showing. Let each coat dry for a minute before going over it.

(Fig. 13.45) The very edge of the figure reflection is reapplied. The water surface is put in with a semi-transparent white mix and a centre white highlight in the middle, and further light blue reflections are added on the neck. Darker blue (a mix of Payne's Grey with blue and a little white) is added for neck reflections.

(Figs 13.46 and 13.47) A final detailing is required with the round 222 detail brush on the handle, which was removed in the process of adding semi-opaque reflections. The figure reflection required a stronger tone and a blue bias to go with the background and the body shadow colour.

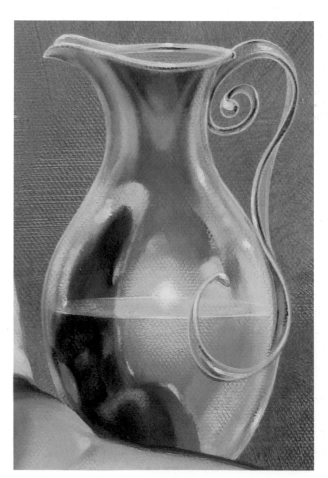

Fig. 13.47.

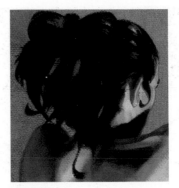

Fig. 13.49.

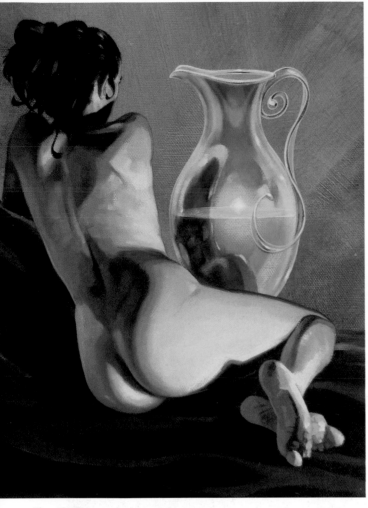

Fig. 13.48.

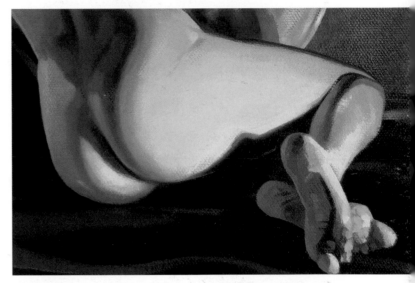

Fig. 13.50.

FINAL DETAILS BEFORE THE BIG TINT

Before the final tint it's best to finalize any details, especially light-coloured ones (Fig. 13.48). Dark areas will be adjustable to a point, but once the image is bathed in green light, that hopefully concludes the painting. Of course the beauty of acrylics is that if it still needs amendments it is still possible to re-do those areas.

(Figs 13.49 and 13.50) Hair curls in black have been added along with hair highlights. A purple material has been over-painted on the red material using a thicker opaque mix. Again it may take two or three coats to hide it. With the flat detail brush add a further thicker coat of the lightest flesh colour on the buttocks and thighs; also a bit of detailing on the feet.

THE BIG GREEN TINT

To do a large tint area requires a large brush, not just for quick coverage, but for fine blending, too, as the paint begins to get dry and tacky. Using the large bristle gesso brush, mix a pool of transparent Viridian Green (Fig. 13.51); have kitchen towel handy to repeatedly remove the excess from the brush. Work flat on a table.

(Figs 13.52 and 13.53) Cover the whole area required with tint. Don't be too generous with the amount. Make long sweeps.

(Fig. 13.54) Almost immediately the wash tint will begin to get tacky as it dries, and as it does so, keep blending the paint to a uniform colour.

(Fig. 13.55) Keep removing the excess paint from your brush often, and re-blend the tint flat using multi-directional brush sweeps.

(Figs 13.56 and 13.57) Use a slightly damp kitchen towel to remove the tint, and then use the wiped dry large tint brush or the ½in-wide synthetic brush to feather the edges. The brushes may need to be slightly damp if the tint has dried too much.

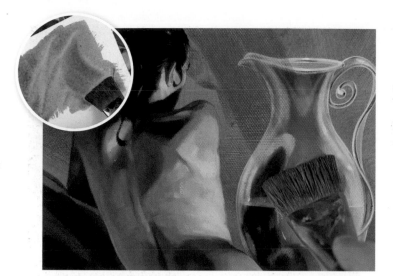

Fig. 13.51 (inset).

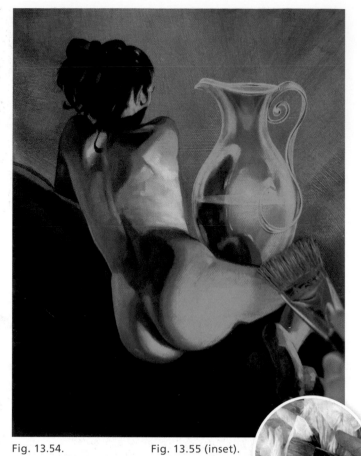

Fig. 13.52.

Fig. 13.54.   Fig. 13.55 (inset).

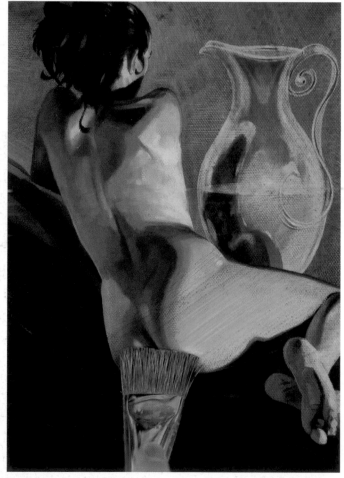

Fig. 13.53.

(Figs 13.58 and 13.59) Using a clean, damp detail brush, remove the tint from the edges of the body and the top of the face.

(Fig. 13.60) If, on reflection, more tint could be added to the back and shoulder blades, then use the same tint process with the detail brush.

(Fig. 13.61) Let the painting dry thoroughly before the final stage of adding a darker background behind the vase. This will have the effect of bringing your eye back to the centre.

(Fig. 13.62) Mix a pool of dark blue and apply on to the dry canvas with the large bristle brush.

(Fig. 13.63) Keep the direction of the strokes sympathetic to the picture by sweeping into the centre behind the vase. Once the colour is on, wipe the excess paint off the brush and blend the outsides of the area thinner.

(Fig. 13.64) Use the main synthetic brush to remove the paint on the vase centre highlight, gently radiating out. If the paint is not coming off, dampen the brush a little more.

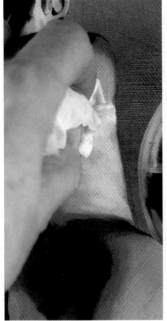
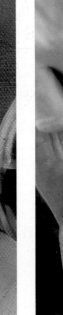

Fig. 13.56.

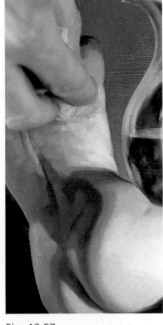

Fig. 13.57.

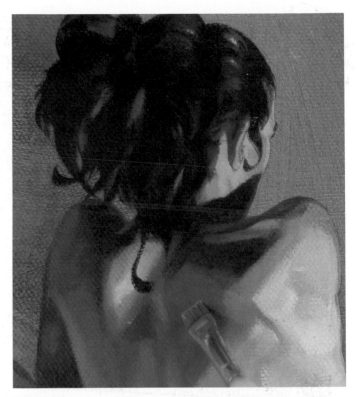

Fig. 13.60.

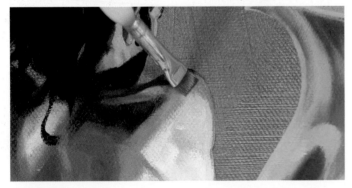

Fig. 13.58.

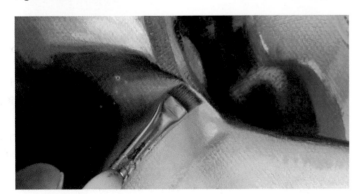

Fig. 13.59.

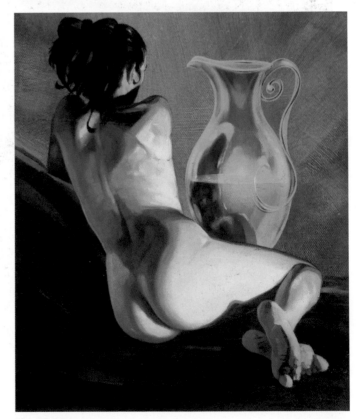

Fig. 13.61.

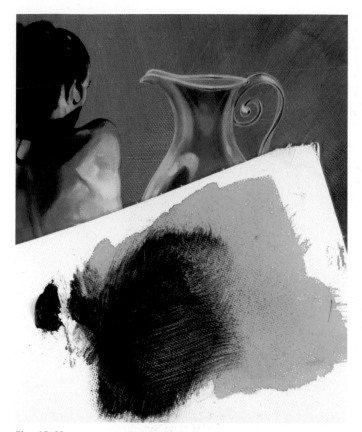

Fig. 13.62.

(Fig. 13.65) With a clean, damp brush, remove the paint on the highlights. Use a drier brush to soften the edges of the removed areas. A wet brush will remove it dramatically back to the original state. Once the paint has dried overnight, the tints will be unmoveable.

(Fig. 13.66) The final picture.

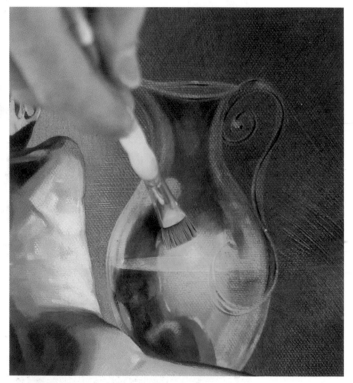

Fig. 13.64.

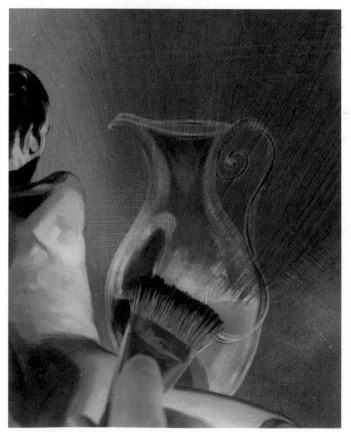

Fig. 13.63.

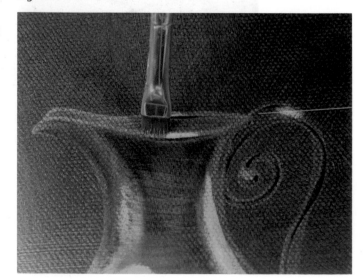

Fig. 13.65.

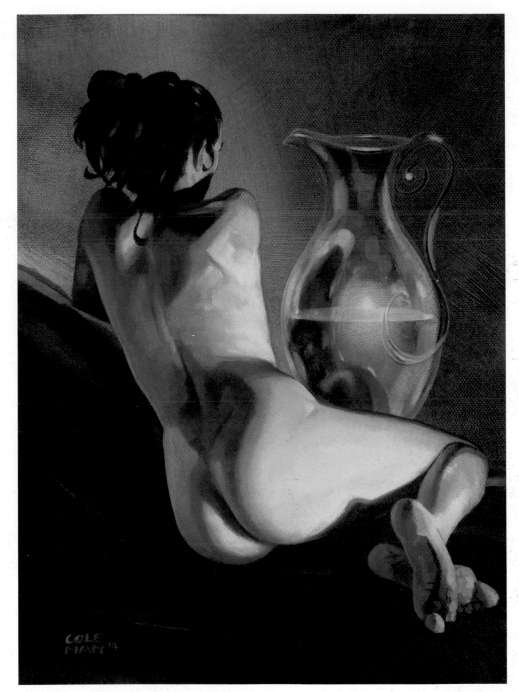

Fig. 13.66 The finished picture.

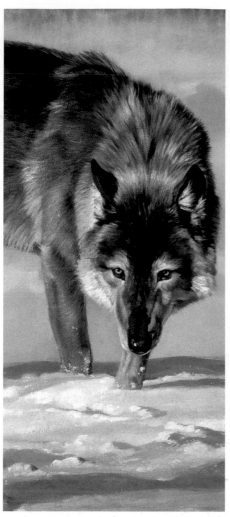

Fig. 13.67.

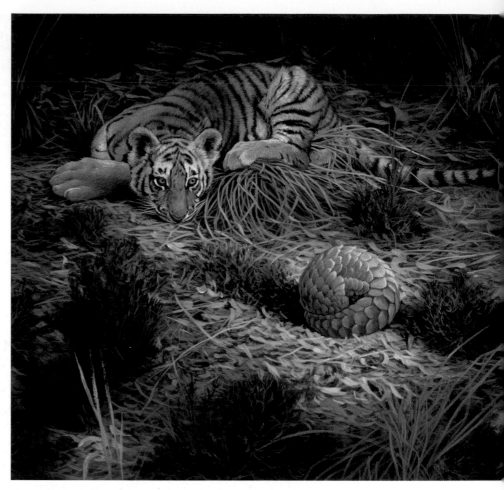

Fig. 13.68.

EXAMPLES OF THIN AND THICK TECHNIQUES

The life drawing described in this chapter incorporates the most common techniques in this type of painting genre. A mixture of thicknesses and transparencies creates all the tones and subtleties required in the work.

The paintings here utilize the same approach in principle, with a bias to either tints or solid colours.

(Fig. 13.67) The wolf has washes of colour on top of thicker opaque paint, with a shadow tint over its back. A little dragging with a dry brush highlights the fur and snow on the leg.

(Fig. 13.68) The Tiger and Pangolin painting uses thick and thin paint on the fur and leaves, with large areas of tinting on the shadows and bushes.

(Figs 13.69 and 13.70) The Hereford bull painting has thinly applied paint everywhere except the bull's hide. Here it is thickly applied with a detail Designer 222 brush and then tinted to achieve a softer graduating shadow.

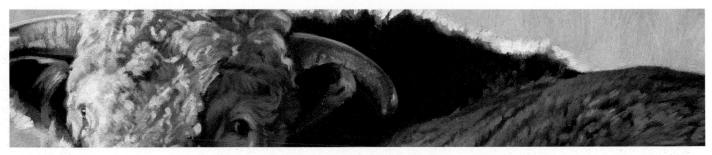

Fig. 13.69.

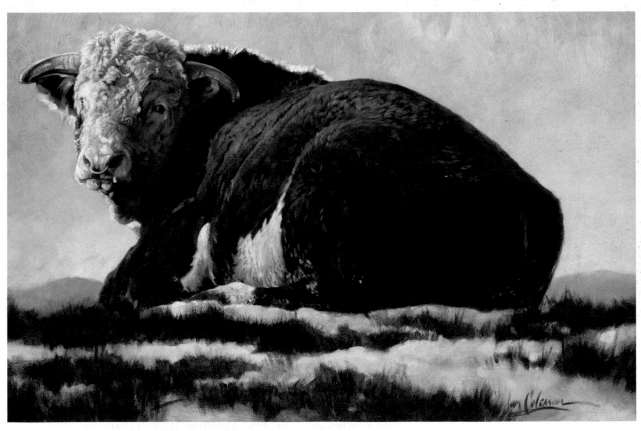

Fig. 13.70.

INDEX

RELATED TITLES FROM CROWOOD

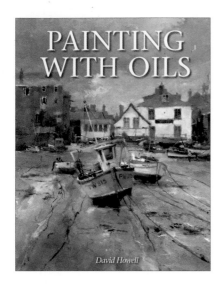

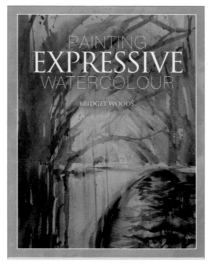

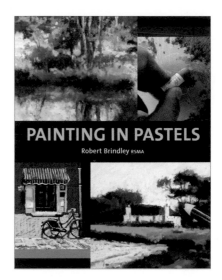

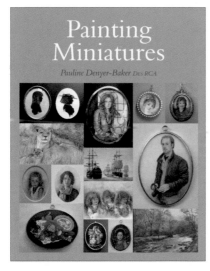

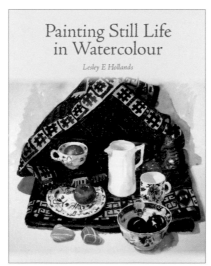

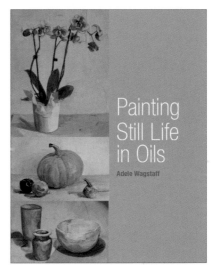

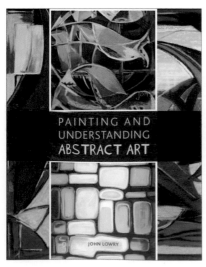

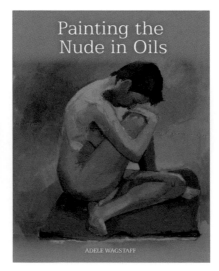

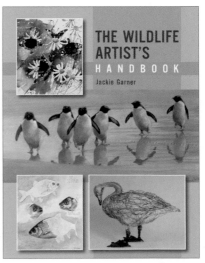